THE SECRET LIFE OF

BARACK HUSSEIN OBAMA

MONDO FRAZIER

THRESHOLD EDITIONS

New York   London   Toronto   Sydney   New Delhi

Threshold Editions
A Division of Simon & Schuster, Inc.
1230 Avenue of the Americas
New York, NY 10020

Copyright © 2011 by Mondo Frazier

First Threshold Editions hardcover edition October 2011

THRESHOLD EDITIONS and colophon are registered trademarks
of Simon & Schuster, Inc.

For information about special discounts for bulk purchases,
please contact Simon & Schuster Special Sales at 1-866-506-1949
or business@simonandschuster.com.

The Simon & Schuster Speakers Bureau can bring authors to your live event.
For more information or to book an event contact the Simon & Schuster Speakers
Bureau at 1-866-248-3049 or visit our website at www.simonspeakers.com.

Designed by Ruth Lee-Mui

Manufactured in the United States of America

1   3   5   7   9   10   8   6   4   2

Library of Congress Cataloging-in-Publication Data

Frazier, Mondo.
The secret life of Barack Hussein Obama / Mondo Frazier.
    p.   cm.
1. Obama, Barack.   2. Presidents—United States—Biography.   I. Title.
E908.F73 2011
973.932092—dc22
[B]   2011013724

ISBN 978-1-4516-3318-4
ISBN 978-1-4516-3320-7 (ebook)

To Elaine,
who picked up the slack when it mattered so I could get this written

Contents

CONTENTS

1

Who Is Barack Hussein Obama?

Oh, what a tangled web we weave
When first we practise to deceive!
—Sir Walter Scott, *Marmion*, Canto VI, XVII (1808)

Who is Barack Hussein Obama?

Nothing in the last fifty years—make that the last 235!—has demonstrated the phenomenon of social mania, the madness of crowds, or the forces of irrational behavior as clearly as the events that led to the election campaign of Barack Hussein Obama.

Obama was the political equivalent of whatever made one feel better, whether it was another cup of coffee or another shot of cocaine. Obama was the "pause that refreshes!"—or at least that was the way he was marketed to the American public. No matter what it was that made a person feel refreshed and alive, it could be experienced by plugging into the cool vibes of Barack Obama.

Weary of George W. Bush, perhaps even more weary of the relentless sniping campaign waged daily against Bush by the Corporate Mainstream Media (CMM), Americans were just plain fatigued and looking for a quick pick-me-up. Barack Hussein Obama and his campaign took full advantage of that mood. They would have said anything; hell, they did say anything. One suspects Team Obama and the CMM would have claimed that support for Barack Obama would result in minty-fresh breath if they could have gotten away with it.

Whatever one was "into"—a run on the beach, a walk in the park, a moonlight stroll, uppers, downers, another beer, or a shot of rye—the feelings of all those things would be duplicated and reproduced merely by listening to the cool, jazzy, rhetorical stylings of Barack Hussein Obama.

Obama had no past, no record, no documents? No problem! Who needed details? The words of Obama were all one needed to discover the truth. What truth one wanted to discover wasn't a problem either: the truth about Bush, about good and evil, about love? Getting behind Barack Obama was the answer to every problem; he would provide relief, soothe anxieties, calm the storm. Barack Obama was going to heal the earth, lower the sea levels. He said so himself—on TV!

Obama was the answer to financial worry. As one excited supporter proclaimed on election night, Obama was going to pay for her mortgage, her car—even her gas!

A vote for Barack Obama would prove to the world that America had thrown off its ugly racist past and was a brand-new country. Casting a vote for Obama was a chance to be one of the cool kids: to vote as famous Hollywood stars and celebrities—

as seen on TV!—would vote. A vote for Barack Obama was obsessive-compulsive behavior made man and woman.

In 2008, Barack Obama was the electoral equivalent of the Hula Hoop; a political Pet Rock; a craze, a fad, an irrational gadget. The latest have-to-have, must-vote-for candidate. Suppose a goldfish-swallowing, disco-dancing smart-phone salesman in a paisley shirt had met a polyester-bell-bottom-jeans-wearing female flagpole-sitter, complete with platform shoes and a Dorothy Hamill haircut, during the intermission at a midnight showing of *The Rocky Horror Picture Show.* Further suppose that the enthralled couple had tripped out to the parking lot, climbed into his Muscle Car, compared mood rings, and then leaped into the backseat to celebrate the Age of Aquarius. Finally, imagine that nine months later that groovy union produced a boy.

That boy couldn't possibly have been a bigger poster child for the power of temporary fad and fashion than Barack Obama during 2008. Barack Hussein Obama became something never before seen in American politics: the presidential impulse-buy item.

Who is Barack Hussein Obama?

He had answered to many names. Was he Barry Soetoro, Barry Obama, Barack Dunham, Barry Dunham, or Barack Hussein Obama? It's no wonder the Corporate Mainstream Media didn't do much investigation into the man: Who knew to which name he'd answer? The number of possibilities might have driven Stephen Hawking mad. Besides, who wanted to know? Hey, Barack Obama's mom spoke twelve different languages, and BHO had a pet monkey when he was a kid!

Pulitzer Prize–winning author Chris Hedges has written about Brand Obama and captured the true flavor of the marketing fraud that was the official Obama Narrative™. Hedges claims Barack Obama is nothing more than "a brand."

> And the Obama brand is designed to make us feel good about our government while corporate overlords loot the Treasury, our elected officials continue to have their palms greased by armies of corporate lobbyists, our corporate media diverts us with gossip and trivia, and our imperial wars expand in the Middle East.

Hedges argues that Brand Obama "entertains," makes us feel "hopeful," and gives us a feeling that the president is "like us." Hedges finishes with a chilling reminder: "But like all branded products spun out from the manipulative world of corporate advertising, we are being duped into doing and supporting a lot of things that are not in our interest."

Which is all true—with one important difference. If Brand Obama had been an inanimate object instead of flesh and blood, all of the campaign's leaders would have been thrown in jail for false advertising. If Barack Obama had been a prescription drug, he never would have made it out of the clinical trials.

Barack Obama was not the product to cure all ills—but that didn't stop his campaign from spinning it that way. The illusion that Barack Obama could be whatever a person desired him to be didn't stop with his election. After the election Barack Obama continued to be (fill in the blank). However, after the campaign was over, it was the CMM that took over running the con. Before he was inaugurated, according to the CMM, Obama was the reincarnation of any number of past American presidents.

Obama was the "New Teddy Roosevelt" and the "New FDR" (*Time* and various newspapers). Obama was the "New Abraham Lincoln" (*Washington Post, Huffington Post, Pravda*). Obama was compared and contrasted with Ronald Reagan (*Washington Post*, Chris Matthews). A T-shirt even proclaimed that Obama was "the New Black." As during the campaign, Obama was still whatever one wished him to be—at least for a little while longer.

Who is Barack Hussein Obama?

Hedges contends that it was the "image" of Barack Obama that appeared "radically individualistic and new"—not the candidate himself. Because all high-level political candidates are products of the corporations and the "vast military-industrial complex," there are no longer different products (candidates); there are only different brands (the way those cookie-cutter candidates are marketed to the voting public, e.g., Brand Obama, Brand Bush). Brand Obama was demanded because the Bush brand had "collapsed." What new brand will be demanded after the relatively quick collapse of the Obama brand is anyone's guess.

Who is Barack Hussein Obama?

Maybe the CMM should have interviewed Chris Hedges before the election; he had Brand Obama nailed. Maybe someone should have quizzed Hedges; it might have been helpful. No one else had the answers.

It hasn't much helped to ask the voters who supported Obama. They didn't know and, in many cases, didn't care. It wasn't much help to look at the meager Obama record. Obama has ensured that most of his records have been impossible to access.

His Occidental College, Columbia University, Harvard University, and medical records have all been sealed by the president himself. In addition, the April 2011 release of a document alleged to be Obama's long-form birth certificate has raised more questions than it has answered. Before Obama's election, his campaign refused to release relevant records, and the CMM declined to press him on the issue.

Private investigations have revealed that Barack Hussein Obama has used more than one Social Security number—and that the SSN currently used has a prefix reserved for residents of Connecticut, a state in which Barack Obama has never resided. This information has not sparked, in a decidedly uncurious press, any inquiries into such curious circumstances.

It hasn't done any good to ask members of the press. While they've provided plenty of opinions, most haven't provided many real answers to Obama's past—because they never asked the hard questions themselves and never followed up on those asked by others outside their ranks. During the campaign, the CMM exhibited a singular lack of curiosity about their Fab Fave candidate and his past, preferring instead to quote from Obama's two memoirs or the campaign's canned answers from the Obama Narrative™.

Inquiries about actual records, which would've helped shed light on Obama's background, were a subject—much like the John Edwards scandal—that remained off-limits in the polite little pieces the CMM substituted for election news. Who wanted hard news anyway? For the corporate media reporters covering Obama, *Tiger Beat* was much more fun than the political beat. Why dig for the hard facts when it was so much easier to provide "Fun Facts"?

It did no good to ask former White House press secretary Robert Gibbs. According to published reports, questions about Obama's post–Columbia University employment with Business International Corporation (BIC) have been strictly verboten—as well as any questions about Obama's withheld records while he was a student at Occidental College or Columbia.

And it hasn't helped to ask Barack Obama himself. Whenever it has been impossible for the CMM to ignore some aspect of Obama's record that has surfaced, he has run from it or insisted that he was unaware of what the record revealed.

Reverend Jeremiah "God Damn America" Wright? After vigorously defending Wright, Obama ran from him, claiming that he sat in Wright's church for twenty years and never heard him say any of those unpleasant things about America.

Former domestic terrorist Bill Ayers? At first, Obama claimed Ayers was "just some guy from the neighborhood" or "one of the thousands of people I know." Bill O'Reilly bought it.

Others didn't. It was shown that Obama had a years-long relationship of working with Ayers, whose views on America ("Every time I think of America, it makes me want to puke") were well-known. Obama spokesmen claimed that Obama didn't know about Ayers's past. Even some in the CMM had trouble swallowing that one.

Obama's relationship with ACORN? The subject was something that Obama spoke of proudly—until ACORN's record of massive voter fraud became better known. Then the Obama camp's position became that Obama "never worked for ACORN."

Who is Barack Hussein Obama?

In 2008, Barack Obama was The Hope; he was The Change. To his opponents, BHO represented the triumph of wishful thinking, the belief that unicorns existed and fairy dust was a real-world commodity. "Who is Barack Obama?" was a new national parlor game in which there was no wrong answer. Barack Obama was more than the sizzle that sold the steak: He was the sizzle all by itself. Who needed steak anyway? Obama would feed anyone who got hungry—probably with steak.

The Obama campaign naturally encouraged this "promise of the empty vessel." In *The Audacity of Hope*, Obama wrote: "I serve as a blank screen on which people of vastly different political stripes project their own views." Barack Obama truly was whatever supporters wanted him to be—even he knew it.

With few records to actually consult and with little relevant experience in public service—Obama had served only 143 working days in the U.S. Senate before announcing his campaign for president—Barack Obama offered the American public few clues to who he actually was. Those interested in learning more had nowhere to go other than the Obama campaign. The CMM churned out a steady stream of puffery. An examination of the hyped hagiography, slobbering puff pieces, and messianic ballyhoo seldom revealed much that proved helpful.

In the end, Barack Obama became electoral Silly Putty for 2008. But Obama's fifteen minutes of marketing fame ended, not with warehouses full of unsought knickknacks or toys that consumers no longer wanted; it ended with a neophyte with no real-world, practical experience in the White House.

At a little before 10:30 P.M. local time on November 4, 2008, CNN declared Barack Obama the winner of the presidential election. A self-congratulatory celebration then began around the country. It erupted into a national three-piece toga party, as Obama Nation celebrated not so much the election of Obama himself as the Idea of Obama— and it was captured live on national television so all the world could watch and feel part of the fun.

The festivities were narrated by many of the same media commentators who had worked so hard the previous twenty-one months in order to ensure that this long-imagined magic moment became a reality. Network coverage revealed a night when Hope! reigned triumphant over Reality. For 52 percent of the American electorate, November 4, 2008, was the Wild Night Out, the Last Great Fling, the Ultimate Bachelor Party, a One-Night Stand, and Girls Gone Wild all rolled into one.

On January 21, 2009, the country woke up with what looked to be a four-year-long national hangover. The CMM has already suggested a little "hair of the dog" for 2012. All of which might or might not have been prevented, if only some enterprising members of the press had resolved to answer the question: Who is Barack Hussein Obama?

2

Twenty Things Most Americans Don't
Know about Barack Hussein Obama

The Obama Quiz

Whether one was warning family and friends of the coming
Barackalypse or was a True Believer chanting "Yes We Can!" in
the front row of a Hope and Change rally, one has to admit:
There's not much that's undisputedly known about our forty-
fourth president. Even the most basic of Barack Obama's records have been fodder for speculation—because no one,
outside of the president and a few choice insiders, has seen
them.

There are, however, some things that *are* known about
Obama—though the press coverage of our president's pec-
cadilloes has been spotty at best. A random sample of twenty
such items—from among the hundreds of presidential tidbits

THE SECRET LIFE OF BARACK HUSSEIN OBAMA

considered—has been collected in this chapter for the reader's entertainment or education.

Because there is so little room and there are so many Obama idiosyncrasies, some that didn't make this list appear elsewhere in this book. After settling on twenty items for this list—because twenty is a nice, round number—it was decided to present them in the form of a quiz. Thus, the Obama Quiz was born.

Sure, an Obama Quiz is so—corny. But go on: Who can resist matching wits or even halfwits with other collectors of Obamalania? How many of the following items was the reader previously aware of? Scoring is simple: If aware or even semi-aware of an item, the reader scores one point. Easy, huh?

And yes, as with most quizzes, there is a scoring chart at the end to allow readers to gauge their level of Obamafication.

1. **Luck is where you find it.** Many people are superstitious and carry good luck charms. Barack Obama apparently believed he could use all the luck he could get. During the 2008 presidential campaign, BHO depended on more than one talisman to bring him good fortune. It was reported that the president carried two such charms with him: a tiny Madonna-and-child statue and a bracelet that belonged to a soldier in Iraq.

   These weren't the only Obama charms. A photograph published in September 2008 displayed the contents of Obama's pocket the day the photo was taken. One item in the photo was a small statue of the four-armed Hindu monkey god, Lord Hanuman. Hanuman means "broken

— 11 —

jaw," and he is described as a mischievous god who "ignited his stretched prehensile monkey tail and thrashed it around Rakshasas' city." *Hindu Blog* explained, "Millions of Hindus worship Hanuman. But those alien to Hindu culture, especially the Western media and Christian Missionaries, quite often use Hanuman to ridicule Hindu culture and malign it."

The discovery of Lord Hanuman brings the number of Obama good luck charms to three—which is itself considered a lucky number by some. Perhaps that brings the total to—four?

Maybe all of those good luck charms really worked. Two days before the photo of Obama carrying the small Hindu monkey god appeared, polling data reported that Barack Obama's "bump" from the Democratic National Convention was gone. After months of being in the lead, Obama was tied with Senator John McCain. Subsequent polling had BHO falling behind—until a once-in-a-generation financial crisis at the end of September. Which, luckily for Obama, propelled him back into a lead he maintained until election day. The president has never publicly attributed his good luck to any particular charm.

2. **Barack Hussein Obama was elected president on November 4, 2008. The next day, the announced winning number in Obama's home state of Illinois Lottery Pick Three evening contest was 666.** Of course, this number is the "number of the Beast" in the Bible's "The Revelation of Jesus Christ." In Revela-

tion, the Beast is associated with Satan and the end of the world as we know it.

But Obama's 666 was not the best-known 666 winning lottery pick. Probably the most famous 666 winning lottery number was the infamous "Triple Six Fix," the 1980 Pennsylvania Lottery Scandal. That event involved an elaborate scheme in which lottery insiders, who included lottery show announcer Nick Perry, placed weights in all of the balls except those with the numbers six and four. The lighter balls with sixes and fours were the only balls the vacuum machine was able to pick up.

According to *Wikipedia*, "The scheme was successful in that 666, an expected result, was drawn on April 24, 1980; however, the unusual betting patterns alerted authorities to the matter. The chief conspirators were sent to prison, and most of the fraudulently acquired winnings were never paid out."

There was no scandal involved in the Illinois Lottery 666. In fact, it was the fourteenth time that particular combination of numbers had been drawn in the history of the game. It's just one of those coincidences that stick in people's memories—particularly those compiling lists of little-known Barack Obamalania.

3. **Is that a Constitution in your pocket or are you just happy to see me?** When he was sworn in, photos of the ceremony showed that there was a bulge in Obama's pants pocket. It was later reported that the bulge was caused by a white kata (silk scarf) "blessed by his holiness

the Dalai Lama." Reportedly, Richard Blum, the husband of California senator Dianne Feinstein, offered the scarf to the president-elect before the ceremony and Obama stuffed it into his pocket.

According to the website *DharmaShop*, which specializes in Tibetan goods, the kata "lends a positive note to the start of any enterprise or relationship and indicates the good intentions of the person offering it. Katas are offered to religious images, such as statues of the Buddha, and to lamas and government officials prior to requesting their help in the form of prayers or other services. The offering of the kata indicates that the request is not marred by corrupt thoughts or ulterior motives."

Perhaps America's forty-fourth president wanted to hedge his bets: His hand may have been on the Bible, but just to be sure, he had a kata in his pocket.

4. **In 2010, Obama became the first president to set up his reelection campaign outside Washington, D.C.** If America has a city that's known for corruption, sweetheart deals, and scandal—other than Washington, D.C.—Chicago is the clear winner. The city is also Barack Obama's adopted hometown. Coincidentally, Chicago is where former Obama chief of staff Rahm Emanuel is the city's mayor.

Corporate media reported that Chicago is also the "likely" headquarters of Barack Obama's reelection campaign. This would mark the first time that a sitting president has located his campaign headquarters outside the Washington, D.C., area. The move has been attributed to a desire by Team Obama to portray the president as an "outsider" in 2012.

The move has already been trumpeted in the Corporate Mainstream Media (CMM) as a savvy ploy. It remains to be seen how many Americans will believe that the president of the United States, one of the world's most powerful men, will be transformed into an "outsider" by virtue of his campaign's being centered in the ultimate City of Insiders.

5. **Wild thing.** In the days leading up to Barack Obama's inauguration, various lists of information about the incoming president appeared in newspapers all over the world. Most of these pieces featured headlines on the order of "50 Fun Facts about Barack Obama" or "Barack Obama: 25 Interesting Facts." These articles were reminiscent of those found in publications—such as *Tiger Beat*—that feature objects of teen affection. While none of the Fun Facts revealed Obama's favorite color, quite a few of those lists were rife with the mundane.

Several of the most often repeated facts concerned Obama's boyhood in Indonesia. Obama's time in Indonesia wasn't often taken up by the CMM before the election. Actually, the subject was consigned to the "birther pile," as it was assumed that anyone who asked questions about that period was only attempting to stir up trouble over Obama's citizenship. However, once the election was safely over, "Obama in Indonesia" morphed into appropriate fodder for "Fun Facts."

One of the most popular Fun Facts from Obama's

days in Indonesia: "Whilst living in Indonesia he ate local delicacies such as dog meat, snake meat, and roasted grasshopper." Another was: "He kept a pet ape called Tata." Before the election, these Fun Facts would have been a sign that the writer was trying to paint Barack Obama as an unknown foreigner. After the election, they were signs that Barack Obama came from an exciting, exotic, and—dare it be said?—fun world.

6. **Obama is related to everybody else.** The family tree of Barack Obama revealed that our forty-fourth president is truly a part of some grand mosaic. According to various genealogists, including one from Utah-based *Ancestry .com*, Obama's the ninth cousin of Brad Pitt and eighth cousin of former vice president Dick Cheney.

Obama's also the relative of a number of well-known conservatives, if such reports are to be believed. Both Sarah Palin and Barack Obama are tenth cousins through a common ancestor named John Smith, a pastor and early settler in seventeenth-century Massachusetts. Obama is related to Smith through his mother, as is Palin, according to Anastasia Tyler, the genealogist at *Ancestry.com*.

Obama's bête noire, Rush Limbaugh, is also a tenth cousin of the president—one time removed—"through a common ancestor named Richmond Terrell" from Virginia. The site also reported that President George W. Bush is related to both Obama and Palin. The two presidents are eleventh cousins through common ancestor Samuel Hinckly, John Smith's (remember him?) father-in-law. Bush and Palin are tenth cousins once removed.

To those conspiracy theorists who write on the subject of "Illuminati bloodlines" (if this term draws a blank, a quick Google search will provide enlightenment), this information is confirmation of their idea that the world's leaders don't really have a family tree—it's more like just a few family branches. The news that President Obama is also distantly related through his mother to U.S. president Harry S. Truman and Wallis Simpson (who married King Edward VIII of England) can't be of any comfort to the conspiracy-minded.

7. **A CMM first.** If the following remark had been uttered by conservative radio host Rush Limbaugh, one can only imagine the media mayhem that would have ensued. Since it issued from former *CBS Evening News* anchorman Dan Rather, the CMM assumed that, though his quotation was colorful, his motives were pure. Rather's observation may have been the first flat-out declaration by an important CMM personality that a human flaw had been discovered in our forty-fourth president.

Listen, he's [Obama] a nice person, he's very articulate—this is what's been used against him, but he couldn't sell watermelons if . . . you gave him the state troopers to flag down the traffic.

—Dan Rather, on syndicated
Chris Matthews show, March 9, 2010

8. **Ice Cream Man.** Remember those "Fun Facts" so favored by publications, both in the United States and

abroad, around January 20, 2009? One fact featured the claim that Obama "doesn't like ice cream." What likely made this particular fact "fun" was the additional claim that his dislike of the popular tasty treat stemmed from a job he once held in a Baskin-Robbins as a teenager. Supposedly, it was "fun" that ordinary common people can savor the joys of ice cream, while our president, due to the evils of capitalism during his formative years, was prevented from joining in the fun. Or something.

What's less fun—at least for the Fun Fact–finding people—are the many published photos showing the president enjoying not only ice cream cones but the sugary goodness of snow cones as well. Maybe this is confirmation that when a narrative of a person's history has to be created almost from scratch, no one can keep track of all the details.

9. **Sorcerer's Apprentice.** The *Telegraph* (UK) reported that President Obama "has read every Harry Potter book." In addition, it's been widely reported that "every night when he is at home he reads the Harry Potter books to his oldest daughter, Malia." While this may be just another Fun Fact for some, it's not helpful to his standing in the fundamentalist Christian community—where the Harry Potter books are synonymous with witchcraft, the occult, and other evil. The next item isn't likely to help with that particular problem either.

10. **Indisputable evidence that Obama is sinister.** It's undisputed that Barack Obama is left-handed—the sixth postwar president to be so digitally inclined. One of the

meanings of the word *sinister* is "on the left side" or "left-handedness." According to *Wikipedia*, "In the Middle Ages it was believed that when a person was writing with their left hand they were possessed by the Devil. (This was uncommon, particularly as there were fewer literate people.) Left-handed people were therefore considered to be evil."

If ever, in the midst of a heated debate, additional proof is needed to illustrate the Evil of Obama, here it is: indisputable evidence that Barack Hussein Obama is sinister—which is just another word for "evil." Remember where you heard it first.

11. **Have teleprompter, will travel.** Obama's reliance on his teleprompter (the device the president reads from when speaking) is legendary; it's the subject of jokes, and many people are well aware of this particular Obama dependency problem. However, what many may not be aware of is the unprecedented extent to which the president relies on the device.

Obama's teleprompter accompanies him everywhere. Obama was the first president to use a teleprompter when addressing a gathering of grade-school children. Obama also took along his teleprompter for its historic debut in India's parliament building. When Obama addressed India's parliament, he reportedly was the first person in the building's history to use a teleprompter.

"Used to the machine-gun delivery of Indian politicians who are never at a loss for words, officials here were a bit perplexed when the U.S. embassy broached the topic," says the *Calcutta Telegraph*. "We assumed that Obama, being such a brilliant orator, delivers speeches extempore," said one official. Another speculated that the president was "probably" asking for electronic help "to avoid Bushisms."

USA Today explained the grade-school teleprompter incident by suggesting that the device was at the school for the president's remarks to the media afterward. One wag then rhetorically wondered, "What's the difference between a bunch of sixth-graders and an adoring White House press corps?" There are some pundits who refer to Barack Obama as the "TOTUS—Teleprompter of the United States." While that may be uncharitable, the above events show that the charge is not totally baseless.

12. **Those days are long gone.** In the summer of 2008, a series of stories appeared in the media reporting the nation's comedians had a perplexing problem: There was no way to make a joke about Barack Obama. Various reasons were given. Comedian Damon Wayans went so far as to claim that it's hard to joke about Obama because "he's trying to do good."

"The thing is, he's not buffoonish in any way," said Mike Barry, a writer for David Letterman who started writing political jokes during the Johnny Carson days. "He's not a comical figure," Barry said.

Those days are long gone. Barack Obama is now a staple in all of the late-night comics' repertoire. Because it's unlikely that readers have heard all of these (mostly) one-liners, here are ten random jokes taken from the late-night talk shows:

- President Obama lit the national Christmas tree, a forty-foot Colorado spruce. Republicans don't believe it's really from Colorado, and they want to see a birth certificate.

  —Jay Leno

- It's been reported that President Obama's speech on Tuesday about Afghanistan helped give NBC its best ratings in a long time. So look out this spring for NBC's new shows: *Afghanistan's Got Talent*, *Law & Order: Kabul*, and *The Tonight Show with Hamid O'Karzai*.

  —Conan O'Brien

- Treasury Secretary Timothy Geithner had to go to the hospital today because of a kidney stone. On the bright side, the stone was the first thing in months passed by a member of the Obama administration.

  —Jimmy Fallon

- A lot of people don't understand why President Obama won the Peace Prize. You know something, look around you. Peaceful. Went to the mall this week. Peaceful. Open house by my house. Not one person came in. It's a peaceful economy we live in.

  —Jay Leno

- I've noticed fewer sidewalk Santas this year. Then I remembered that President Obama sent the Salvation Army to Afghanistan this year.

  —David Letterman

- President Obama says that Congress is very close to getting a new health-care plan but due to compromises it "won't include everything that everybody wants." For instance, it covers everything except trips to the doctor or the hospital.

  —Conan O'Brien

- President Obama met with the CEOs of top companies about creating more jobs for Americans. After the meeting, the CEOs went home to China.

  —Conan O'Brien

- Two feet of snow in the Midwest. But the good news is, these are the first shovel-ready jobs Obama has come up with since becoming president.

  —Jay Leno

- A new food bill has been signed into law. It's part of our war against doughnuts. If we're not vigilant, the doughnuts will win. After signing the law, President Obama said our government shows it is serious about setting a good example for children's health. Then he went outside to smoke a cigarette.

  —Craig Ferguson

- Because of a printing error, a billion new hundred-dollar bills have to be destroyed. They're going to burn $100 billion—just like they did with the last stimulus program.

—Jay Leno

The United States has been running deficits of more than $1 trillion per year since Obama has been in office—with no end in sight. But at least a solution for the Obama comedy deficit seems to have been found.

13. **Marlboro Man.** The press has always had time for one more story about Obama's battles with his smoking habit. The topic has been the subject of many a press report. The reports run along the lines of girls whispering in the restroom: Is he or isn't he?

Obama has quit, wants to quit, has started smoking again, has quit—this time for real—or has resolved to quit again. It seems a bit strange that a White House press corps that has never gotten around to asking the president exactly what his intentions were with his civilian defense force always had time for one more "Obama is smoking again" story. One question they've forgotten to ask the president: "Mr. President, are you breaking White House regulations?" After all, there is a nonsmoking policy in the White House.

While there's been no mention of the president's favorite smokes from the White House press, according to a 2004 Chicago interview, Obama smokes Marlboro Reds.

14. **Scrooge lives at 1600 Pennsylvania Avenue.** Reportedly any day at the Obama White House is a good excuse

for a party or celebration—unless that day is Christmas. In a July 2008 *People* magazine interview, it was revealed that Obama "and his wife, Michelle, do not give Christmas or birthday presents to their two young daughters." In fact, this tradition wasn't just a guideline; Barack Obama said that it's a "steadfast rule."

Obama had earlier admitted that he and his wife do spend "hundreds" of dollars on birthday slumber parties— but nothing for Christmas. The then-senator told *People* that the First Couple adhere to their unusual custom because they "want to teach some limits." Another Christmas custom not on the list of those celebrated by the Obama family is a visit to Christmas Eve church services.

All the White House Christmas news wasn't grim: Obama did admit that Santa Claus was permitted to deliver "seasonal [note that he didn't call them "Christmas"] gifts." The First Lady then confided: "Malia says, 'I know there is a Santa because there's no way you'd buy me all that stuff.'"

15. **Isn't there someone who is supposed to check on these things?** According to city regulations, the cottage that President Obama rented for his 2010 Christmas vacation in Hawaii was an illegal rental. Obama did not break the law by staying at the house, but according to local reports, "The property owner who rented his house to the Obamas does not have the permit that would allow a stay of fewer than thirty days." Which begs the question: Who is in charge of making sure the president doesn't break any laws and regulations, even one of the

thousands that his administration enacted during his first two years in office? Is that same person in charge of enforcing the White House no-smoking policy?

16. **Gone in sixty seconds.** The story was widely publicized: Barack Obama walked out of a D.C. press conference in December 2010 and let Bill Clinton "take over." What wasn't widely reported: This was the first time in history that a president walked out of his own press conference—because he was afraid of being late for a party.

On December 9, 2010, the president held a press conference to explain his agreement to extend the Bush tax cuts for another two years. After speaking with reporters, Obama turned the press conference over to former president Bill Clinton. About halfway through Clinton's remarks, Obama left, saying that he had several holiday parties to attend. More than one publication ran headlines that included the word "weird" to describe the unprecedented happening.

A more sober observation might be that Barack Hussein Obama was "a man on a mission" that evening—and leave it at that.

17. **Bet the committee didn't include the Obama Girl.** While at Harvard Law School, Barack Obama applied to appear in a black pinup calendar. He was rejected by the all-female committee. Any number of possible comments to this news were auditioned for inclusion here—and rejected—by the author. The decision was finally made to leave that task to the imagination of the readers.

18. **Notable quotable Michelle Obama!** Few presidents have had a wife as consistently quotable as Michelle Obama. Many readers may have heard several "outrageous" Michelle quotations. But who can keep up with them all? Any readers familiar with all seven of these statements by the First Lady may award themselves one bonus point to their score at the end of this chapter.

"The truth is, in order to get things like universal health care and a revamped education system, then someone is going to have to give up a piece of their pie so that someone else can have more."

"America is just downright mean."

"The realities are that, you know, as a black man, you know, Barack can get shot going to the gas station, you know." (Gas station security in the tony Chicago neighborhood where the Obamas live must be a lot tougher than it is in most locales around the country. One bonus point to those who picked up on Michelle's three "you know" tics.)

"Even if we give parents all the information they need and we improve school meals and build brand-new supermarkets on every corner, none of that matters if, when families step into a restaurant, they can't make a healthy choice."

"For the first time in my adult lifetime, I am really proud of my country."

"Because sometimes it's easier to hold on to your own stereotypes and misconceptions. It makes you feel justified in your own ignorance. . . . That's America."

"When we took our trip to Africa and visited his home country in Kenya, uhh, we took a public HIV test—for the very point of showing folks in Kenya that there is nothing to be embarrassed about in getting tested." (Michelle Obama, speech to gay, lesbian, bisexual, and transgender Democrats, August 28, 2008. This last quotation includes source information because of its importance to later chapters.)

19. **An egg in the hand is worth . . .** Barack Obama keeps a carving of a wooden hand holding an egg on his desk. Several reports have stated that the carving is Kenyan and represents the "fragility of life." But that is not a universal interpretation. Another description of a similar carving from Ghana suggests a hand holding an egg symbolizes "that leadership is fragile and, like an egg, it must be handled with care."

So, there's some discussion about what the egg in the hand on the desk of Barack Obama really symbolizes. This author, after a fair amount of research, can state that reports that "Barack Obama has the heart of a small child" are true. It's rumored he keeps it in a little box in that same desk.

20. **Pick 'em.** For the last item on this list there are two candidates. The reader gets full credit if he is familiar with either. If familiar with both, add one bonus point to the score.

a. **In high school he was known as O'Bomber for his skill at basketball.** At least that was the way the "Fun Factsters" presented this bit of information to the world.

People who had actually played alongside Barack Obama confirmed that, yes, the O'Bomber moniker was correct. But as one former teammate put it, "It was because he stood outside the circle and threw up a lot of shots."

b. **He's a travelin' man.** Barack Obama didn't spend a lot of time in the White House during his first two years, compared with every other president before him. According to figures compiled by Ed Morrissey, at the website *Hot Air*, Obama spent 48 percent of the first half of his term outside Washington, D.C. This means that during his time in office, President Obama has frequently been someplace other than that office. Some would note that when the president's away from Washington, less gets done—which is a good thing.

How many of these was the reader previously aware of? Be honest. Here's how to score.

0–3 **Woefully ignorant:** You've lived in a cave or have had no contact with the outside world over the last three years. However, your lot is improving: In spite of past history, you now hold this book in your hands!

4–9 **Average news consumer:** Most likely, you gather most of your information through one of the Corporate Mainstream Media organizations. Again, your progress is apparent because you're reading this!

10–14 **Political junkie:** You regularly surf the Internet and frequent political websites and blogs. You generally know what's going on, and why—or at least you vaguely remember something about it. Most people you know consult you when Obama news breaks to get your "take"!

15–18 **Confirmed:** You are either a confirmed Obamaphobe or a confirmed Obamaphile. The guy fascinates you either in a "Bringer of Light" or "God Who Failed" sort of way. Regardless, you're the local king of Obama trivia!

19–20 **Paid investigator:** Most likely you're employed as either a private investigator, an opposition researcher, or a member of the White House staff. Chances are you're reading this book to find out how much more Obama information has been discovered!

3

The Media and the Messiah

In the past, radio shock jock Howard Stern has jokingly referred to himself as "the King of All Media." After 2008, Stern had to vacate his title: There was a new "King of All Media" and his name was Barack Obama. Obama was on every channel, on every TV; his face beamed from every magazine; his voice dripped from every speaker. During Campaign 2008, every medium was the message—and that message was Barack Hussein Obama, broadcasting 24/7 around the dial.

Every channel became the Obama Channel, a televised part of a CMM whole that continually celebrated their chosen candidate. Former media favorites—such as Hillary Clinton during the Democratic primaries—were tossed aside, but only after a good and proper bruising from the malicious minions of the CMM overlords.

Barack Obama received the blessing of every large corporate media empire. Those readers who believe that Fox News was particularly hard on Barack Obama are wrong: Fox News didn't attack Obama with the same savagery that MSNBC, CBS, and the rest of the CMM attacked either Sarah Palin or Hillary Clinton. But maybe the CMM deserves a break. After all, religion has never been its strong suit, and with Barack Obama, corporate media thought it had a real-life political messiah on its hands. That's a once-in-a-lifetime bonanza. Think of the ratings!

Even Fox News featured a steady diet of Barack Obama: You can't bash him unless you rehash him. Fox News's coverage of Obama was certainly less friendly, but in fall 2008, even Fox featured Brand Obama every hour, on the hour. Regardless, the CMM's multimillion-dollar ad campaign worked: On November 4, 2008, Brand Obama became President Obama.

The Obama Channel: Broadcasting 24/7 on Every TV

Without a doubt, Barack Obama has been the most televised president the United States has ever had. Really, could it have happened any differently? The media gets a messiah only once in a blue moon. President Obama appeared on more than sixty different television shows in his first twenty-two months in office. During his first nine months, Obama appeared on TV more times than most sitcom stars.

For those magical first nine months in office, the White House motto seemingly was "All Obama, All the Time." During that nine-month period, Barack Obama outperformed every previous president by a wide margin in the number of televised interviews given by participating in sixty-six televised interviews—including appearances on five political talk shows on the same Sunday in September 2009.

By comparison, George W. Bush, over the same period, had given sixteen interviews and Bill Clinton, six. If TV interviews were jobs, the United States would have had full employment by October 2009. The president's favorite venue has been NBC's the *Today* show, with sixteen appearances. Three shows are tied for second with five Obama appearances each: *The Daily Show with Jon Stewart, Late Show with David Letterman,* and *NBC Nightly News.*

While not seen as much as Vince, the ShamWow guy, or now-deceased pitchman Billy Mays, Obama was on the tube. A lot. The following is a list of the shows on which Barack Obama has made guest appearances. Most occurred during his first two years in office; four appearances were as a candidate from May 2007. A single TV appearance occurred in May 2006, on *Face the Nation.*

Anderson Cooper 360°
Teen Choice Awards
Meet the Press (three times)
60 Minutes
Fox Saturday Baseball Game of the Week
The Daily Show with Jon Stewart (five times)

Channel One News

WWE Monday Night RAW King of the Ring

WNBA on NBA TV

TMZ on TV

The Tonight Show with Jay Leno
 (with Maggie Gyllenhaal and Taylor Hicks)

The Rachel Maddow Show

The View

The Colbert Report

NCAA March Madness

NBA on TNT

MLB Tonight

Late Night with Conan O'Brien

Countdown with Keith Olbermann (three times)

Face the Nation (two times)

Late Show with David Letterman (five times)

NBC Nightly News (five times)

Saturday Night Live (two times)

The Ellen DeGeneres Show (three times, appearing once with
 Reese Witherspoon and Jim Cramer, and appearing once
 with Jimmy Fallon, Kelli Williams, and Trace Adkins)

Tavis Smiley (three times)

This Week (three times)

Today (sixteen times)

In addition, according to CBS News's Mark Knoller, Barack Obama gave fifty-two addresses or statements specifically on his health-care proposals during his first year in office and used a teleprompter 177 times. He conducted forty-two news conferences, gave 158 interviews (including ninety that were televised), and was out of the public eye only twenty-one days.

If one didn't see Barack Obama on television during his first two years in office, it wasn't because the president wasn't trying.

Cover Boy

Television wasn't the only medium that crammed BHO down the throats of consumers. Dozens of magazines featured Obama on their covers. Barack Obama made it onto ten *Time* covers in the forty-two weeks preceding October 16, 2008, and fourteen in all during 2008—twenty-five if you count the skybox at the top of the magazine. This was almost half of the *Time* covers in 2008.

Time might have been the publication most guilty of Obamaphilia, but it was hardly alone. *Newsweek* had Obama on the cover twelve of forty-nine issues in 2008. By contrast, Obama's opponent, John McCain, appeared on five *Time* covers—including one with Obama in 2008. Obama and his family were also featured on the cover of *People* magazine.

While Obama was also a cover boy for *Rolling Stone, GQ, Vanity Fair,* and *Men's Vogue,* he dominated the covers of *Time.* How often was Barack Obama on the cover of *Time* in 2008? Plenty: He appeared on the cover of *Time* roughly once every four weeks during the last ten months before the election. Was *Time* biased? No way! All one had to do was ask them.

The media were miffed at the charges of bias. They pointed out that much of their coverage had a simple explanation: They were biased toward whoever had the most commercial appeal.

They were featuring Barack Obama on nearly every issue's cover because the public demanded it.

The "commercial appeal" defense was one used by *Newsweek* against the charge of bias. The magazine did so well commercially under its all-Obama-all-the-time format that twenty-one months after the election, the Washington Post Company, the owners of *Newsweek,* sold it for a buck. That was about eight cents for every time they ran a Barack Obama cover in 2008. One doesn't want to contemplate what the sales price for the newsweekly might have been if not for all that "commercial appeal" of Barack Obama.

"Commercial" considerations were the defense *Time* used to justify its obsession with Obama in 2008 as well. *Time* would know all about what sells. In the last twelve years, *Time* has lost nearly three-quarters of a million subscribers.

"*Time* covers both parties and candidates equally," magazine spokesman Daniel Kile claimed—presumably while maintaining a straight face. Still, the public seemed to be onto the game. If there had been no Corporate Mainsteam Media in 2008, Barack Obama might very well have still triumphed. Nevertheless, even with practically every media outlet securely in the campaign's pocket, Obama managed to attract only 52.9 percent of the popular vote.

The media trumpeted this victory as a "landslide," and it was—for a Democratic candidate. It was only the second time in forty-four years that a Democrat received more than 50 percent of the popular vote. Obama's margin of victory was the eighteenth-largest among presidential victories.

After the election, both *Newsweek* and the *Washington Post* made startling admissions—for them. They had favored Barack Obama in their coverage. The yawns were deafening. Tell us something we don't know.

In 2008, corporate media went to the dogs. Team Obama used access to their candidate like Scooby Snacks—and the public watched as yapping CMM poodles jumped through the campaign's hoops to get another treat. Media watchdogs were out; media lapdogs were in—and used the leg of Chris Matthews instead of a fire hydrant. Like Pavlov's dog, the CMM slobbered every time Barack Obama spoke. It was hard to watch and many Americans didn't: They turned it off and signed on to Facebook.

In 2008 the mask came off the Corporate Mainstream Media, once and for all. Ironically enough, it was corporate media's Golden Boy, Barack Obama, who did the unmasking—and Obama not only pulled off the mask of what was maintained to be objective journalism, he ripped it to shreds. After 2008, the CMM would never be able to wear that false face again. By 2010, Barack Obama, King of All Media, had morphed into Barack the Destroyer.

Serves 'em right: That's what they get for putting all of their media eggs in a messianic basket.

4

The Missing Obama Records

In an age in which seemingly every facet of a person's life is recorded, on file, and increasingly available on the Internet, the total absence of Barack Obama's vital records is an almost singularly unique phenomenon. This situation would be odd even if Barack Obama was an eighty-year-old stonemason from rural Tennessee who had been born in a rustic cabin and never traveled more than twenty-five miles from his home during his life.

One suspects that if the CMM wanted to perform a thorough vetting of that imaginary stoneworker, more information would have been unearthed in a single week than has come to light in the six years that Barack Hussein Obama has served as either a U.S. senator or the president of the United States.

In Obama's case, the records either don't exist, haven't been released, or have disappeared. In the matter of his long-form birth certificate, much energy, time, and money—reportedly more than $2 million in legal fees alone—was expended in order to keep the documents from a curious public, truly a remarkable situation for a man who holds the highest office in the land. The release of Obama's so-called long-form birth certificate in April 2011 has done little to stem either the debate or the public's curiosity. Because "you can't tell the players without a scorecard," the following is a list of unrevealed Obama records; it's provided to be both helpful and enlightening.

Obama Records: Not Released

- Barack Obama original long-form birth certificate*
- Soetoro/Dunham marriage license
- Soetoro adoption records
- Punahou School records
- Columbia College records
- Columbia thesis (reportedly on "Soviet Nuclear Disarmament")
- Harvard College records
- Occidental College records
- Medical records
- Law practice client list
- Illinois bar records
- Barack Obama passport records (his official government passport files may have been scrubbed clean by officials

---

*The White House released what it claimed was BHO's "long form birth certificate" in April 2011. Some experts quickly labeled it a "forgery"—and not a particularly good forgery at that.

now working in the Obama administration; in the saga of the missing Obama files—as with much about Obama's past—coincidence has its role to play)

- Stanley Ann Dunham passport records (her official government passport files were first reported to be "lost"—possibly they, too, were scrubbed clean; Dunham's pre-1968 passport records were later reported to have been "destroyed" by the State Department, which is odd only because the State Department is not in the business of destroying past passport records)

Obama Records: Lost

- Illinois State Senate calendar and schedule
- Noelani Elementary School kindergarten records—"unable to locate"

Obama Records: Never Did or No Longer Exist

- *Harvard Law Review* articles—none
- Baptism certificate—none
- University of Chicago scholarly articles—none
- Annenberg Challenge Board minutes—none
- Illinois State Senate records—none

Obama Records: Released

- St. Francis of Assisi School, Jakarta, Indonesia—obtained by private investigators
- Besuki Primary School, Jakarta, Indonesia—obtained by AP

- Soetoro/Dunham divorce—released by independent investigators
- Selective Service registration—released with questions surrounding the date on which Obama registered
- Barack Obama Social Security number—released by independent investigators who have found more than one SSN used by Barack Obama and other anomalies, which to date have not been explained by the president or his spokesmen

In addition, on January 21, 2009, as his very first official act upon being sworn into office, President Barack Hussein Obama signed Executive Order 13489, which officially sealed all of his records.

As readers can surmise from the lists above, information on our forty-fourth president is not only hard to come by, but even the most elementary information has been "unavailable." What other modern politician has assumed the highest office in the land without the press badgering him for his medical, school, university, birth, and previous political records? In fact, what previous politician has operated in the 24/7 cable news environment without the public's gaining such elementary knowledge? What modern president has the CMM so studiously defended from any and all who desired to peer into the president's past history?

Who is Barack Hussein Obama?

"Journalists" in the employ of the Corporate Mainstream Media checked their professional curiosity at the door of Barack Obama's campaign headquarters. If the CMM was not interested in such an easily checked story as Obama's past relationship with former domestic terrorist Bill "Every time I think of America, it makes me want to puke" Ayers, why would anyone suppose it would expend much effort to dig into the unexpectedly more difficult task of bringing the missing Obama records to light?

Beginning in 2007, the CMM evolved into a sort of Royal Society of Professional Obama Apologists. Its first order of business was to ignore all calls for information on the man running for president. Its next—when ignoring questions didn't work—was to leap into attack mode. No story questioning the official Obama Narrative™ was too small to escape its notice and its condescendingly arrogant replies. The CMM never responded to questions about Obama. Instead, it attacked any messenger bearing inconvenient revelations—if the information was acknowledged at all.

When questions arose about Barack Obama's birth certificate, the CMM consulted the Obama campaign for answers. The campaign posted a Certification of Live Birth on its website and claimed that this was the candidate's birth certificate. When it was pointed out that the Certification of Live Birth was routinely issued to foreigners who took up residence in Hawaii, the *Los Angeles Times* quoted the Obama campaign's Ben LaBolt: "I can confirm that that is Senator Obama's birth certificate."

Oh.

Ben LaBolt was also helpful about the odd fact that not many people remembered our gregarious president while he was enrolled at Columbia University. According to the *New York Times*, LaBolt said, "He [Obama] doesn't remember the names of a lot of people in his life."

A couple of fascinating books examining the Columbia period of Obama's life are *Obama: The Postmodern Coup—Making of a Manchurian Candidate* by Webster Griffin Tarpley and *The Manchurian President: Barack Obama's Ties to Communists, Socialists and Other Anti-American Extremists* by Aaron Klein and Brenda J. Elliott. Both focus on the subjects of the missing records and the missing years of Barack Obama's time at Columbia to an extent that is far beyond the scope offered in this chapter.

The *Los Angeles Times* responded to a mild uprising in the comments section of its first Obama birth certificate whitewash by ratcheting up the rhetoric against nonbelievers in an August 2008 piece. To this writer, the *Los Angeles Times* piece sounded not just exasperated but slightly unhinged.

> In Obama's case, there has been rampant online speculation that his birth certificate is forged or altered somehow. Well, the folks at *FactCheck.org* say they have seen the certificate, touched and vouched it—Obama is as American as baseball, apple pie, and, these days, burritos, pasta, and kung pao chicken.
>
> So that should settle it . . . unless . . . wait . . . the people at *FactCheck.org* use computers, with keypads, that have the letters r-e-z-k-o on them, which just happened to spell the name of one of Obama's disgraced former backers . . . and they were in Chicago to see the birth certificate at . . . Obama headquarters . . . CONNECT THE DOTS, PEOPLE!

Does this sound like an objective reporter straining to get to the bottom of a subject that obviously concerned many of his readers? Asking questions was no longer the mark of an informed electorate; it was considered bad form. Asking questions became synonymous with "attack politics" and a sign of "racism."

The *Los Angeles Times*, it will be remembered, did not report on Senator John Edwards, who at the time was reportedly on Barack Obama's short list as a vice-presidential prospect, when Edwards was chased and cornered in a public restroom of the Beverly Hilton after visiting his mistress and their love child. This happened under the nose of the *Los Angeles Times* and was the subject of a memo "suggesting" to the *Times*'s bloggers not to mention the event to its readers.

The curious response of the fact-checking website *Fact Check.org* is also a clue to how a supposedly neutral "fact-checker" responded to questions about Obama's missing long-form birth certificate. *FactCheck* was cited repeatedly by the CMM as the last word on questions about Obama's birth certificate:

> We also note that so far none of those questioning the authenticity of the document have produced a shred of evidence that the information on it is incorrect. Instead, some speculate that somehow, maybe, he was born in another country and doesn't meet the Constitution's requirement that the president be a "natural-born citizen."
>
> We think our colleagues at *PolitiFact.com*, who also dug into some of these loopy theories, put it pretty well: "It is possible that Obama conspired his way to the precipice of the world's biggest job, involving a vast network of people and

government agencies over decades of lies. Anything's possible. But step back and look at the overwhelming evidence to the contrary and your sense of what's reasonable has to take over."

The strategy exhibited seemed to be "Nothing like a little professional sneering from the credentialed media class to put the rubes in their place." The *PolitiFact.com* cited by *FactCheck.org* was also a good example of the incestuous, circular nature of the CMM appeal to each other's authority. The *Los Angeles Times* cited *FactCheck*, which referenced *PolitiFact*, which cited the Obama Campaign, which asked Ben LaBolt and other staffers, who consulted the Obama Narrative™, which usually drew from Obama's memoir, *Dreams from My Father*. Lather, rinse, repeat.

Rarely did the questions ever get so far as to be put directly to Barack Obama himself, thus sparing the candidate any statements that could be checked later by a truly neutral third party.

This might be the time to point out that *PolitiFact.com* is not some website dedicated to a higher truth, maintained by disinterested scholars poring over texts to ascertain the answers to partisan questions. It is maintained by and is a part of the liberal Florida newspaper the *St. Petersburg Times*. The fact that *Politi Fact* is a "Pulitzer Prize Winner" is prominently displayed at the top of the site. One suspects that the Pulitzer was a reward for clever rebranding of a busted media product into something the public might more easily believe.

PolitiFact.com is staffed by the same writers who worked at the *St. Petersburg Times* before the rebranding; it still reflects the biases of the editorial staff. The only difference is that now the *St. Petersburg Times* has a brand that masquerades as a neutral fact checker—as opposed to the old way of simply publishing that same information in the form of left-wing editorials readers had stopped accepting blindly.

If the *St. Petersburg Times* had written, in its editorial page, "It is possible that Obama conspired his way to the precipice of the world's biggest job, involving a vast network of people and government agencies over decades of lies. Anything's possible. But step back and look at the overwhelming evidence to the contrary and your sense of what's reasonable has to take over," it's quite possible it would have been dismissed out of hand by the skeptical. But the same words, posted at the same website under the *PolitiFact* brand, were supposedly more believable, by virtue of having appeared under the aegis of the Pulitzer Prize Winner, *PolitiFact.com*.

At some point, it should have been apparent to progressives that it was in their interest to uncover this information as well. Just as conservatives were persuaded to support George W. Bush as the electoral lesser of two evils, progressives were persuaded to support a candidate about whom little was known outside the carefully constructed narrative of the Obama campaign. As it turned out, Obama's branding as the "Non-Bush" was enough to win the full-throated support of the progressive left. No records were required.

Obama's Missing Records: A Collection of Queer and Curious Notes

Supporters in 2008 asserted that Obama had released his medical records. They were mistaken. They could be excused, though, due to pieces that appeared in the CMM which attempted to confuse the matter. On May 30, 2008, the *Los Angeles Times* said:

> Although he hasn't had a physical in 16 months, Democratic presidential candidate Barack Obama has been in excellent health—and is physically ready to serve as president, his longtime physician wrote in a letter released by the campaign today.
>
> The letter contained relatively few details but noted that Obama has a family history of cancer—his mother died of ovarian cancer and a grandfather of prostate cancer. A prostate-specific antigen test detected no issues for Obama, however.
>
> The overview was contained in a one-page letter with no supporting documentation. With no surgery or hospital stays, this is a complete summary of his doctor visits and medical records for the past two decades, said campaign spokeswoman Jen Psaki.

Contrast the *Los Angeles Times*'s gentle treatment of the missing Obama medical records—the campaign told the press that the doctor who had written the letter cited by the *Times* "would not be made available to the press"—with what was written about Obama's opponent John McCain's release of past medical history. McCain made the decision to let a selected group of reporters spend three hours with his health records.

The CMM's response? McCain was criticized for not allowing enough time for the reporters to go through the nearly twelve hundred pages of the records provided. Twelve hundred pages versus a brief one-page summary letter.

Like much in the missing records, Obama's health was an article of faith, something to be accepted by press and public alike. Although ABC News did report, "The release of a scant one-page summary for 21 years of care brought some criticism to the Obama campaign—especially when compared to the thousands of pages of medical records released by McCain." Most of the press, nevertheless, bought it.

Candidate Obama had been known, according to a lawsuit brought by Philip J. Berg, former deputy attorney general for Pennsylvania, by five different legal names: Barack Hussein Obama, Barry Soetoro, Barry Obama, Barack Dunham, and Barry Dunham. This was unprecedented by a candidate running for president. To the CMM, however, it was unremarkable.

The *New York Times* in May 2008 on John McCain's medical records:

> No presidential candidate should get to the point that he has locked up his party's nomination without public vetting of his health.

The *New York Times* in May 2008 on Barack Obama's medical records:

> The letter is the first publicly released information about Mr. Obama's medical history or current condition. The six-paragraph, one-page statement summarized the senator's health for the last 21 years and was signed by Dr. David L. Scheiner,

who said he has been Mr. Obama's primary care physician since March 23, 1987. The undated letter was released less than a week after Senator John McCain of Arizona, the presumptive Republican nominee, released his medical records.

A spokesman for Mr. Obama said his campaign would not make Dr. Scheiner available for a telephone interview.

Why the Medical Records of Presidents and Candidates Are Important

In the past, White House physicians have been known to lie; candidates for president or nominees have been known to evade the truth, distort the facts, or lie. You've got Woodrow Wilson with a stroke and his wife allegedly running the affairs of the country; you've got Franklin Roosevelt who may or may not have been told how deathly ill he was in his last term, and certainly nothing was told to the country about it; you've got Kennedy every which way not acknowledging that he had Addison's disease; you had [Thomas] Eagleton who had to leave the [Democratic] ticket in '72 because he didn't tell [George] McGovern about his past history of electric-shock therapy and depression; and there was [Paul] Tsongas in the mid-1990s and the fact that he had a recurrence after they had maintained that he was cured of cancer.

—Lawrence Altman, "Covering Candidates' Medical Records"

The CMM interest in George Bush's records was so intense in 2004, it led CBS News and Dan Rather to report on forged records—though they weren't identified as such until the blogosphere pointed out the forgery. The remarkable lack of curiosity in the same corporate media just four years later concerning Obama's records has never been explained in a rational or satisfactory manner.

When Stanley Kurtz was finally allowed access to the Chicago Annenberg Challenge records, they revealed a load of things the Obama campaign would have rather not talked about—and the CMM didn't, except to whitewash the Bill Ayers connection that the records documented. As a reader asked, "How did Obama's time on the Annenberg Challenge board go from being a key bulletpoint in his resume—by his own accounting—to one the media refuses to even mention?"

> Every time somebody turns over a rock of Barack Obama's
> past, something unpleasant crawls out.
>> —RE Bierce, in email to *DBKP—Death By 1000 Papercuts*

Why weren't the media interested in the missing Obama records? In the *Chicago Tribune's* case, it's because it had a vested interest: The *Tribune* had asked Obama to run for president in 2006. Obama's campaign mastermind, David Axelrod, was a former employee of the *Chicago Tribune*. One would assume he still had a few friends who worked at the paper. And, presumably, friends do favors for friends.

In October 2008, *Newsmax* magazine investigated the claims made on Obama's *Fightthesmears.com* website and found that the "smears" about Obama were largely true. A number of what the Obama campaign had branded as "smears" were questions about various missing documents or years from Obama's life. "Smear" was also the word for any uncomfortable information that surfaced in the media or on the Internet that the Obama Narrative™ found difficult to ignore or explain away.

Obama's campaign started a website to combat rumors: *Fightthesmears.com*. The only problem? It didn't. Picking and choosing mostly straw men, the website was a brilliant concept: Label inconvenient information that didn't fit the Obama Narrative™ "smears."

The Obama campaign used its Internet site to discredit other Internet sites with which it disagreed. Stories that threatened to gain traction were branded "smears" and relegated to *Fightthesmears.com*, where Obama's thin résumé/record was repackaged as Internet fact, wrapped with a nice ribbon of indignation at having been bothered in the first place.

Harkening back to the 1990s, it's remembered that the "conspiracy theorist" label was applied to publications (notably *American Spectator*) that uncovered uncomfortable information about Bill and Hillary Clinton's past.

When Hillary Clinton ran for the Democratic nomination for president, a now pro-Obama CMM—which had previously derided those with questions over Hillary's cattle futures and other bits and pieces from Arkansas during the Clintons' stay in the White House—suddenly became interested in those same stories ten to fifteen years after the fact, a truly remarkable rehabilitation by the CMM of what previously was a "conspiracy theory."

The only trace of Barack Obama at Occidental College that the public has been allowed to see has been a few of Obama's efforts at poetry that were offered on the college's website. Occidental's website informed the curious, "Transcripts of his poems are available upon request."

There were some who felt that the inclusion of Obama's kindergarten records among the missing Obama records was unfair. Obama attended kindergarten at Noelani Elementary School on the Hawaiian island of Oahu during the 1966–67 school year, according to the *Maui News*.

Furthermore, in a report at *World Net Daily*, "According to the Hawaii Department of Education, students must submit a birth certificate to register. Parents may bring a passport or student visa if the child is from a foreign country." School records from elementary school are usually considered no big deal as far as presidential records go, but in this case it's been pointed out that release of the Noelani Elementary records would be a pain-free way for Barack Obama to document that he is a U.S. citizen.

Or not. Obama has never released his elementary school records and *WND* reported, "Noelani Elementary School officials have not responded to *WND*'s request for comment."

In 2008, Senator Barack Obama's campaign stated that it would bring a new level of honesty and transparency to the White House. Obama proudly boasted that he passed a law requiring more transparency via a public database of all federal spending. One suspects that readers who paid attention to the words and contradictory actions of candidate Obama on the subject of "transparency" were not surprised when the words of President Obama did not match his actions on the same subject upon gaining the White House.

During the Democratic primary season, Barack Obama

complained that the Bush administration was "one of the most secretive administrations in our history." In addition, Obama criticized his primary opponent, Hillary Clinton, for not releasing records of her White House schedules. This is mentioned only for comedic relief.

The difference between a Hawaiian *Certificate* of Live Birth and a Hawaiian *Certification* of Live Birth is much like the difference Mark Twain described between the right word and the almost right word: "[It] is really a large matter—it's the difference between the lightning bug and the lightning."

The *Certificate* of Live Birth is a legal document that provides much more information about the individual named on the certificate. This is a document that Obama has not released. The *Certification* of Live Birth is a much more generic-type document. One need not be born in the State of Hawaii to obtain one. The *Certification* of Live Birth is the document that Obama has released.

Obama himself commented on his birth certificate on page 26 of *Dreams from My Father,* noting that he "discovered this article, folded away among my birth certificate and old vaccination forms, when I was in high school." So, we do know that the president had access to more than just the *Certification* of Live Birth he offered the public in 2008. This prompted reporter Kenneth Timmerman to observe, "This, to me, presents a question as to why it was necessary for Obama to provide an obviously laser-printed, recent copy of his birth records in the first place. If he had his original, tucked in among articles and old vaccination forms, why not just provide that one?"

Obama's Selective Service records descrve a few obser-
vations. Obama made a few remarks about his having had to
register for Selective Service during a September 7, 2008, appearance on ABC's *This Week* with George Stephanopoulos.

GEORGE STEPHANOPOULOS: *One of our viewers wrote in—
you talk about service—and asked, Brenda Godfrey Bryan,
Marietta, Georgia: Did you ever consider joining the armed
services to protect and serve our country? If not, why?*
BARACK OBAMA: *You know, I actually did.*
STEPHANOPOULOS: *When?*
BARACK OBAMA: *You know, I had to sign up for Selective
Service when I graduated from high school. And I was
growing up in Hawaii, and I had friends whose parents
were in the military, there were a lot of Army, military bases
there. And I always actually thought of the military as
some ennobling and honorable option. But keep in mind:
I graduated in 1979. The Vietnam War had come to an
end. We weren't engaged in an active military conflict at
that point. So it's not an option that I ever decided to
pursue.*

"You know, I had to sign up for Selective Service when I
graduated from high school. . . . But keep in mind: I graduated
in 1979." This particular point is curious because there was no
requirement—nor was it even possible—to sign up for Selective
Service when Obama graduated from high school. According to
Wikipedia:

On March 29, 1975, President Ford signed Proclamation 4360, Terminating Registration Procedures Under Military Selective Service Act, eliminating the registration requirement for all 18–25 year old male citizens.

On July 2, 1980, however, President Carter signed Proclamation 4771, Registration Under the Military Selective Service Act, retroactively re-establishing the Selective Service registration requirement for all 18–26 year old male citizens born on or after January 1, 1960. Only men born between March 29, 1957, and December 31, 1959, were completely exempt from Selective Service registration. The first registrations after Proclamation 4771 took place on Monday, July 21, 1980, for those men born in January, February and March 1960 at U.S. Post Offices. Tuesdays, Wednesdays and Thursdays were reserved for men born in the later quarters of the year, and registration for men born in 1961 began the following week.

A small group of investigators have concerned themselves with the discrepancies found in Barack Obama's Selective Service records, most notably Debbie Schlussel. "Through an FOIA document request, a retired federal agent has obtained Obama's Selective Service Registration card and its accompanying DLN printout sheet. The former agent, Stephen Coffman, points out that the Selective Service System Data Management Center's FOIA response was fulfilled prior to his actual request. The dates on the documents do not follow any logical sequence, nor do they match the dates when Coffman brought these issues to the attention of Selective Service officials."

It's beyond the scope of this work to examine in depth all of the many contentions surrounding the Selective Service records of Barack Obama. Readers interested in learning more should conduct a Google search of "Obama Selective Service registration" and be prepared for a long period of reading: The search returns some 180,000 results. Schlussel's website, *Debbie Schlussel.com,* isn't a bad place to start.

5

Has Anyone Seen My Birth Certificate?

Barack Obama is arguably the least known of any American president; missing or sealed are his kindergarten records, Punahou School records, Occidental College records, Columbia University records, Columbia thesis, Harvard Law School records, *Harvard Law Review* articles, scholarly articles from the University of Chicago, passport, files schedule/calendar from his years as an Illinois state senator, his Illinois State Bar Association records, medical records, any baptism records, and his adoption records.

But the one document MIA that has fired up the most controversy by far is the president's original long-form birth certificate.

The United States Constitution requires that the president

be a natural-born citizen of the United States. Since 2008, questions about whether President Barack Obama was actually born in Hawaii have refused to go away. Obama has rejected all demands for the release of his original long-form Hawaiian birth certificate, which would include the actual hospital that performed the delivery and the name of the attending physician.

Why would anyone even question whether the forty-fourth president was born in the United States?

NOTE: The release of a document alleged to be Barack Obama's long-form birth certificate finally occurred in April 2011. Almost immediately, various experts wrote that there were problems with the document's authenticity. Some wondered how the president had procured such a document in April 2011, when various officials from the State of Hawaii had assured the public in 2010 that the very same document no longer existed.

Regardless of its validity, the release of this document still leaves unanswered the many questions that have surrounded the curious case of Barack Obama's long-form birth certificate since the spring of 2008. This chapter details many of those still unanswered questions, along with a few other assorted oddities.

Before continuing, it might be helpful to remind the reader to keep an open mind.

This writer first heard the contentions of the "birthers"—the clever word coined by the media to identify those who had questions as conspiracy theorists and kooks and thereby invalidate any discussion of those questions—in spring 2008. In the daily rush of pursuing other stories at the time, a few cursory looks at various sites on the Internet satisfied what little personal curiosity existed. The supposedly neutral authority of the partisan

PolitiFact and *FactCheck.org* websites was used by many of the sources consulted by the author at that time.

Revisiting the issue three or four months later led to the discovery of an unlikely string of curious circumstances and coincidences surrounding the long-form birth certificate of Barack Hussein Obama. The number of curious circumstances have not decreased in the months since then. If anything, they have increased.

"Keeping an open mind can never be bad advice" was the lesson learned.

The following are a few facts that have helped fuel the controversy, the curious circumstances surrounding the birth of Barack Hussein Obama.

- Obama's paternal grandmother, Sarah Obama, has stated that Obama was born in Kenya—and that she was present at his birth. A Kenyan Anabaptist minister has testified that a civil registrar affirmed Obama's birth at Coast Province Hospital in Mombosa, Kenya. Peter Ogego, Kenya's ambassador to the United States, affirmed Obama's birth in Kenya immediately after election day in a November 2008 radio interview. While some have maintained that the translation of what Sarah Obama said was botched, no one has disputed Ogego's claim.
- Michelle Obama, at a 2007 fund-raiser, described her husband as "Kenyan." The statement from the now–First Lady is in addition to another, earlier statement in which she described Kenya as Barack Obama's "home country." Videos of both statements can easily be found online at such sites

as *YouTube*. No one in the media has asked the First Lady to clarify or expand on these remarks, nor has she ever repudiated them.

- The "Obama for America" PAC paid $1,066,691.90 to the Perkins Coie law firm between October 16, 2008, and March 30, 2009, to fight every single request to release Obama's original birth records. This legal team continues its work, battling lawsuits all over the country that seek to force the president to produce a valid long-form birth certificate. Estimated legal costs reportedly now total $2.7 million—and counting.

   While realizing that lawyers have to eat, too, the question remains: Has this been a wise use of Obama's monetary resources? Since the defense team's efforts continue, the only answer to that question has to be "Yes." The question then becomes "Why?"

- In April 2010, U.S. Supreme Court Justice Clarence Thomas told a House subcommittee that the high court is "evading" the issue of determining whether a person born outside the fifty states can serve as U.S. president. Has anyone in the press bothered to ask Justice Thomas to explain how and why the court is "evading" this issue?

- A 2008 National Public Radio report for a program titled "Tell Me More" described then-senator Barack Obama as "Kenyan-born" and a "son of Africa." After the report was cited by *World Net Daily* investigators, NPR scrubbed the "Kenyan-born" reference from its website, but not before screenshots of the original NPR report had been taken. They can be viewed on the Internet, particularly at *World*

Net Daily. This is not the first reference that has been found in older media reports referring to Barack Obama as "foreign-" or "Kenyan-born." Many of these reports have been "corrected" or "updated" or have disappeared altogether. The question here is: Have the media been that sloppy in reporting on Barack Obama? Whether the answer is "Yes" or "No," then the question again becomes "Why?"

- Tim Adams, a college professor who had access to state birth records when he worked as a senior elections clerk for the City and County of Honolulu in 2008, stated during the 2008 presidential election that Barack Obama was not born in Hawaii and that no long-form birth certificate exists for Obama. The State of Hawaii subsequently verified that Tim Adams did indeed work as a senior elections clerk in 2008. Since the initial interviews that aired his claims, Tim Adams has been incommunicado on the subject.

- An article in the January 8, 2006, *Honolulu Advertiser* stated that Barack Obama was, like Tammy Duckworth, "born outside the country." "Duckworth is happy to point out that she and Hawai'i-raised Punahou graduate Obama have 'a kama'aina connection.' Both were born outside the country—Obama in Indonesia, Duckworth in Thailand—and graduated from high school in Honolulu—Punahou and McKinley, respectively." The *Advertiser* since has updated its article to reflect "that Barack Obama was born in Hawaii." Was Tammy Duckworth, who is the assistant secretary for public and intergovernmental affairs in the United States Department of Veterans Affairs, misquoted?

In which of the instances was the *Advertiser* guilty of sloppy reporting: the reporting of the original quotation or the later update?

- Michelle Obama, during a July 2008 round table at the University of Missouri, remarked that Stanley Ann Dunham, Obama's mother, was "very young and very single when she had him." Why has this quotation, which is clearly at odds with the official version of Obama's history from the Obama Narrative™, not elicited any curiosity in the decidedly uncurious Corporate Mainstream Media? Isn't this continued and studious incuriosity a matter of curiosity itself?

  "He understands them [the struggles of low-income families] because he was raised by strong women. He is the product of two great women in his life: his mother and his grandmother. Barack saw his mother, who was very young and very single when she had him, and he saw her work hard to complete her education and try to raise he and his sister."

  Again, these statements completely contradict the official Obama narrative that his mother was married to Barack Obama, Sr., at the time of his birth. Actually, it would change the entire narrative of Obama's first memoir, *Dreams from My Father.*

- Conflicting reports have been published (*Washington Post*, ABC News) that Obama had been born at the Queen's Medical Center in Honolulu, as well as the Kapiolani Medical Center for Women and Children across town. In 2008, members of the Obama campaign provided the names of both hospitals at the same time. ABC News later reported, "Obama was born in Kapiolani Maternity and Gynecological Hospital in Honolulu on Aug. 4, 1961." Which of these media reports is correct? Why has the media organization that published the wrong information not issued a retraction?

Not a single person came forth to vouch for the fact that Obama was born in Hawaii in August 1961: no doctor, nurse, hospital administrator, friends, neighbors, or acquaintances. Author Ron Jacob has claimed that he spoke with the attending physician. No corroborating evidence of Jacob's claim has been located to date. Kapiolani Hospital has repeatedly refused to confirm or deny the truth of the claim or to provide a copy of a hospital birth certificate or record. Why has this easily resolved question remained unresolved?

- On April 30, 2008, the Senate approved Senate Resolution 511, recognizing that John Sidney McCain III was a "natural-born citizen" under Article II, Section 1, of the Constitution. At the same time the Senate confirmed one candidate's bona fides, it was silent about whether candidate Barack Obama was "natural-born." By April 2008, enough questions had surfaced about Obama's birth circumstances to prompt many articles in the media on the matter. Why didn't the Senate kill two birds with one stone, so to speak?

- Perkins Coie has begun every legal challenge to an Obama birth-certificate lawsuit with a letter to the plaintiffs threatening financial sanctions if their case is not withdrawn. "Should you decline to withdraw this frivolous appeal, please be informed that we intend to pursue sanctions, including costs, expenses, and attorneys' fees. . . ."

- Army Lieutenant Colonel Terrence Lakin has risked a court-martial in order to determine whether President Obama is eligible to serve as POTUS and commander in chief. Lieutenant Colonel Lakin is the "lead flight surgeon charged with caring for Army Chief of Staff General George W. Casey's flight crew."

  Lieutenant Colonel Lakin is trying to get the same verification from the president that Lakin has been asked to provide for many jobs, and to obtain a security clearance for the U.S. Air Force. After months of seeking answers, he has not received a definitive response that would assure him of the president's constitutional eligibility.

  NOTE: Lieutenant Colonel Lakin pleaded guilty in December 2010 for failing to obey. Lakin faces up to eighteen months in prison and dishonorable discharge. Lakin has pointed out that "the minimal invasion to any politician's privacy from having to show an original signed birth certificate is far less than the harms to our country caused by someone not qualified whose election would thus subvert the law and the truth."

- Two other members of the military earlier mounted challenges to Obama's qualifications to serve as commander in chief, refusing to serve overseas. The military canceled their assignments rather than try their cases.

- An archived 2004 article from the *Sunday Standard* in Kenya that reported on Barack Obama's run for the U.S. Senate in Illinois described the political newcomer as "Kenyan-born."
- On August 28, 2008, Nancy Pelosi, as chair of the Democratic National Convention, and Alice Travis Germond, secretary of the Democratic National Convention, signed two forms certifying that Barack Obama and Joe Biden were the Democratic candidates for president and vice president.

    The first document certified that Barack Obama was constitutionally eligible to serve as president of the United States. The second version, which was the one sent to the secretaries of state of the fifty states, omitted any certification of constitutional standing for the office of president. The question here is: Is it normal procedure for the DNC to prepare two such certifications?
- Leo Donofrio of New Jersey filed a lawsuit claiming that Obama's dual citizenship disqualified him from serving as president. His case was one of two that was considered in conference by the U.S. Supreme Court but denied a full hearing.

These are by no means all of the curious circumstances surrounding Obama's birth certificate and his records. While far from being complete, they do constitute a representative sample.

Quiz time for readers.

Let's say you're the president of the United States.

You're the Most Powerful Man in the World™. The mainstream press generally covers for you—but there have been whispers about whether you are constitutionally qualified.

More than fifty fellow Americans, including a prominent Pennsylvania Democrat, have filed suit in various state and federal courts asking you to provide proof that you are constitutionally qualified to hold the office of president—to settle the matter once and for all.

What do you do?

- A. Provide the court with your long-form birth certificate and go back to shaking hands, making promises and smiling for the cameras, and preparing for another run in 2012.
- B. Provide images of a document to a friendly website to post, but not to the court.
- C. First, ignore the requests. Then spend in excess of $2 million to fight the requests, in lieu of providing the proof.
- D. Quietly post a notice at your campaign website, *Fight thesmears.com*, at the height of the questions, during the 2008 campaign, about your having dual citizenship with Kenya.

Time's up. What do you do?

Most readers sensibly chose A.

But, if you're Barack Obama, you chose answers B, C, and D.

Readers may reasonably ask, "Why?"

What's the big deal? Regular folks provide their birth certificates every day for any number of reasons—obtaining a driver's license or marriage license come to mind. Heck, even kids have to provide a certified copy of their birth certificates to register for kindergarten or to join a sports league in many locales.

Most people do it—if they're able—without much grumbling.

And they're not even the president of the United States of America.

Another very reasonable question that has never been answered: If Barack Obama has nothing to hide, why is everyone involved going to such lengths to hide it?

Attorney Philip Berg filed what would prove to be the first of many birth-certificate lawsuits, asking the court to force Obama to prove he was an American citizen.

That seemed reasonable. There were questions. Why not get some answers and put the matter to rest?

Obama merely has to do what thousands of Americans do each day—especially after 9/11: Provide a birth certificate or proof of U.S. citizenship. It's a minor inconvenience, but they do it.

Berg, a prominent Philadelphia attorney and Hillary Clinton supporter, filed suit in the U.S. District Court for the Eastern District of Pennsylvania on August 22, 2008, against Illinois Senator Barack Obama and the Democratic National Committee. The action sought an injunction preventing the senator from continuing his candidacy and a court order enjoining the DNC from nominating him at the following week's Democratic National Convention—all on grounds that Senator Obama was constitutionally ineligible to run for and hold the office of president of the United States.

Berg is a former gubernatorial and U.S. senatorial candidate, former chair of the Democratic Party in Montgomery County, former member of the Democratic State Committee, and former deputy attorney general of Pennsylvania. According to Berg, he filed the suit—just days before the DNC was to hold its 2008 nominating convention in Denver—for the health of the Democratic Party. "I filed this action at this time," Berg stated, "to avoid the obvious problems that will occur when the Republican Party raises these issues after Obama is nominated."

The suit asked for three documents:

- A certified copy of Obama's "vault" (original long version) birth certificate
- A certified copy of Obama's certificate of citizenship
- A certified copy of the oath of allegiance taken by Obama at the age of majority

Attorneys for Barack Obama responded by filing motions fighting the lawsuit.

That seems like curious behavior for a candidate anxious to dispel rumors about his qualifications and citizenship.

Why would that be?

Philip Berg explained: "It's my belief that he [Barack Obama] can't produce the documents. If Obama cannot produce a certificate of citizenship, that would make him an illegal alien. In that case, he should be arrested, tried, and deported. Senator Obama could put this whole thing to rest by providing an official 'vault copy' birth certificate. The fact that he's fighting it shows me that he can't produce the documents."

Again, that sounded reasonable.

On September 24, 2008, the day before Obama posted his dual citizenship admission on *Fightthesmears.com*, his legal team filed (along with the DNC's lawyers) a joint motion for a protective order to stay discovery pending a decision on the motion to dismiss.

Berg said that this action "outraged" him.

"This is another attempt to hide the truth from the public; it is obvious that documents do not exist to prove that Obama is qualified to be president.

"Their joint motion indicates a concerted effort to avoid the truth by attempting to delay the judicial process, although legal, by not resolving the issue presented: that is, whether Barack Obama meets the qualifications to be president."

The author asked Berg: Why would Obama do this? Why not just produce the documents? Why delay discovery— effectively ensuring that the documents will not have to be produced until after the election?

"I can only assume that if Obama wins, they will then claim that you cannot sue a sitting president."

Oh.

What about dual citizenship? With that constitutional question gaining traction, the Obama campaign did another curious thing.

On September 25, 2008, on Obama's *Fightthesmears.com*, the campaign admitted that Barack Obama had had dual citizenship, that he had been a citizen of both the United States and Kenya.

Obama defenders have especially cited the *Annenberg Polit-*

ical Fact Check/FactCheck.org statement—which coincidentally was the exact position of the Obama campaign:

> When Barack Obama Jr. was born on Aug. 4, 1961, in Hono-
> lulu, Kenya was a British colony, still part of the United King-
> dom's dwindling empire. As a Kenyan native, Barack Obama
> Sr. was a British subject whose citizenship status was gov-
> erned by The British Nationality Act of 1948. That same act
> governed the status of Obama Sr.'s children.
>
> Since Senator Obama has neither renounced his U.S. cit-
> izenship nor sworn an oath of allegiance to Kenya, his Kenyan
> citizenship automatically expired on Aug. 4, 1982.

For someone involved in a lawsuit over citizenship, ad-
mitting that Obama had had dual citizenship at this juncture
didn't seem particularly helpful—or likely to quiet those asking
questions.

We asked Berg about this.

"The dual citizenship with Kenya—that's a smokescreen.
Kenya allows dual citizenship. Kenya is not the issue.

"The Obama campaign never mentions Indonesia—and
won't. That's a problem. When Obama moved to Indonesia
and attended school, he was adopted or acknowledged by Lolo
Soetoro; Indonesia didn't allow dual citizenship."

As Berg wrote in his court filing, *Berg* v. *Obama,* No.
08-cv-04083:

> Obama lost his U.S. citizenship when his mother married an
> Indonesian citizen, Lolo Soetoro, who legally "acknowledged"

Obama as his son in Indonesia and/or "adopted" Obama, which caused Obama to become a "natural" Indonesian citizen. Stanley Ann Dunham Soetoro relocated herself and Obama to Indonesia wherein Obama's mother naturalized in Indonesia. This is proven by Obama's school record with the student's name as "Barry Soetoro," Father's name: Lolo Soetoro, M.A., and Citizenship: Indonesia.

Hmmm. And what did the Obama campaign have to say about all of this?

Nothing.

One begins to understand why Obama's lawyers chose to file motions instead of producing the documents in question.

Berg: "We got him. The fact that he's not produced any of the documents settles it."

Unfortunately for Berg—and others interested in seeing Obama's super-secret birth certificate—the case was dismissed for a "lack of standing." The court heard no arguments about the merits of the case.

A few reasonable questions about the elusive—and hidden from public view—birth certificate of Barack Obama:

1. Why won't the Obama campaign provide Obama's birth certificate to just one judge? The judge could verify that the president was constitutionally qualified. Instead, the Obama campaign—later, the Obama administration— and the DNC filed multiple motions to dismiss. Never once has a state or federal court heard the merits of an Obama birth-certificate lawsuit.

2. Why has the Obama campaign provided digital images of a Certification of Live Birth, claiming it to be a "birth certificate," to *FactCheck.org* that had been altered—either by the campaign or *FactCheck.org*—and why did *Fact Check.org* state that the images had never been altered? Evidence was quickly provided that they had been.

3. Why did *FactCheck.org* have to later fact-check its own June 12, 2008, fact-checking post on the Obama birth certificate? That is curious behavior for a site that is supposedly a neutral referee on political questions. NOTE: The two original posts have since been merged into one and updated many times.

4. Why did the Obama campaign and, later, the Obama administration fight every attempt to force the president to produce a valid original long-form birth certificate?

5. Why is it that the document Obama's lawyers have shown to *FactCheck.org* has not been shown to others in the media—outside of a few digital images to friendly CMM papers? There are certainly enough Corporate Mainstream Media organizations that are Obama-friendly—they would be more than happy to pronounce their satisfaction with it.

Since the questions first arose during the 2008 election campaign, those representing Barack Obama have offered inquiring minds three things.

One: A computer-generated "Certification of Live Birth." That may seem to answer the question for the casual reader, but COLBs are normally given if one gives birth at home or while traveling overseas. There is a large percentage of Asians in Hawaii. It's quite common for people to come to Hawaii and receive a Certification of Live Birth. The COLB is also needed to get a Hawaiian driver's license and is routinely given to residents who've moved to the state from elsewhere.

Until recently, even the Hawaiian state government refused to accept a short-form COLB—the document touted by Obama's defenders—as proof of a Hawaiian birth required for eligibility in state programs. The Hawaiian Home Lands program, for example, required a "long-form birth certificate" filled out in the hospital with details such as the name of the hospital and the attending physician.

Obama's own state wouldn't accept the Certification of Live Birth as proof someone had been born in Hawaii. Yet everyone in the other forty-nine states has been expected to stop asking questions whenever an image Obama's Certification of Live Birth appears at a few media organizations.

Two: A copy of a birth announcement that appeared in the *Honolulu Advertiser* and *Honolulu Star-Bulletin* in 1961. Again, this is a great response for the casual reader. But the birth announcements offer no proof of citizenship, because they might reflect nothing more than information a family filed with the Hawaii Department of Health to obtain a state Certification of Live Birth for a baby born outside Hawaii. Any parents presumably would see the benefit of securing American citizenship for their child.

What are the problems with accepting the birth announcement as "proof"? Actually, plenty—and it didn't take a conspiracy theorist to uncover them.

- Neither newspaper had an editor to vet birth announcements; neither newspaper independently checked the truthfulness or accuracy of birth announcement information derived from Hawaii Department of Health vital statistics records.

- Both newspapers merely published birth announcements, as received, from information published in Hawaii's Department of Health vital statistics announcements.

- Hawaiian hospitals did not report to newspapers any birth information.

- Errors and misstatements in birth announcements published in the two Hawaiian newspapers have been documented, stemming from incorrect information recorded by the Hawaiian Department of Health.

Three: A healthy dose of ridicule for anyone asking questions about Barack Obama's birth records. To date, no media organizations have investigated these inconsistencies; instead, the media have deflected questions about Obama's birth with a mixture of the COLB, the birth announcements, and especially, sneering ridicule for anyone who dared raise the issue.

Former White House press secretary Robert Gibbs mostly ignored the infrequent questions on the topic. When he did answer, it was to laugh off the entire issue and ridicule the odd questioner.

"Are you looking for the president's birth certificate?" he asked incredulously at one 2009 press briefing when the issue was raised. "Lester, this question in many ways continues to astound me. The state of Hawaii provided a copy with the seal of the president's birth.

"I know there are apparently at least four hundred thousand people [laughter] that continue to doubt the existence of and the certification by the state of Hawaii of the president's birth there, but it's on the Internet because we put it on the Internet for each of those four hundred thousand to download. I certainly hope by the fourth year of our administration that we'll have dealt with this burgeoning birth controversy."

The "Lester" referred to by Gibbs was Lester Kinsolving of *World Net Daily*, which has remained the most steadfast of media organizations in demanding to see Barack Obama's long-form birth certificate.

Still, why all of the curious behavior: by Barack Obama, the Obama administration, the Obama defense team, the Obama campaign, the DNC, Obama's legal team, *FactCheck.org*, and a compliant CMM?

Seems simple: Production of the document would make the issue go away. Barack Obama could go back to promising a chicken in every pot and ObamaCare for every garage and playing one more round of golf.

New Media can go back to asking questions about "Just who exactly is Barack Obama and why are so many of his past associations shrouded in secrecy and his past documents so difficult to obtain?"

Is Barack Obama constitutionally qualified to be the president of the United States of America?

Who knows? One thing is certain: Barack Obama and his

legal team have produced no proof that would silence future questions—or the lawsuits that continue to be filed.

Until such time as they do produce that elusive, original birth certificate, the question "Why is Barack Obama not doing what thousands of Americans have to do every day?" will continue to be asked—both in court and outside it.

Nancy Salvato with *BasicsProject.org* summed up the curious attitude of Barack Hussein Obama:

What perturbs the rest of us is that President Obama has failed to produce a legitimate birth certificate. He has a team of lawyers who are opposing the examination of his sealed records in Hawaii. What he produced was a certificate of live birth . . . not a birth certificate. The rest of us are appalled at the lack of media examination surrounding the fact that there is no law requiring that a candidate for the highest office in our land produce an authentic birth certificate which proves natural citizenship.

There are other questions about the Obama birth certificate that have arisen in the last twenty months. A small army of private investigators, political operatives, and ordinary citizen journalists have continued the tedious sifting of archives and old newspaper articles. Their work has revealed even more explosive information that has been more difficult to laugh away or explain.

What they have found has sparked legislators from at least a dozen states to introduce legislation to settle future constitutional questions once and for all. These efforts at the state level have been tenaciously fought by supporters of our forty-fourth president. Why?

Various Odd Obama Birth-Certificate Notes

- A website that does a good job of exploring the claims and questions of the "birthers" is *Obama Conspiracy Theories.* The site does a nice job of presenting contrary evidence in a straightforward manner with a minimum of ridicule. The site describes itself: *"Obama Conspiracy Theories* is your one-stop destination for conspiracy theories and fringe views about Barack Obama." While this writer many times doesn't agree with all of *OCT*'s conclusions, he does appreciate the continuing efforts by the site's proprietor, "Dr. Conspiracy," to provide contrary documentation, efforts that the CMM should have undertaken since 2007.

- By far the largest collection of online articles investigating the Obama birth-certificate controversy from the other perspective can be accessed at *World Net Daily.* Most progressives, as well as some conservatives, have derided *WND*'s efforts, but this doesn't in any way invalidate the results of its investigations. Any readers wanting to learn more will find the archives on the matter at *World Net Daily* an invaluable resource.

- Billing itself as a "conservative" website is no guarantee that the site will cover the issue of Obama's lack of documents any differently from how the CMM has—that is, not at all or badly. Readers—who naturally expect such conservative media to devote precious resources to investigating this important question—shouldn't judge too harshly. Some sites are simply anxious about being accused of racism, bigotry, or cheap scaremongering.

- Lou Dobbs, once a popular host at CNN, was probably the most prominent voice in the CMM to ask questions about the Obama birth certificate. "I believe Barack Obama is a citizen of the United States, folks, don't you? But I do have a couple of little questions, like you. Why not just provide a copy of the birth certificate? That's entirely within the president's power to do so. One would think the president would want to get rid of this nonsense. But he doesn't— and so, none of us knows what the reality is."

  Seems a reasonable enough view to many. But Dobbs is no longer at CNN; a campaign was mounted by a far-left, George-Soros-funded group, Media Matters, to remove Dobbs from CNN.

  According to *Wikipedia*, "On October 5, 2009, a bullet struck Dobbs's home as Dobbs and his wife stood outside it. The bullet struck the vinyl siding of their attic and fell to the ground without penetrating the vinyl. Dobbs attributed the incident to his stance against amnesty for illegal immigrants." Dobbs left CNN a month later.

  Since the time Dobbs left CNN, he has stayed mostly silent on the Obama birth-certificate controversy. It's been reported that Dobbs is considering a run for the U.S. Senate from New Jersey in 2012.

- One point that has been raised about the Certification of Live Birth presented by the Obama defenders as "proof":

The document lists the race of Barack Obama, Sr., as "African," a term that was not in use in 1961. The common description until more recently was "Negro." No explanation of this discrepancy has been offered by Team Obama.

- A photograph has surfaced of Ann Dunham, supposedly taken on Waikiki Beach during the summer of 1961. This photo of Obama's mother, shown wearing a bikini, is interesting but not that convincing as "evidence." The degree to which a woman appears pregnant is judged differently by various individuals. It's mentioned here because the photo exists. Readers who are interested will have to form their own judgment of what it does or does not show.

This chapter and the questions posed here are in no way a comprehensive treatment of this controversial subject. One suspects that an exhaustive study would be a project that could easily span several volumes. There are literally hundreds of Internet websites that are basically dedicated to this one particular question. Readers have seen the highlights, but these are only the beginning of an issue that hasn't gone away: the case of Barack Obama and his mysterious birth certificate.

6

A Birther Is a Racist Is a Truther Is a Nazi

In late December 2010, a trio of stories propelled Obama's birth certificate back into the news. Also back in the news was the favorite PC term for those who didn't wish to seriously engage in the discussion: "birther." "Birther" was just another politically correct term designed to substitute ridicule for debate.

The topic of the elusive birth certificate of Barack Obama has been thrust back into the news, primarily via two stories: Chris Matthews asking, "Why doesn't Obama show his birth certificate?" and the new governor of Hawaii telling tales of Obama's parents, who were apparently two of his pals from the past.

A third, though less-noticed, item also unintentionally contributed to the discussion: the sudden revelation by the Associated Press—without citing a source for its discovery—of the particular Hawaiian hospital with the honor of hosting our forty-fourth president's entry into this world.

Obama himself has never publicly revealed that information, so one would think that the AP would be anxious to declare where it got the previously undiscovered information in its piece. But the AP did not make a big deal of it. It just slipped it into its article—probably for "flavor."

Matthews and his guest panel wondered—two years after Matthews abrogated his constitutionally protected duty to investigate the question—why BHO hadn't gotten around to producing his long-form birth certificate? Actually, the correct question would be: "Why hasn't BHO gotten around to producing his long-form birth certificate and instead spent upward of $2 million in court over the question?"

Which really makes this story about why Chris Matthews has suddenly become curious. Why has Matthews apparently decided that being tied to the progressive wolfsbane of "birther" is no longer any big deal? Does it all have to do with Neil Abercrombie's peculiar statements?

Neil Abercrombie is Hawaii's new governor. As Elaine Marlow discovered in her earlier post, "Hawaii Governor Neil Abercrombie Adds Fuel to Obama Birth Certificate Fire," Neil Abercrombie was *Time*'s go-to guy for Obamabilia back in April 2008.

On April 9, 2008, *Time* published "The Story of Barack Obama's Mother." *Time* magazine managed to find only one person for the interview who knew both of Barack Obama's parents, Neil Abercrombie.

Here we are almost two years later and guess who's the governor of Hawaii? Neil Abercrombie! Son of a gun! Only now, he remembers seeing Barack Sr. and Obama's mother with "their child at social events."

Abercrombie surely knew that he would have to have seen the happy Obama family within a two-week window: Stanley Ann Dunham was enrolled in classes in Washington State fifteen days after Barack Obama was supposedly born. Obama Sr. left Hawaii some months later, while Ann Dunham was still a student on the mainland. The couple was divorced soon thereafter. Which is funny, because a copy of their marriage license has never been found.

No big deal: just another day on the Obama's Missing Records beat.

To continue, Neil Abercrombie was one serendipitous guy. He happened to be at those "social events" during that window. But Abercrombie had to be aware of how far-fetched his timeline appeared—while also aware that others would be aware of it. It's a matter of what little public record is available for our most private of presidents.

Abercrombie was the author of another queer quote: "Maybe I'm the only one in the country that can look you in the eye and say that I was here when that baby was born." What does that even mean? Why is he the only one in the country? How odd.

Also odd: Why is Abercrombie bringing up the subject of Obama's birth certificate now—and doing so with statements sure to invite more speculation? It's amazing the discussion that can be sparked by a couple of progressives with a platform. If only that had occurred back in 2008.

And why was this discussion even being held? There's absolutely no reason for it: Barack Obama—like Dorothy in *The Wizard of Oz*—has always had the power to click his heels three times and make the whole issue disappear.

The entire discussion, its timing and the reason for it, is beyond absurd.

Which brings us to another point: From the beginning, anyone who exhibited any curiosity about such a mundane matter got tagged with the very latest in PC thought control, the infamous "birther" label.

Inconvenient, unanswered questions? Shout "BIRTHER!" and end the debate!

Just like shouting "CONSPIRACY THEORIST!"

Just like shouting "NAZI!"

Just like shouting "TRUTHER!"

Just like shouting "RACIST!"

It's Godwin for Dummies. It's also as passé as Che. Tactics are most effective when the other side isn't aware of them. That's why PC is so 1980s college campus: Most who are serious immediately see the game and call it BS.

It's also a tired tactic. The repeated use of "racist" by the Corporate Mainstream Media to describe the concerns of the Tea Party cheapened both that term and the tactic itself.

"BIRTHER," however, is used at least as much by conservative writers as by progressives—maybe that's the reason it's not been called out as an attempt to limit the debate. That doesn't make it any less a garden-variety, politically correct trick resorted to by those too lazy to address the issue. It has become shorthand for "I don't have time or inclination to seriously address the points of the matter."

Why argue the merits when it's much easier and quicker to substitute smug arrogance and a handy pejorative for what's sure to be tedious research.

It's so easy, anyone can do it—and boy, have they!

Instead of writing, "I'm busy and have a lot of other issues occupying my time," or taking a pass altogether, why do some pundits feel compelled to throw a headline, a link, and a suitable derogatory adjective for "BIRTHER!" together on the subject as a substitute for reasoned thought?

Actually, it makes them sound like they're card-carrying members of the CMM. Maybe that's their point? Speech codes are coming under increased fire on college campuses, but they're alive and well in the media—and "BIRTHER!" is evidence of that!

PUNDIT CHALLENGE 1: Next time you're about to write "BIRTHER!" substitute the word "RACIST!" and read it back. Does it sound silly? It should.

PUNDIT CHALLENGE 2: Next time you're filled with the righteous anger that comes only from well-meaning people being smeared with the "RACIST!" label, substitute the word "BIRTHER!" in the offensive article. Are you still angry?

You should be—because it's the same thought-control PC tactic used successfully for years by progressives. Why have a discussion when you can avoid it altogether with one little word. For a time, "NAZI!" also worked well.

Another good discussion squasher is "CONSPIRACY THE-ORIST!" For ten months, that was one of the favorite phrases used to describe this writer when the news blackout was under way over all things relating to the John Edwards/Rielle Hunter scandal. It's enough to make one believe that one definition of a conspiracy theorist might be "someone who is better informed than their detractors."

Don't present counterarguments, present scorn. Don't answer inconvenient information, ridicule it. Saul Alinsky would have approved of—even if he would be a bit disappointed by—Chris Matthews and Neil Abercrombie.

(This piece appeared largely in the form seen here on December 30, 2010, as "A Birther Is a Racist Is a Truther Is a Nazi" by Mondo Frazier at *DBKP—Death By 1000 Papercuts.com.*)

7

Columbia, the Obama Narrative™, and Other Conspiracy Theories

> My Administration is committed to creating an unprecedented level of openness in Government. We will work together to ensure the public trust and establish a system of transparency, public participation, and collaboration. Openness will strengthen our democracy and promote efficiency and effectiveness in Government.
>
> —memorandum, President Barack Obama

"Transparency" was an Obama buzzword in 2008 and all of the cool kids were using it. Obama used it, too, and proposed himself as the leader of "the most transparent administration in history." So how did a president who ran as an open book become the target of so much speculation and so many theories—some of which could be categorized as "conspiratorial"—about his past and his motives?

Other words the cool kids were using that year were "Hope" and "Change." Like most buzzwords from the Obama Narrative™, Team Obama selected the words because they meant whatever the listener chose to believe they meant. Any connection with "hope" and "change" as understood by Barack Obama was purely coincidental. Much of Obama's past is a similar construct: Any relationship between Obama's past and the fairy tales collected in the Obama Narrative™ was purely coincidental. Who's to say what the past was? It's so open to—shall we say?—personal interpretation. Particularly the years Obama spent at Columbia University after transferring from Occidental College in Los Angeles.

Obama's years at Columbia have proved fertile ground indeed for the seeds of conspiracy. One of the most outlandish of the conspiracy theories about Obama's time at Columbia comes from Barack Obama himself. Basically, it goes like this: Barack Obama transferred from Occidental College to Columbia University in New York City to allow him wider access to his political awakening and to experience the wonders of a more diverse environment.

In spite of grades that "weren't very good" (Obama's words), he was admitted to the Ivy League school and moved to New York. Before Columbia, Obama was almost universally described as "outgoing" and "gregarious," but upon arriving in NYC, he promptly hid from the world in the school's library. The young student flew so far under the radar that no one remembered his being there. Later, after news accounts publicized this strange situation, several people came forward to claim that "I knew Barack Obama." At least one of those long-lost pals can't be found in the pages of Columbia yearbooks or public records as being a student.

Despite a "monklike" devotion to his studies while hidden in the library, the "brilliant" Obama managed to haul down a final grade point average of somewhere between 2.0 and 3.2. In Political Science. A few years later, this sterling record of achievement was the basis of his gaining admittance to Harvard Law School. This is the theory of events as provided by the Obama Narrative™.

During the 2008 primary season, reporters who wanted to learn about Barack Obama consulted the largest record available about a man with little other public record: *Dreams from My Father*, a bit of Obama autobiographical stream-of-consciousness, supplied lots of narratives and motives—and relatively little verifiable information about certain periods of Barack Obama's past. One of the periods that Obama skipped over was his time at Columbia University. Another was his time spent in Pakistan—but that's another chapter.

A CMM that found it hard to pose hard questions *to* Barack Obama also found it easy to ask questions about those who had questions *about* Barack Obama. In comparison, the interview questions put to Republican vice-presidential candidate Sarah Palin were straight out of an Imperial Chinese Confucian examination. Most of the questions posed by our fierce watchdogs in the press to Barack Obama ran something on the order of "How you feel today, Champ?"

Barack Obama showed up in Joe "the Plumber" Wurzelbacher's neighborhood. Joe asked Obama a question and Obama's answer revealed an unpleasant fact: Obama wanted to "spread

[Joe's] wealth around." Obama partisans in Joe's home state of Ohio used state government computers to look into Joe's supposedly private records. They then leaked the ill-gotten information to a CMM that was only too eager to spread it around. If Joe had been running for president on the Democratic ticket, one suspects, the press would have thrown themselves in front of a bus if that would have prevented the leakers from divulging Joe's records.

Since the CMM often didn't press Barack Obama about these formative years, speculation has been substituted by those attempting to explain "what makes Obama tick."

Did Barack Obama Really Attend Columbia University?

In the days before election day 2008, much of Barack Obama's past still remained shrouded in secrecy. The same press that could tell readers how much Sarah Palin's shoes cost and the name of the designer handbag one of her daughters was seen carrying couldn't seem to muster much curiosity over large gaps of time in the Obama Narrative™. When someone at the *New York Times* did work up the courage to ask Obama about his Columbia years, he refused to answer. The *Times*'s outraged response?

"Okay."

Indeed, portions of the CMM were more intent on hiding information than on publishing it. This situation reached a climax when it was discovered that Barack Obama was a guest at a send-off dinner for a controversial Palestinian apologist, Rashid

Khalidi. Obama, who at the time was trying to portray himself as an unflinching friend of Israel in order to secure the Jewish vote, had not quite sealed the deal when it was discovered that the *Los Angeles Times* had in its possession a videotape of the Khalidi event. The *Times* confirmed that it had the videotape, and that it had no intention of letting the public see it.

The *Times* then went through a convoluted evolution of excuses about why it would not make the video of the event available. The few remaining customers of the *Los Angeles Times* were then treated to the spectacle of the newspaper making news by its refusal to report the news—a familiar position for the paper.

In July 2008, even though John Edwards was caught by reporters from the *National Enquirer* after visiting his mistress and their love child at the Beverly Hilton—and it was confirmed a few days later by Fox News—the *Los Angeles Times* instructed its reporters NOT to write on the paper's blogs about Edwards's mishap. So, readers of the *Los Angeles Times* were used to being kept in the dark. The Obama-Khalidi video was just one more instance.

It's helpful to know the facts of the matter. Yes, there are cold, hard facts of Obama's Columbia period—just not very many of them. Obama himself hasn't been very helpful in adding to this body of knowledge, as the reader will see. The CMM has done a little work, which demonstrates that it *could* do a proper job of reporting if it chose to do it. It just didn't make that choice very often. Let's take a look at what is known about Obama's years at Columbia University.

Barack Obama transferred to Columbia University, located

in New York City, in August 1981 from Occidental College in Los Angeles. Obama majored in political science with a specialty in international relations and graduated with a B.A. in 1983. Obama wrote in *Dreams from My Father* that his grades at Occidental College were "not so good." Despite this, he was admitted to Columbia University.

In a 2007 *Los Angeles Times* article about Obama's time at Occidental College, many classmates and professors were interviewed about their memories of "Barry Obama." At least a dozen were featured in the *Times* article. In 2008, the *Wall Street Journal* reported, "Fox News contacted some 400 of his classmates at Columbia and found no one who remembered him."

The *New York Times* asked Barack Obama about his years at Columbia and reported that he "declined repeated requests to talk about his New York years, release his Columbia transcript, or identify even a single fellow student, co-worker, roommate, or friend from those years."

The *New York Sun* asked the Obama campaign for information for a 2008 article, "Obama's Years at Columbia Are a Mystery." Their answer? "The Obama campaign declined to comment for this article and did not offer an explanation for why his transcript has not been released."

The *New York Times* tried again in February 2008—unsuccessfully—to wrest some information about Obama's Columbia period. "Mr. Obama declined to be interviewed for this article." A campaign spokesman, Tommy Vietor, referred the paper to the Official Book of the Obama Narrative™, *Dreams from My Father*, calling the book "a candid and personal account of what Senator Obama was experiencing and thinking at the time."

Vietor had a ready-made answer prepared—in case the *Times* dug up past Obama acquaintances with accounts different from the Narrative. He even hazarded a guess about why those at Columbia might not be able to recall the man *Newsweek*'s Evan Thomas later described as "sort of God": "It's not surprising that his friends from high school and college wouldn't recall personal experiences and struggles that happened more than twenty years ago in the same way, and to the same extent, that he does."

Which was to say: If anyone remembered anything about Columbia, of course it would be a different version from Obama's, who recalled practically nothing. Another Obama spokesman, Ben LaBolt, told the *New York Times*, "He doesn't remember the names of many people from earlier in his life."

The Associated Press attempted to pry some information out of the Obama campaign for a May 2008 article and got nowhere, reporting, "The Obama campaign declined to discuss Obama's time at Columbia and his friendships in general. It won't, for example, release his transcripts or name his friends."

In September 2008, Lysandra Ohrstrom, in the *New York Observer*, wrote, "No one from the library in the School of International Public Affairs, the building he would have had most of his classes in as a political science major, remembered him. The chairman of the Political Science Department when Senator Obama was an undergraduate, Mark Chalmers, wrote in an e-mail that he did not remember him, and the two alumni

I managed to reach from the class of '83 refused to answer any questions about their old classmate."

Several 2008 press accounts identified several individuals who claimed that they knew Barack Obama during his Columbia years: a roommate, who was a Pakistani illegal, Sohale Siddiqi; a former professor, Michael Baron; and Michael Wolf, a classmate of Obama's who went on to become president of MTV Networks.

More than a year later, in 2009, CBS News's Declan McCullagh, writing about the "conspiracy theories" surrounding Obama's time at Columbia University, identified those same three people—and no one else—while observing, "Remarkably few people seem to remember a student named Barack Obama; two possible reasons are that he transferred from Occidental College in Los Angeles as a junior (therefore missing freshman orientation and the related socializing), and that he lived off-campus in a densely populated urban environment." Whether McCullagh attributed his failure to get to the bottom of the "conspiracy theories" to a lack of ambition, being outwitted by his subject, or a possible conspiracy is unknown.

In a March 2008 *DBKP* interview, Libertarian presidential candidate Wayne Allyn Root mentioned "my college classmate Columbia University Class of '83." However, it was while talking to *Reason* six months later that Root really opened up about his memories of Barack Obama while at Columbia:

I think the most dangerous thing you should know about Barack Obama is that I don't know a single person at Columbia that knows him, and they all know me. I don't have a classmate who ever knew Barack Obama at Columbia. Ever! . . . Nobody recalls him. I'm not exaggerating, I'm not kidding.

Root and Obama were in the same class with the same major.

Class of '83 political science, pre-law Columbia University. You don't get more exact than that. Never met him in my life, don't know anyone who ever met him. At the class reunion, our 20th reunion five years ago, 20th reunion, who was asked to be the speaker of the class? Me. No one ever heard of Barack! Who was he, and five years ago, nobody even knew who he was.

I didn't know him. I don't think anybody knew him. But I know that the guy who writes the class notes, who's kind of the, as we say in New York, the *macha* who knows everybody, has yet to find a person, a human who ever met him. Is that not strange? It's very strange.

It's been written that "Columbia University proudly claims Obama as a 1983 graduate." The university magazine, *Columbia College Today,* profiled him in 2005. However, he's not in the yearbook and Columbia hasn't been able to produce a picture of him at school.

Root's memories sparked further discussion, to say the least. Finally, in 2009, the *New York Times* eventually did locate someone who knew Obama at Columbia: another roommate by the name of Phil Boerner. The *Times* also published two addresses listed for a "Barack Hussein Obama" in the Columbia 1982–83 student directory. Also included was a reference to a campus publication, *The Sundial*, that included a March 10, 1983, article titled "Breaking the War Mentality" by Barack Obama.

By 2010, two other former classmates of Obama's surfaced who remembered him. *FactCheck.org* published a letter from a woman who claimed she had played pickup soccer with Barack Obama while at Columbia. Cathy M. Currie, Ph.D., wrote, "He was a serious guy, but always had a ready laugh or twinkle in his eye."

Jim Davidson (Columbia '85) left a comment on an article at the *Agitator* that read in part, "I was a student at Columbia, I met Barack Obama, I knew he was a student, and he and I talked, among other things, about my involvement in Students Against Militarism, my discomfort with its connection to Maoists and Stalinists on campus, and my favourite hat with political buttons all over it."

Barack Obama did not graduate with honors, which means that his GPA was between 2.0 and 3.2. Despite this relatively low GPA, he was accepted in 1988 at Harvard.

Except for a few references in *Dreams from My Father* about Obama living off-campus, this is the sum total of what is certainly known about Barack Obama during his years at Columbia. In an attempt to fill in the blanks, there's been no end of speculation. If Obama released his Columbia records, such speculation—well-reasoned as it is—would simply stop. Pundits could write about Obama's redistributive policies instead.

Which might be one of the reasons Obama has never released his Columbia records or attempted to clear up the mysteries of his Columbia past. Would he really be eager for pundits to speculate about his policies even more than they do now? Maybe all the secrecy surrounding Obama is really just high-level strategy aimed at controlling the media. Of course, Obama didn't need any strategy to control the corporate media. The CMM did that without any prompting. Regardless, Barack Obama is the only major-party nominee since 2000 who has not released information about his or her college performance—or had it leaked.

Obama's Columbia years continue to remain mysterious for several reasons. One, his records remain off-limits to the public. Two, by almost all accounts, during every other period of his life, Obama has been described as an outgoing and charismatic young man. Both his name and his looks were somewhat memorable, according to accounts published by the press. Plus, Obama's the president of the United States. One would think that fact alone would draw people out of the woodwork eager to recall memories and share events with the press.

As one wag put it, "What is the chance that a budding young politician of undeniable talent and promise spends his junior and senior years at Columbia, and no one remembers him?"

How can it be that in 2011, we still know so little of Barack Obama's missing years at Columbia? One answer: The CMM operates under its very own "Don't Ask, Don't Tell" policy when it comes to Barack Obama's past; the press has been perfectly satisfied to be kept in the dark. By contrast, in 2004, CBS News had such a burning desire to see George Bush's Texas Air Guard service records that it foisted forged documents on its viewers.

Perhaps that explains why CBS News has exhibited no curiosity about unreleased Obama records. Maybe they're still gun-shy?

The absence of a press fulfilling its adversarial role as it related to Barack Obama has led to speculation. Absent the Obama records—which the president has refused to release—speculation is not only to be expected, it's the only course of action for those seeking clues about the American commander in chief.

What are the consequences of the actions of Barack Obama, who ran as a "fill-in-the-blanks" candidate, and of the CMM that chose to protect his records from serious scrutiny? What Victor Davis Hanson wrote in 2008, in *The End of Journalism*, sounds prophetic today:

> The media has succeeded in shielding Barack Obama from journalistic scrutiny. It thereby irrevocably destroyed its own reputation and forfeited the trust that generations of others had so carefully acquired. And it will never again be trusted to offer candid and nonpartisan coverage of presidential candidates.
>
> Worse still, the suicide of both print and electronic journalism has ensured that, should Barack Obama be elected president, the public will only then learn what they should have known far earlier about their commander-in-chief—but in circumstances and from sources they may well regret.

Until the Obama records see the light of day, there will be no end of speculation offered as an attempt to fill in the blanks. Those who disagree with the "conspiracy theories" put forward,

no matter how bizarre or unlikely, cannot refute such speculation. They know nothing more than the conspiracy theorists; the
Obama supporters are merely speculating as well. This includes
pundits, talking heads, CMM "journalists," bloviators, commentators, and the millions of Obama supporters lurking in the
comments section at CMM websites.

If No Information Is Available,
Idle Speculation Will Do

So, again, what was Barack Obama actually doing during his
Columbia years if he wasn't really at Columbia? Lord knows—
and He ain't telling. And Obama himself hasn't been very
helpful—some might even say he has been "vague"—about his
Columbia years. As he wrote in *Dreams from My Father:* "I spent
a lot of time in the library. I didn't socialize that much. I was like
a monk."

Obama also wrote that during breaks from his "monklike"
skulking in the library, he was somewhat involved with the Black
Student Organization and antiapartheid activities. But Mark
Attiah, a former VP of the Black Students Organization, was
"shocked to learn that Obama was even a member of the BSO."
Obama was not only not in the 1983 Columbia BSO photo, he's
not even listed as being absent. There is no evidence, other than
Barack Obama's claim, that he was involved in the BSO while
at Columbia University. Just another part of the mysteriously
marvelous Obama Narrative™ that fits together like a grand
mosaic—until one looks closely at the individual pieces.

All of the gaps and contradictory claims leave us, once more, largely with speculation, which falls along several different lines of reasoning, each at least as plausible as the picture of a messianic young black man wandering around an Ivy League campus for two years during the early eighties, enthralling all he met as he simultaneously performed a Vulcan Mind Wipe—all with a "twinkle in his eye," as Dr. Currie recalls it.

One theory is that Barack Obama was in New York, but instead of attending classes at Columbia, he was learning the ropes about becoming a black revolutionary. Because he was a "red diaper doper baby," and a social climber, Obama wanted to climb the black Marxist social ladder. While doing so, the theory goes, he crossed paths with former Weather Underground honcho Bill Ayers—who really was "just another guy in the neighborhood" in New York and Columbia, as he would be years later in Chicago. What a coincidence! What a country!

Because Ayers was one of the superstars of the movement during those days and had lots of connections, was he not able to plant a file or pull some strings and get Barack Obama a degree from Columbia? Mencius Moldburg asks two other relevant questions: "And would someone who blows up police stations blanch at planting a file? Honestly, can we even be confident that the staff at Columbia looked at the file?"

Obama claimed that Bill Ayers was "just another guy in the neighborhood" when the media first inquired on the subject. But Obama not only held his first political fund-raiser in Bill Ayers's house, he was at Columbia during the infamous 1981 Brinks robbery. The robbery, in which two police officers and a guard were killed, sent Weather Underground member and Ayers associate Kathy Boudin to federal prison. Ayers and his wife, Bernadine Dohrn, raised Boudin's child while she was in prison. Her child was still living with Ayers and Dohrn when they hosted the Obama fund-raiser. As the Walt Disney song put it, "It is a small world after all."

One of the more speculative theories proposed is the following: Barack Obama had moved to New York to become involved in political causes célèbres, only to practically barricade himself in the library once he arrived. He only took the occasional break from his monklike vow of inconspicuousness to sneak out and play the odd game of pickup soccer "in front of Butler."

Despite all the library time logged by Obama—who later would be almost universally described as a "gifted student"—he still managed to graduate without honors in political science. This in itself has been one of the most unbelievable claims that the speculators have made.

Incredible.

However, that's the theory floated by Barack Obama himself.

Whatever else Obama was doing, apparently he spent some time moving around. There are a number of addresses given for him during his stay at Columbia. In *Dreams from My Father*, Obama wrote that for a brief time he lived at "109th Street and Broadway in Spanish Harlem." A 2008 Fox News documentary stated that Obama lived at Ninety-sixth Street and First Avenue. The 2009 *New York Times* article gave addresses at 142 West 109th Street #3B and 339 East 94th Street #6A.

The AP added to the list when it reported in 2008 that the Obama campaign listed "five locations where Obama lived during his four years [in New York]: three on Manhattan's Upper West Side and two in Brooklyn—one in Park Slope, the other in

Brooklyn Heights. His memoir mentions two others on Manhattan's Upper East Side. In about 1982, Siddiqi and Obama got an apartment at a sixth-floor walkup on East 94th Street."

So there may be some truth to the assertion that Barack Obama was too busy to make any friends at Columbia—too busy moving. Right? All of these sources—as well as Barack Obama himself—tell us that Obama moved quite frequently while at Columbia. One count of the Obama Columbia addresses puts the figure at seven different ones.

West Coast photojournalist Zombie, writing at the *Zombie-Time* blog, did a nifty bit of detective work that puts all of the above narrative into doubt. Looking back at the phone directories from 1982 to 1985, Zombie produced photographic evidence from the NYC phonebook that Barack Obama "moved into that 94th Street apartment shortly after first arriving, and stayed there the rest of the time while in New York." A "B. Obama" kept the same phone number, according to the directories, while living the entire time at 339 East 94th Street.

Now for a question: What possible reason could Barack Obama have for explaining in *Dreams from My Father* and in various press accounts that he moved around a lot and slept in alleys and with friends, most of the time in cold, drafty, bad habitats? Zombie writes the "only feasible explanation" has to be "that Obama rented the 339 East 94th St. apartment and then moved out while subleasing it to others, still maintaining the apartment and the phone in his name. And while acting as a sort of freelance landlord, collecting rent from his sublessors, he was still broke and kept having to move from place to place himself."

Against that theory is the counterargument that Obama probably just stayed put the entire time, as the phone directories suggested. Perhaps he concocted the entire "frequent mover" story to gain street cred and enhance a rags-to-riches narrative?

There are still other theories surrounding Obama's stint at Columbia. One is that he came, he attended class, he was nothing to write home about as a student, and he graduated. The reason he has not released his records is that they will show that, in spite of his middling grades, he was admitted to Columbia and Harvard—as an affirmative action case. As he writes in *Dreams from My Father*:

> To avoid being mistaken for a sellout, I chose my friends carefully. The more politically active black students. The foreign students. The Chicanos. The Marxist professors and structural feminists and punk-rock performance poets. We smoked cigarettes and wore leather jackets. At night, in the dorms, we discussed neocolonialism, Franz [sic] Fanon, Eurocentrism, and patriarchy.

A long 2005 profile in a Columbia alumni magazine included a few vague remarks by Obama about his time at the school, including that he was "somewhat involved" in "antiapartheid activities." The *Los Angeles Times* also reported Obama's "role in protesting college investments in firms doing business in South Africa during the apartheid era" and that "he and others recall a strong speech Obama made at a campus rally urging South Africa divestment." There are also many links between

Obama's South African activism and the Students for a Democratic Society (SDS), which spawned the more violent Marxists who later gravitated to the Weather Underground.

This led to another line of speculation that it was Obama's interest in Marxist political activism that largely determined his move to New York and Columbia University. Of course, according to this line of thinking, it would not do for his participation in Marxist politics to become known. That is why what he really did at Columbia is such a secret.

This leads us to our next chapter: the last, and perhaps wildest, theory of what Barack Hussein Obama was doing during his time at Columbia.

8

Obama and the CIA: Agent Double O Bam!

Was Barack Obama Ever a CIA Asset?

How did Barack Obama spend his time while enrolled at Columbia University? Let me count the ways. But seriously, this is only a chapter in a book; it would take a continuing subscription service to keep up with all the theories, hypotheses, and wild guesses that the complete refusal by our forty-fourth president to release his Columbia University records has spawned.

One of the most entertaining—which is not the same as unbelievable—of the theories of what Barack Obama was really doing while at Columbia posits that Barack Obama was working as a CIA operative. The main, though by no means only, proponent of this theory is Wayne Madsen, editor of the *Wayne Madsen Report*.

Madsen is a former National Security Agency employee and member of the Association of Former Intelligence Officers. From Madsen's *Wikipedia* entry: "Wayne Madsen is a controversial Washington, D.C.–based investigative journalist, author and columnist who has been described by critics including Andrew Sullivan at the Atlantic Monthly, CBS, and Salon as a conspiracy theorist and conspiracy minded blogger. He is the author of the blog *Wayne Madsen Report.*"

A slightly different take on Wayne Madsen can be found at *WMR*:

> In the tradition of Drew Pearson's and Jack Anderson's famous "Washington Merry-Go-Round" syndicated column and I. F. Stone, this online publication tackles the "politically incorrect" and "politically embarrassing" stories and holds government officials accountable for their actions. This web site extends a warm open invitation to whistleblowers and leakers. Business as usual for the crooks and liars in Washington, D.C. is over.

Madsen has claimed that he "discovered CIA files that document the agency's connections to institutions and individuals figuring prominently in the lives of Barack Obama and his mother, father, grandmother, and stepfather." Madsen has written about these findings in a series of reports, some of which are available only to subscribers to the *WMR*.

The starting place for this theory is a company by the name of Business International Corporation, which coincidentally is where Barack Obama went to work upon graduating from Columbia University. Once more, it's helpful to list the information compiled by Madsen et al. and try to determine how much of it can be verified. One thing is for certain: Madsen's information, much like the information contained in the Obama Narrative™, is based on documents that the public has not seen.

Obama at Business International Corporation

MADSEN CLAIM: After Barack Obama graduated from Columbia, he went to work for a company called Business International Corporation (BIC).

OBAMA CLAIM: Continuing his practice of not divulging unnecessary information about his past—especially any that concerns his time in New York City—Obama wrote in *Dreams from My Father* that "eventually a consulting house to multinational corporations agreed to hire me as a research assistant." He didn't say when he worked there or name the company but others who worked with Obama came forward later and named BIC as his place of employment.

OTHER SOURCES: The University of Chicago Law School's website, which has Barack Obama listed as a "Senior Lecturer in Law," contained a little helpful information. Most likely, this information was provided to the school by Barack Obama. "Barack Obama—Business International Corporation; January 1984–January 1985."

An August 2008 *Boston Globe* article also reported on Obama's first report written for a BIC newsletter that was "concerned with how investing in gold futures in Sao Paulo and London could be used to hedge against the fluctuating value of Brazilian cruzeiros." In the report, the *Globe* named BIC as Obama's place of employment at the time.

VERDICT: Barack Obama worked for Business International Corporation for about a year after graduating from Columbia. So far, so good. Almost everyone's on the same page. It's after these elementary facts that the claims diverge.

Business International Corporation Was a CIA Front

MADSEN CLAIM: Madsen has claimed that BIC was a CIA front that supposedly held meetings and seminars that involved some of the world's "most powerful leaders and used journalists as agents abroad."

OBAMA CLAIM: Understandably, Obama doesn't mention that BIC is a CIA front in *Dreams from My Father*. Is this one reason BIC was never named in his book? Interestingly enough, Obama did mention in his book that he felt like "a spy behind enemy lines, I arrived every day at my mid-Manhattan office and sat at my computer terminal, checking the Reuters machine that blinked bright emerald messages from across the globe." Was this perhaps a Freudian slip?

OTHER SOURCES: Others who worked with Barack Obama at BIC have come forth in print, mostly to dispute his version of events in *Dreams from My Father*. Several of those former coworkers have documented their different memories of that time. One was Dan Armstrong, who wrote about what he remembered in a 2005 piece at *Analyze This*, an Internet blog. A reunion of sorts broke out in the comments section, and others who claimed to have worked at BIC during that time shared their own Obama BIC memories—most of them centering on how Obama had embellished his role at BIC in *Dreams from My Father*. Armstrong confirmed that the company had correspondents who filed reports from different countries.

In 1977, the *New York Times* ran an article in which the co-founder of BIC told the paper that "Eldridge Haynes [the other founder] had provided cover for four CIA employees in various countries between 1955 and 1960."

Australian journalist and filmmaker John Pilger is a progressive based in London who twice won Britain's Journalist of the Year award. Pilger has stated publicly that Business International has a "long history of providing cover for the CIA with covert action and infiltrating unions on the Left." Pilger claims he knows this "because [BIC] was especially active in my home country of Australia."

In 1987, *Lobster* magazine, published in the United Kingdom, identified BIC as a CIA front. *Lobster*'s philosophy was stated as, "If you generally accept the government line, that there is a 'national interest,' and believe what you read in the newspapers, then *Lobster* is probably not for you."

Perhaps the most surprising revelation appeared in a 1969 book, *The Strawberry Statement*. In it, a former student protester, James Kunen, wrote of a remark about Business International by an unnamed Students for a Democratic Society conference attendee in 1968. The attendee, referred to by Kunen as "the kid," claimed the company offered to finance SDS demonstrations in Chicago. Business International is described as "the left wing of the ruling class" and as desiring a Gene McCarthy presidency. Which is surprising, because if one accepts that Business International was a CIA front, "the CIA" and "left wing" are not terms one normally finds associated in the same sentence.

Many of the more violent Weather Underground participants—founded by Obama mentor Bill Ayers—had their beginnings in the SDS, providing evidence that it really is "a small world after all." If this information is true, can this mean anything other than that the CIA was in the business of funding the far left and communist organizations? Or that there's a division of the CIA that was so engaged? It's been a contention of several progressive writers, particularly Sherman Skolnick, that the CIA has used liberal foundations and corporations to funnel money from right-wing contributors and has used CIA fronts that acted as "gatekeepers" to prevent real left grassroots activism.

VERDICT: No less an authority than the *New York Times* has reported that BIC was used as a CIA front. Since the *Times* reported this fact in 1977, the normal caveats concerning *New York Times* reporting on Barack Obama do not apply. Since there are other sources as well, it appears that Wayne Madsen's contention is correct: Business International Corporation has been used in the past as a CIA front.

What Obama Did at Business International Corporation

OBAMA CLAIM: From *Dreams from My Father*: "Eventually a consulting house to multinational corporations agreed to hire me as a research assistant."

OTHER SOURCES: The information on the University of Chicago Law School website—again, who would have supplied this information but Obama himself—lists Barack Obama's duties while at BIC as "Writer/Financial Analyst, January 1984–January 1985."

Dan Armstrong says that Obama inflated his duties. "First, it wasn't a consulting house; it was a small company that published newsletters on international business. Like most newsletter publishers, it was a bit of a sweatshop. I'm sure we all wished that we were high-priced consultants to multinational corporations . . . essentially the job was copyediting."

"Jeannie" from the comments on the Armstrong article notes: "I worked with Dan and Barack at Business International. I too read Barack Obama's account of his work at Business International and immediately thought this was not the same place I worked! It was not a high level consulting firm. As today's NYT article states, it was hardly an upscale environment."

Many responses in the comments section were by people who claimed to have worked at BIC when Barack Obama was there, and all agreed that his account of the place in his book was grossly overstated, both regarding what the place was (a consulting house) and regarding what Obama's duties were.

At one point, Obama wrote that "the company promoted me to the position of financial writer. I had my own office, my own secretary; money in the bank. Sometimes, coming out of an interview with Japanese financiers or German bond traders, I would catch my reflection in the elevator door—see myself in a suit and tie, a briefcase in my hand—and for a split second I would imagine myself as a captain of industry, barking out orders, closing the deal, before I remembered who it was that I had told myself I wanted to be and felt pangs of guilt for my lack of resolve."

The claims that Obama had his own secretary or was promoted were roundly ridiculed, both in Armstrong's article and in the comments. To Obama's contention that he was an expert on "interest rate swaps" as he had portrayed in *Dreams from My Father*, Bill Millar's response was: "I remember trying to explain the nuance of these instruments to him in the cramped three Wang terminal space we called the bull pen. In contrast to his liberal arts background, I had a degree in finance and Wall Street experience, so I knew what I was talking about. But rather than learn from a City College kid, the Ivy Leaguer just sort of rolled his eyes. Condescendingly. I'll never forget it. God forbid he leave the impression that a mere editor like myself knew more about something than did Barack."

Eventually, it appears that Obama did write a few articles on his own. In August 2010, Dr. Stuart Jeanne Bramhall wrote that Obama's job consisted of research and "to write for two BIC publications, *Financing Foreign Operations* and *Business International Money Report,* a weekly newsletter."

VERDICT: Barack Obama inflated his résumé account of what he did at Business International Corporation. This is hardly unheard of, but the inclusion of such grandiose claims in *Dreams from My Father* elevates the action from "résumé inflation" into the category of "myth making." Perhaps it could be represented as "narrative making," particularly when Obama wrote about almost being sucked into the evil, greedy world of capitalist corporations—only to be rescued by his long-lost half-sister and an almost mythical "calling" to be a community organizer. Easy enough to see through these days, but many progressives bought into the charade during the heady days before January 21, 2009.

A few notes before moving on. Wayne Madsen has claimed that BIC tried to "recruit those on the left as CIA agents and assets" and used its contact among liberal leaders to do so. This would seem to corroborate James Kunen's account of BIC's offer to finance the SDS demonstrations in Chicago. Madsen has further claimed that any questions about Obama's employment with BIC have been "off-limits to the White House press corps."

Reporters attempting to bring the subject up during press briefings risk dismissal from the press pool, according to Madsen.

Wayne Madsen's hypothesis is that the reason no one remembers Barack Obama's time at Columbia is that he was not at Columbia during this time. He was working for the CIA, and part of his payment was a graduation diploma from Columbia. Of course, that's speculation, but it sounds about as plausible as some of the speculation presented in the Obama Narrative™.

Stanley Ann Dunham: International Mom of Mystery

Barack Obama's mother, Stanley Ann Dunham, had quite an interesting life, shot through with coincidences. Stanley Ann was some mom—and by some mom, it's meant that she was a globetrotting, oil-rep-marrying, CIA-front-employed, twelve-language-speaking, International Mom of Mystery. It's fairly well known that Dunham met Obama Sr. in a Russian language class at the University of Hawaii. A *Time* piece reported that she could speak Urdu, and it's also known that she spoke Indonesian, Dutch, and English as well.

Even in the most cursory of studies of Barack Obama's mother—and the prepublic years of Barack Obama—one is struck by two things: that peculiar occurrence called coincidence and the mad proliferation of such occurrences. The long-winded dictionary definition of *coincidence* runs something on the order of "A coincidence is the occurring of an event in conjunction with certain conditions, e.g. another event. As such, a coincidence occurs when something uncanny, accidental and unexpected happens under conditions named, but not under a defined relationship."

A shorter, more easily remembered version might be that whenever two seemingly nonrelated events occur that cause the casual observer to think, "Isn't that odd?" a coincidence probably has occurred. As for quantifying those odd occurrences, it's hard.

There are no known physical dimensions ascribed to a coincidence, but if there were and the ones surrounding Stanley Ann Dunham and Barack Obama were stacked, one atop the other, one would be well advised to be sure that ObamaCare covers severe nosebleeds before attempting to climb to the top. The shaky edifice may even offer a high enough vantage point to be able to see where the president's original long-form birth certificate has been stashed.

Back to Stanley Ann Dunham, International Mom of Mystery.

Some sources put the number of languages she spoke at a dozen. Which is handy when one travels the world as Stanley Ann Dunham did. Put the two of those together: a proficiency in a number of foreign languages—including Urdu!—and a well-seasoned international traveler. She was a CIA recruiter's wet dream.

For some reason, Dunham was always traveling to the world's hot spots just before or as things got hot. Indonesia after the bloody 1965 Suharto coup—which was instigated by the CIA—was one of them. Pakistan—that's where the Urdu would come in handy—was another. Stanley Ann ostensibly had reason to travel to Djakarta, along with her Mobil Oil executive husband, Lolo Soetoro—who was the liaison between Mobil Oil and General Suharto, who took power after the CIA-backed coup.

Stanley Ann Dunham's stay in Pakistan was a bit stranger. A Pakistani newspaper, *Daily Waqt,* reported that while in Pakistan, Dunham stayed for five years in the Hilton International Hotel (now the Avari Hotel) in Lahore and "traveled daily from Lahore to Gujranwalla." Apparently, Stanley Ann had quite the job! Five years in a Hilton International seems like a big hotel bill, even in Pakistan. Of course, by this time, it was only for one person: Dunham and Soetoro had divorced.

But it gets even weirder. The same article reported that when Barack Obama visited in 1981, he "stayed in the same hotel." At the time, Obama tells readers in *Dreams from My Fa-*

ther, he was wearing thrift-store clothing. Maybe the Hilton International had a Dunham-Obama Discount Plan? This leaves hanging the question of how Obama scraped the cash together to afford his 1981 Pakistani getaway in the first place. More on that in a moment.

Stanley Ann Dunham traveled the world in the employ of several different organizations, including the U.S. Agency for International Development (USAID), the Ford Foundation, and the East-West Center at the University of Hawaii. A bit of Stanley Ann Dunham trivia: Her passport records for the years before 1968 were somehow destroyed by the State Department—even though the State Department does not normally destroy passport records. Isn't that strange?

Maybe it was just a coincidence that Stanley Ann Dunham happened to be in Indonesia and Pakistan at a time when the CIA's presence in those countries was especially strong. Maybe it was just further coincidence that Obama's mother was always employed by foundations or organizations known to have strong ties to the CIA. Maybe it was a coincidence that Stanley Ann Dunham was married to the one guy who was the go-between for Mobil Oil and the newly installed regime of General Suharto when she was in Indonesia. After all, Obama Sr. was at one time employed by Shell Oil. Maybe she had a thing for oilmen?

According to old friends who grew up with Stanley Ann Dunham, she became a serious student of Communist and Marxist theories back in high school. One profile even named a few of her radical teachers and administrators at Mercer High, which Dunham attended, whose classrooms formed part of what was called "anarchy alley." What sounds strange is that this avant-garde, supposedly idealistic communist-thinking student of the left met a major oil company executive during the radical 1960s, and not only found him *not* to be a repulsively evil money-grubbing capitalist pig, but was so taken in by his Big Oil company/military charm that she married him.

Okay, so maybe that's not coincidence. Maybe that's just the power of love.

Maybe it was just a coincidence that Stanley Ann Dunham's pre-1968 passport records happened to be destroyed. Maybe it was a coincidence that Stanley Ann Dunham lived at the Hilton International in Lahore for five years—the same swanky digs used by her son in 1981 when he visited the country as a penniless youth.

If a reader exists who believes in such a string of coincidences, congratulations! You have just been identified as one of the few people left in America who still have faith in the Obama Narrative™. You just might vote for Barack Obama in 2012.

Spooky Business

In a 2007 *Chicago Tribune* interview, Barack Obama referred to his mother as "the dominant figure in my formative years. . . . The values she taught me continue to be my touchstone when it comes to how I go about the world of politics." Unlike many of Obama's utterances, that particular one's not hard to believe.

Barack Obama also has had a string of coincidences occur throughout his lifetime—just like those associated with his mother. While at Columbia, one of Obama's professors was reportedly former national security advisor for Jimmy Carter

Zbigniew Brzezinski. Brzezinski appeared on MSNBC in March 2008 to sing Obama's praises, mentioning a 2002 speech the future president had given opposing the Iraq War. Brzezinski claimed credit as the source of the arguments Obama had used in that 2002 speech.

Isn't it odd that Brzezinski would be supplying talking points about the Iraq War to an Illinois state senator?

An even more bizarre string of coincidences surrounds a trip taken by then-senator Obama in 2005 to Russia as part of a fact-finding tour that included Senator Richard Lugar (R-IN). Perhaps it's not unusual for a newly minted U.S. senator to be invited to be part of a Russian fact-finding tour that inspected a nuclear weapons site in Perm, Siberia.

This was a base where mobile launch missiles were being destroyed under the Cooperative Threat Reduction program (CTR), which also went by the name of the Nunn-Lugar program. The program, shot through with corruption, traded massive amounts of U.S. currency for nukes that were supposed to be destroyed by the Russians. A GAO report revealed that some of the money, which totaled more than $6 billion, was used to destroy obsolete weapons that Moscow was going to replace with more sophisticated upgrades. The U.S. money also provided salaries for Russian scientists.

What is unusual is that Americans weren't told of Obama's 2004 inspection of a Russian nuke plant in 2008—when candidate Obama was so desperate to demonstrate foreign policy experience that his campaign scheduled a grand speaking tour of Israel and Europe. Wouldn't most politicians in Obama's shoes have been trumpeting that Russian experience?

But wait—there's more!

After inspecting the Russian facility, the U.S. delegation was held up by the Russians for three hours at the airport while Russian authorities detained Obama and Lugar. The Russians examined their passports and wanted to search their plane. Some reports stated that the Russians accused Obama of being a spy. *Bellona Web* reported that the "seemingly bureaucratic misunderstanding escalated, ultimately involving the White House, the State Department, and a host of military officials in Washington and each of their Russian counterparts in Moscow, an official at the US Embassy said." An official report from Lugar's office about the trip never mentioned the incident. Neither did Barack Obama in 2008.

One account of this trip was posted on the website *Cloakand dagger.de* on August 28, 2005, shortly after the Russian incident occurred. The site is no longer functioning, but other websites cited the story, which reported that the Russians had accused Senator Barack Obama of being a *British* spy. The report, by Sherman Skolnick, a Chicago-area activist, carried the interesting headline, "CLOAK'S EXCLUSIVE AUGUST 2005 STORY EXPOSING OBAMA'S KENYAN BIRTHPLACE FORCES OBAMA TO SANITIZE HIS PASSPORT FILE." This is double-plus interesting because it appeared three years before questions about Barack Obama's birth narrative were floated elsewhere.

Barack Obama's Excellent Pakistani Adventure

Another set of coincidences intersect at Obama's 1981 trip to Pakistan. As stated, it was during this time that Obama said he was living in poverty and wearing thrift-store clothing. Yet he somehow managed to find the cash to finance a two-week trip to Pakistan. Which he never talked about. Which in itself is odd: Here's a guy who wrote two autobiographies that explored events, real, imagined, and totally fictional, that supposedly forged the modern-day Barack Obama from his humble beginnings. That's according to the Obama Narrative™.

But Obama doesn't mention his 1981 two-week jaunt to Pakistan in any of the 830-plus pages of two separate autobiographies. Again, doesn't that seem just a little odd? Neither did candidate Obama—again, supposedly desperate for foreign policy credibility during the 2008 election—mention his 1981 trip to Pakistan to the press. Until other factors forced his hand. More on that later.

Maybe the trip slipped his mind; after all, it was the first overseas trip undertaken by Barack Obama as an adult. Perhaps nothing of note happened in Pakistan—surely staying at the Hilton International was no big deal and held no special memories for a man who paid particular attention in *Dreams from My Father* to detailing the Third World living conditions he endured while attending Columbia. Who would remember sleeping in the Hilton International in Lahore, Pakistan, in June and then sleeping in an alley in New York City a few months later? It's not like it's a contrast that a young writer might use when recalling that time.

Maybe nothing of note happened to Barack Obama on that 1981 trip to the other side of the world? Perhaps that's why he never mentioned it? It was finally reported that young Obama traveled with a college friend from Pakistan. Perhaps the whole trip was one of those "Lost Weekend" types where the participants remembered nothing but the beer and the girls? Pakistan 1981: beer, girls, and martial law.

Martial law?

Who would remember traveling around a country—Pakistan during the summer Obama visited—that was under martial law? Travel by Americans to Pakistan at the time was discouraged by the U.S. State Department—there was a travel advisory for Americans in effect—but Obama went anyway. Who would remember that youthful act of defiance?

Passport Services/Bureau of Consular Affa[irs]
Department of State/Washington, D.C. 205_

AUGUST 17, 1981

TRAVEL TO PAKISTAN

BEFORE TRAVELING TO PAKISTAN, AMERICAN CITIZENS SHOULD BE AWARE OF THE FOLLO[WING] UPDATED VISA REQUIREMENTS: 30 DAY VISAS ARE AVAILABLE AT PAKISTANI AIRPORTS [FOR] TOURISTS ONLY. AS THESE VISAS ARE RARELY EXTENDED BEYOND THE 30 DAY TIME PER[IOD,] TOURISTS PLANNING TO STAY LONGER SHOULD SECURE VISAS

*BEFORE COMING TO PAKIS[TAN.] ANY TRAVELER
COMING INTO PAKISTAN OVERLAND FROM INDIA
MUST REPEAT MUST HA[VE A] VALID VISA, AS 30
DAY VISAS ARE NOT REPEAT NOT ISSUED AT THE
OVERLAND BOR[DER] CROSSING POINT AT WAGHA.*

*ANY NON-OFFICIAL AMERICAN WHO IS
IN PAKISTAN FOR MORE THAN 30 DAYS MUST
REGIS[TER] WITH THE GOVERNMENT'S FOREIGNER
REGISTRATION OFFICE. EXIT PERMITS ARE
REQUI[RED] FOR THOSE WHO HAVE STAYED
LONGER THAN 30 DAYS BEFORE THEY ARE
ALLOWED TO LE[AVE T]HE COUNTRY. ALL
AMERICANS TRAVELING TO PAKISTAN ON OFFICIAL
BUSINESS OR [FOR] PRIVATE EMPLOYMENT ARE
REQUIRED TO HAVE A VISA BEFORE ARRIVAL, AND,
AS [THE] GOVERNMENT OF PAKISTAN'S CLEARANCE
PROCESS IS OFTEN QUITE LENGTHY, WE WOULD
URGE TH[OSE] COMING TO APPLY AT THE NEAREST
PAKISTANI EMBASSY OR CONSULATE AS FAR IN
ADVA[NCE] OF THEIR SCHEDULED ARRIVAL AS
POSSIBLE.*

*THIS SUPERSEDED REQUIREMENTS SET FORTH
IN DEPARTMENT PUBLICATION M-264, [VISA]
REQUIREMENTS OF FOREIGN GOVERNMENTS.*

EXPIRATION DATE: INDEFINITE.

Barbara Crossette described in a June 14, 1981, *New York Times* travel article some of the conditions Barack Obama would have found in Lahore once he arrived:

Lahore is quiet now: The reputation for carousing that Rudyard Kipling touched on in his brief autobiography, *Something of Myself,* has been obliterated by the martial-law government's Islamization program. . . . The Soviet presence in Afghanistan has closed the overland route from Kabul to Delhi and Calcutta, reducing the number of foreign travelers. The war between Iran and Iraq has further deterred tourists.

Joseph Cannon, who has written a series of entertaining and informative articles on this matter at his *Cannonfire* website, has wondered:

During his days at Occidental, Barack Obama apparently came to know a Political Science professor who was also a key CIA consultant on Soviet matters. . . . At the very least, we can say that a trip to a strife-torn forbidden zone would have constituted quite an adventure for any young man. So why does Obama refuse to mention this adventure in his books? Think about it: If you were writing an autobiographical work, wouldn't you want to fill it with dramatic incident?

Cannon has pointed out good questions, as have others. Pakistan at that time was a hotbed of CIA activity. The Soviets had invaded Afghanistan in December 1979 and through the CIA, the United States eventually committed more than $600 million in clandestine aid, much of it to the Afghan mujahideen resistance fighters. Most of this aid went through Pakistan. It's easy to understand why none of this made an impression on the young, impressionable Obama.

There's also the matter of Obama's passport: Did he still have an Indonesian passport, as some have alleged? That certainly would have made traveling to Pakistan a lot easier in those days. The public has no way of knowing, as Obama's passport records have been declared strictly off-limits by the one person who could clear up a lot of speculation: Barack Obama himself. The CMM hasn't pressed him on the issue—or any other issue that concerns the sealing of the vast document dump that is his past life.

One clarification on the matter of how difficult it was for Americans to travel to Pakistan at that time is appropriate here. It has been reported at various sites that "travel to Pakistan during the time Barack Obama made his trip was banned; therefore, it would not have been possible for BHO to have entered the country on an American passport"—or some variation on this "fact."

Actually, travel to Pakistan was difficult for Americans—but not proscribed by either government. According to the Crossette piece in the *New York Times*:

> It is possible to cross from India to Pakistan by train from Amritsar and Delhi, but border procedures can be long and complicated. A road crossing at Wagah is also open for a few daylight hours. Check schedules, and allow several extra hours for border formalities.
>
> Tourists can obtain a free, 30-day visa (necessary for Americans) at border crossings and airports. Transportation within Lahore is plentiful, with taxis, scooter rickshaws

and horse-drawn tongas (especially in the old city) readily available.

Time for one more coincidence. In March 2008, it was widely reported that the passport files of John McCain, Hillary Clinton, and Barack Obama were accessed and perhaps tampered with by unnamed State Department employees. Two weeks after this reporting, Barack Obama suddenly remembered his Most Excellent Pakistani Adventure and mentioned it to the press. Eleven days after that, a key witness in the federal probe investigating the passport file tampering was murdered in front of a D.C. church. The *Washington Times* noted, "Lt. Quarles Harris Jr., who had been cooperating with a federal investigator, was found late Thursday night slumped dead inside a car." As noted, probably just one more coincidence.

Oh, and by the way, while in Pakistan, Obama traveled to Jacobabad where he was the guest of the Soomro family. In 2008, it was reported in the Pakistani press that "Muhammad-mian Soomro confirmed this information, stating it was his first meeting with Obama." Obama even went partridge hunting with Soomro—who coincidentally became prime minister, and then president of Pakistan in 2007.

Who would remember that? What candidate searching for a way to embellish his foreign policy résumé could resist bragging that as a youth he'd hung out with the future president of Pakistan? What this means is that for perhaps the only time in his life, Barack Hussein Obama resisted the urge to polish his record—at a time when it needed polishing. In fact, he never mentioned a word of any of this in either his autobiographies or on the campaign trail.

Isn't that odd?

So, a penniless Obama traveled to a country under martial law, where the U.S. State Department had issued a travel advisory. Obama then ignored the millions of Afghan refugees in Pakistan, checked into the Hilton International, showered, shaved, and changed into a fresh set of thrift-store clothing to go bird hunting with the country's future prime minister.

It is true that the material presented in this chapter is a lot of coincidences and odd bits of information that have leaked from sources other than the Obama Narrative™. There is no public record of Barack Obama's (or Stanley Ann Dunham's) being in the employ of the CIA. Perhaps he was, perhaps he wasn't. The reader may consider the information and, based on background, life experiences, and ability to keep an open mind, may come to either conclusion.

But any explanation of why Barack Obama would not have mentioned a word of his Most Excellent Pakistani Adventure in either of his two autobiographies requires a conspiracy theory that might cast doubt on either the sanity or the sincerity of the person proposing it.

9

Obama the Socialist

socialist: *noun* 'sō-sh(ə-)list\ **1** : one who advocates or practices socialism

2 *cap* : a member of a party or political group advocating socialism

socialism: *noun* 'sō-shə-,li-zəm\ **1** : any of various economic and political theories advocating collective or governmental ownership and administration of the means of production and distribution of goods

2 a : a system of society or group living in which there is no private property **b :** a system or condition of society in which the means of production are owned and controlled by the state

3 : a stage of society in Marxist theory transitional between capitalism and communism and distinguished by unequal distribution of goods and pay according to work done

—from the Merriam-Webster online dictionary

Is Barack Obama a Socialist?

This question was one posed mainly by conservative media during the 2008 presidential campaign. It probably wasn't exactly the right question to ask, but since the Corporate Mainstream Media avoided probing candidate Barack Hussein Obama's past at all costs, it was the logical one to pose.

Some more revealing questions might have been:

"Why have you had so many Marxists and Communists in your past?"

"Why are all of your past writing efforts off-limits to the public—especially those from your college years, when your political philosophy and views were being formed?"

"Why do so many of your supporters seem to be seen with Soviet flags, Che Guevara posters and shirts; and other communist symbolism?"

"You stated in your book *Dreams from My Father*, 'To avoid being mistaken for a sellout, I chose my friends carefully. The more politically active black students. The foreign students. The Chicanos. The Marxist professors and the structural feminists and punk-rock performance poets. We smoked cigarettes and wore leather jackets. At night in the dorms, we discussed neocolonialism, Frantz [*sic*] Fanon, Eurocentrism, and patriarchy. When we ground out our cigarettes in the hallway carpet or set our stereos so loud that the walls began to shake, we were resisting bourgeois society's stifling constraints. We weren't indifferent or careless or insecure. We were alienated.'"

A number of questions might have proved helpful at this point: "Do you still feel alienated?" "What made you feel alienated in those days?" "Are you still resisting 'bourgeois society's stifling constraints'?" "What are a few of those 'constraints'?" "Who were your Marxist professors and what did you learn from them?" "When you were wearing your leather jacket and smoking your cigarettes, what exactly were your positions on 'Eurocentrism' and 'patriarchy'?" "Did you know that those two words are considered buzzwords on the far left?" "What brand of cigarettes were you smoking?"

Except for the last question, it would have been helpful if the American electorate had had some answers to those questions—instead of waiting to discover the answers when Obama led the federal government in a takeover of General Motors and Chrysler, for example. Or when Obama repeatedly broke his pledge "I won't raise taxes one thin dime . . . on anyone not making $250,000 a year." During the election campaign, many voters gave Obama the benefit of the doubt. After all, no true-believing socialist would have made that pledge, right?

Maybe not, but a Chicago machine politician with socialist lust in his heart would have—and did.

Fortunately, unlike the CMM, conservatives figured "better an inexact question than no question at all." Unfortunately, neither the Obama campaign nor the CMM ever paid any attention to the questions coming from conservatives unless Barack Obama himself, in an unguarded moment, brought up the subject.

Whenever the enterprising—and therefore rare—CMM "journalist" did make inquiries of the Obama campaign that couldn't be answered by that day's talking points, reporters were referred to one of three sources to search for answers:

1. The Obama Narrative™, the official mythology constructed by Team Obama that chronicled the blessed Barack in his heroic struggles as he transcended the evil capitalistic country in which his corporeal body had been imprisoned since birth.
2. The *First Book of Obama*, or, as it was better known, *Dreams from My Father*. This was the foundation upon which much of the Obama Narrative™ rested.
3. Whatever was written by the editorial staff of the *New York Times* on any particular day, who had already consulted numbers 1 and 2.

Since none of the Obama source material mentioned anything very helpful about Barack Obama and socialism, not many questions of that sort were answered. Again, not many questions were even asked—aside from the aforementioned conservative press. That poorly funded, numerically small group of journalists did ask the question: Is Barack Obama a socialist?

The Obama campaign not only wasn't saying, it wasn't allowing anyone who even thought the question near their candidate while the cameras were rolling. Still, the question was posed—and some interesting information turned up that shed light on the answer, based on past actions of Barack Obama that had somehow never made it into the Obama Narrative™.

In late May 2008, Jeff Dunetz, writing at the *Yid With Lid* website, revealed that "Senator Obama's Old party was called the New Party"—as in the socialist New Party, a Marxist party coalition that had endorsed Barack Obama in his run for the Illinois state senate in 1996. Most New Party members were from the Democratic Socialists of America and ACORN. At the time, ACORN was not yet synonymous in the general public's mind with corruption and voter fraud. According to Dunetz, the New Party's short-term goal was to move the Democrats leftward and help bring about a Marxist major third party. Who wouldn't want that on their résumé?

Here was information that required no interpretation of events, no reading of the political tea leaves of Obama's past. The New Party was largely composed of Marxists, socialists, Communists, and hardcore left-wingers—and Barack Obama had not only sought out the New Party endorsement, he recruited New Party volunteers to work on his campaign.

But the information languished, while CMM political commentators maintained the fiction that Obama was a center-left politician, as much a part of the American mainstream as apple pie. During that same time period, Stanley Kurtz, writing at *National Review*, was investigating Obama's Chicago ties to ACORN and Bill Ayers and incidentally mentioned Obama's connections to the New Party. Kurtz was stonewalled while attempting to research the public records of the Chicago Annenberg Challenge, a group in which Obama and Bill Ayers had worked closely together for years—even as candidate Obama was disingenuously distancing himself from his many connections with Ayers.

Except for a post at *Red State* and several pieces by Rick Moran at *Right Wing Nuthouse* and *American Thinker*, the story was absolutely, totally ignored. In fact, it was reported that when Obama sought the New Party endorsement, he was required to sign a contract that he wouldn't dump the Marxists after the election. In effect, in exchange for the New Party endorsement, Obama promised that he would continue his relationship with the New Party after the election. None of this interested the major media commentators.

The United States of America had a man running for the highest office in the land who had been allied with a political party composed of Marxists, communists, and socialists—and this was of absolutely no interest to the major media organizations? How can that be?

But not one major media commentator wrote a single word on the subject of Obama's ties to the New Party. While the CMM asked rhetorical questions about Senator Obama's political possibilities, not a question was asked or a word written about Obama's past endorsement by a Marxist political party.

Summer stretched into fall. Barack Obama was anointed as the Democratic Party's standard bearer and delivered his acceptance speech in front of two huge Styrofoam Greek columns in Denver, John McCain selected the little-known governor of Alaska as his running mate and secured the Republican nomination, and the campaign moved into the last month before the election. Then, in early October, Obama's New Party ties and the question of whether he was a socialist became news once more.

On October 8, on a small blog by the name of *Politically Drunk On Power*, Jarid Brown wrote a piece on Obama and the New Party. Unlike the pieces in late May, Brown's provided graphic proof of an October 1996 New Party newsletter that boasted of three Illinois New Party members who won Democratic primary elections, including Barack Obama:

New Party members are busy knocking on doors, hammering down lawn signs, and phoning voters to support NP candidates this fall. Here are some of our key races. . . .

Illinois: Three NP-members won Democratic primaries last Spring and face off against Republican opponents on election day: Danny Davis (U.S. House), Barack Obama (State Senate) and Patricia Martin (Cook County Judiciary).

Brown discovered the New Party publication in the online files of the nonprofit Internet Archive after it had disappeared from the organization's website. Brown introduced the material with a tempting lead-in:

After allegations surfaced in early summer over the "New Party's" endorsement of Obama, the Obama campaign along with the remnants of the New Party and Democratic Socialists of America claimed that Obama was never a member of either organization. The DSA and "New Party" then systematically attempted to cover up any ties between Obama and the Socialist Organizations. However, it now appears that Barack Obama was indeed a certified and acknowledged member of the DSA's New Party.

On Tuesday, I discovered a web page that had been scrubbed from the New Party's website. The web page, which was published in October 1996, was an internet newsletter update on that year's congressional races. Although the web page was deleted from the New Party's website, the non-profit Internet Archive Organization had archived the page.

Brown's piece, with its graphic proof of Obama's membership in the New Party, was widely disseminated throughout the conservative blogosphere—but again, the CMM remained silent on the matter. Finally, a few days later, Obama himself forced the issue of socialism into the news in such a way that even the CMM couldn't ignore it.

On a widely covered visit to Toledo, Ohio, three days before the final presidential debate between Obama and McCain, Obama had his October 12 encounter with Samuel Joseph "Joe the Plumber" Wurzelbacher. With the cameras rolling, Obama strolled through Wurzelbacher's neighborhood, making small talk and taking questions from the residents. One of those questions came from a man who had been out in his yard when Obama appeared, a man who quickly became known as "Joe the Plumber."

So a humble plumber trod where CMM journalists had feared to go.

"I'm getting ready to buy a company that makes 250 to 280 thousand dollars a year. Your new tax plan's going to tax me more, isn't it?"

Obama's answer to Wurzelbacher's question immediately thrust the issue of socialism—and the Democratic nominee's views on it—front and center into the public and media debate. Obama answered:

"It's not that I want to punish your success. I just want to make sure that everybody who is behind you, that they've got a chance at success, too. . . . My attitude is that if the economy's good for folks from the bottom up, it's gonna be good for everybody. If you've got a plumbing business, you're gonna be better off . . . if you've got a whole bunch of customers who can afford to hire you, and right now everybody's so pinched that business is bad for everybody and I think when you spread the wealth around, it's good for everybody."

Spread the wealth around.

Four little words: That off-the-cuff phrase quickly became shorthand for "socialism"—or rather, "Obama is really a social-ist." This should scarcely have been surprising to anyone who had access to Obama's meager voting record while he was in the U.S. Senate. But most Americans are not political junkies. Many voters got their news from the Corporate Mainstream Media and were ignorant of the debate that had occurred on the Internet.

Previously, Obama's campaign team had carefully guarded their candidate's specific views on capitalism and the free mar-ket. Obama's "spread the wealth around" comment pushed a de-bate over the candidate's views that had previously played out only in the conservative media—mostly on conservative web-sites and on talk radio—into the CMM where many millions of less-informed Americans still got their news. Worse still, Obama had made the remark while many TV cameras were recording it, so there was no denying or downplaying it. Millions of Ameri-cans now wondered, "Is Barack Obama a socialist?"

An objective look at Obama's short record didn't help him or his campaign narrative. During his short stint in the U.S. Sen-ate, Barack Obama, according to *National Journal*, compiled the most liberal—as in the farthest left—voting record in that body. This accomplishment is all the more remarkable because the U.S. Senate contains one avowed socialist, Bernie Sanders of Vermont. Yet, despite his Senate votes, the Corporate Mainstream Media in the fall of 2008 seemed more intent on allaying fears in the American electorate that Barack Hussein Obama might be a socialist than seriously examining Obama's record to determine if he actually was one.

Most of these pieces used a couple of different defenses or some variation thereof. The first defense consisted of having a writer read the political tea leaves from Obama's past and conclude that Obama was "not a socialist." The second CMM ploy was an appeal to socialist authority: interview an actual socialist, who would deny that Barack Obama was "one of them."

In the days after Obama's encounter with Joe the Plumber, readers were treated to more crack investigative work into Wurzelbacher's background than was expended during the entire campaign on the man running for president. Wurzelbacher's divorce records, tax records, and driving records became public knowledge because he'd asked an inconvenient question of Barack Obama. Meanwhile, the CMM couldn't bring itself to badger Obama for any of *his* records.

The corporate media kept pounding the "Obama is not a socialist" theme for months after the November election. In March 2009, the *Washington Post* contributed "Obama's No Socialist. I Should Know" by Billy Wharton, editor of the Socialist Party USA's magazine, *The Socialist*. Even the *Wall Street Journal* weighed in on the side of Obama apologia a few weeks later with a piece by Alan Blinder, a professor of economics and public affairs at Princeton University and a former vice chairman of the Federal Reserve Board, entitled "Obama Is No Socialist."

The desocialisting of Obama continues up to the present time. In July 2010, *Politics Daily* featured an interview with

Frank Llewellyn, the national director of the Democratic Socialists of America, the United States' largest socialist organization,
who claimed that "Obama is most definitely not one of them."

Of course, the CMM could have brought up Obama's spon-
sorship of the Global Poverty Act in the Senate. The GPA proposed to take nearly $1 trillion from U.S. taxpayers and give it
to the poor. That was "spreading the wealth around" writ large.
Obama was on record proclaiming the glories of spreading the
wealth of U.S. taxpayers around—but stories about the Global
Poverty Act were a rarity.

One last point: Information about the many connections between Barack Obama and Bill Ayers was available to the CMM.
It was not only not interested in them, it suppressed the information and instead wrote pieces that attacked journalists who
had made inquiries and documented the truth. America was
treated to the spectacle of a portion of the press, which had sat
on its collective ass, browbeating the portion that had actually
put in some legwork. It was the John Edwards scandal all over
again—but this time, the stakes were higher.

Ayers had hired a young lawyer by the name of Barack Hussein Obama to administer his Chicago Annenberg Challenge.
Ayers wrote in his book *Prairie Fire* that his movement was un
abashedly "communist." This was of no interest to a press supposedly intent on answering the question "Is Barack Obama a
socialist?"

The Corporate Mainstream Media—and this many times included both shows on Fox News and articles in the *Wall Street
Journal*—downplayed discussion of the Obama-Ayers connection during the months leading up to the 2008 election. While

the subject of Ayers was avoided principally because of Ayers's past as a leader of the Weather Underground, any such discussion might also have brought up Barack Obama's many past links not only to socialism, but to Marxism as well. If those discussions had been honestly held in the press, then Americans could have answered the question "Is Barack Obama a socialist?" very easily for themselves.

And the CMM and Team Obama couldn't have allowed that to happen, now, could they?

10

The Obama Narrative™

In the beginning was the Word, and the Word was
with God, and the Word was God.

—John 1:1

Every religion has had its sacred texts and every cult its how-
to manuals; 2008 was no exception. Christians had the Bible;
Jews, the Tanakh; Muslims, the Koran; Scientologists, *Dianet-
ics*. The supporters of Barack Hussein Obama had theirs, too:
the Obama Narrative™.

Like any collection of revered words, much of the Obama
Narrative™ had to be taken on faith. It was the complete words,
visions, and history of Barack Hussein Obama—both real and
imagined. At the foundation of the narrative was *Dreams from
My Father*, Barack Obama's first autobiography, or, as it became
known, *The First Book of Barack*. The Obama Narrative™ became "The Greatest Story Ever—LOL!"

His supporters were fired with a fierce determination to

implement, through Barack, "the Change." Detractors ungraciously called their zeal "cultlike." To those supporters, Obama was the Hope and Obama was the Change. Some of them may even have thought that Obama would deliver them from the root of all evil. To his detractors, Obama was "the Messiah" or "the Anointed One," in that year and forever after. While he may not have been a messiah, Obama sure sometimes sounded like one:

> My job is to be so persuasive that if there's anybody left out there who is still not sure whether they will vote, or is still not clear who they will vote for, that a light will shine through that window, a beam of light will come down upon you, you will experience an epiphany . . . and you will suddenly realize that you must go to the polls and vote for Obama. (New Hampshire, Lebanon Opera House, January 7, 2008)

> Because if we are willing to work for it, and fight for it, and believe in it, then I am absolutely certain that generations from now, we will be able to look back and tell our children that this was the moment when we began to provide care for the sick and good jobs to the jobless; this was the moment when the rise of the oceans began to slow and our planet began to heal; this was the moment when we ended a war and secured our nation and restored our image as the last, best hope on Earth. (final primary night, St. Paul, Minnesota, June 3, 2008)

Barack Obama's wasn't a campaign; it was a philosophy, a way to live one's life. Phrases like "the fierce moral urgency of

Change Now!" were heard, tweeted, repeated, and used to spark discussion or settle debates. Obama's words were the words of the Anti-Bush—it didn't matter that Obama's actions, once the election was in the bag, proved many times to be, disturbingly, a mirror image of the Hated Booosh.

Whenever impure thoughts or uncertainty arose, whether in the CMM or in the trenches, the Obama Narrative™ was there to dispel doubt and quiet fears.

Scholars argue over the proper proportion of history and legend contained in the works of Homer. Discussions of a similar spirit bedeviled the Obama Narrative™. Opponents argued that there were no public records to challenge the narrative claims; supporters—especially those from the CMM—countered that this was the Obama Narrative™'s strongest point. Both largely agreed that any similarity of the Obama Narrative™ to events and persons, living or dead, was purely coincidental.

The Obama Narrative™ was one of the most brilliant marketing ploys in political history—maybe in the history of advertising, too. It enabled a campaign to portray a political social climber, a lightweight, a man with no relevant experience, with little relevant background, not merely as a choice in an election, but as the solution to a nation's—the world's—many problems. It had little connection with fact or history, was not tied to reality, and only by appealing to *Dreams from My Father* could it be challenged.

In the end, it didn't matter. There were millions ready to believe, and the Obama Narrative™ gave them all the more reason to believe. It stroked their faces, smoothed their hair, wiped away their tears, and reassured them that everything would be set right—if only their man could mount the presidential po-dium. Didn't Obama himself promise that the earth would heal and the sea levels would fall?

"The fierce moral urgency of Change Now!" was upon them—and the Obama Narrative™ assured them that Now! was their time and their time was Now! Only months later, after the disappointments—and for the right, confirmations—mounted, would anyone bother to check the fine print. By then, it was too late; it was discovered that Barack Obama had been sold "as is."

When the true nature of the transaction became apparent, there was no website on which to log the buyers' dissatisfaction, no need to wonder whether to Press One for English, no Better Political Business Bureau to which to appeal.

Barack Hussein Obama came with no guarantees or war-ranties, either real or implied. There were no surgeon general warnings. This product carried no FDA or other warning labels. No caveat emptor; no "buyer beware." No "Lemon Law" had the power to undo this electoral transaction.

After the adrenaline rush of the Deal, the dulling ennui of buyer's remorse was a real Obummer. Look as hard as they might, former supporters could find nothing in the Obama Nar-rative™ that offered a remedy for this feeling of "being taken."

During the election campaign, it was the right that doubted the series of fairy tales that littered the Obama Narrative™. On the other hand, many on the left happily bought the narrative's fiction lock, stock, and barrel. Their disappointment has been one of important promises broken; it's been the cold disillusionment of the realization that "change" meant "business as usual." Their wake-up call has been a particularly bitter one.

The right never expected much from the product hawked as Brand Obama. It was a completely different story for the left. Since January 21, 2009, when Barack Hussein Obama assumed power, it has been the left that has realized they've been stuck with a president who's revealed himself to be "Barack Obama: Corporate Stooge, Friend of the Military-Industrial Complex, and Bankster Gangsta Gofer."

The young and ignorant didn't care; they were just along for the ride. Some did it for the buzz; some because Obama events were a good place to pick up girls; some did it for the lutz. Most didn't know they had been had and some didn't care. After they had cast their votes, they retreated into insular worlds of video games and smart-phone apps or another episode of *Jackass*.

Which is precisely why Barack Obama's team worked so hard to mobilize them. Because they were just in it for the rush, because they didn't pay much attention to the fine print, these voters suffered less buyer's remorse when the product they bought turned out to be a dud.

They'll be ripe for the picking come 2012, either by Obama or by someone else with an updated narrative and better mythology.

The problems that have surrounded Barack Obama have had nothing to do with messaging or misidentification of the correct message. The real problem has been that at the end of the day, he's still only Barack H. Obama. He's proven to be all ribbons and wrapping paper, and once people discovered this covered an empty box, the game was up. No amount of rebranding can ever put that genie back into the bottle or put Humpty back together again.

This is what his "brain trust," headed by David Axelrod, doesn't understand. Their product is busted and no amount of infomercials can Change the fact. It's not 2008 and potential voters are no longer ready, willing, and eager to be led by the false promises in the Obama Narrative™ and its false prophet. For Team Obama, 2012 will be the "Year of the Cynic." Obama has been outed and his former adherents are furious.

They wanted someone real and Obama has sadly turned out to be anything but. It's 2011 and Barack H. Obama's time has passed. BHO is now retro.

Regardless of how hard the Obama Narrative™ tried to spin its Barack Obama reality into CMM gold, the reality has remained the same. That's the primary problem with the Obama Narrative™: No matter how many more interviews he grants, he's still Barack H. Obama.

Put another way long ago: "You can't make a silk purse out of a sow's ear."

Faith has its limits, and soothing sacred solutions sometimes run up against hard earthly reality. The great appeal of the Obama Narrative™ was its hope, its great promise of the future. Its downfall has been the stark contrast of that vision with current events.

11

Campaign 2008:
The Big Lie and the Obama Narrative™

Popular radio and TV host Sean Hannity repeatedly claimed during the 2008 campaign that "2008 was the year that journalism died." By the time the year was over, events completely vindicated Hannity—and most of those events involved the corporate media's coverage of Barack Hussein Obama.

That Barack Obama benefited from the media coverage during the 2008 election is beyond argument. The CMM covered the candidates in the run-up to the November 4 election in a manner so one-sided that record numbers of Americans noticed it. A July 2008 Rasmussen Reports survey showed nearly 60 percent of voters responded that Obama got better treatment from journalists than his opponents; an August 2008 Rasmussen poll reported that "55 percent believed media bias was more of a problem than campaign cash."

More revealing still, a Zogby/Ziegler Media poll conducted shortly after the election found that the media coverage shaped the opinions of voters about Obama and his opponent, John McCain. When pundits protested that their coverage was objective and professional, another poll, this time by Wilson Research Strategies, was commissioned by John Ziegler to test the results from the Zogby survey.

The findings largely confirmed the findings of the first poll. The WRS survey found that where a voter got his news largely determined who that voter supported with his ballot. Those "exposed" to CNN voted 63–37 for Obama; MSNBC, 73–26 for Obama; ABC, NBC, or CBS network newscasts, 62–37 for Obama; and national newspapers, 64–36 for Obama. John McCain received the majority of votes of those who got their news from Fox News and talk radio, both notable bastions of conservative thought and opinion.

Chris Wilson, CEO of Wilson Research Strategies, summed up the results of the survey:

> There has been a tremendous amount of punditry and debate about whether or not there was mainstream media and popular culture bias during the presidential election and whether or not that led to an overt polarization of the electorate in 2008 and now it is possible to quantitatively illustrate that not only did both of the above take place, but they likely did so at a disservice to the voters.

This wasn't just an election in which supporters of the two major party candidates divided on ideological lines or separate goals for the direction of the nation. It was also an election where the electorate was literally divided by separate realities of the world around them.

As the data from these surveys show, the information believed to be true by, respectively, McCain and Obama voters directly correlates not just to the candidate each voter was likely to support, but also the sources from which the voter received his or her political information.

These polls weren't so much news flashes: They merely confirmed the obvious to disinterested observers. The CMM was "in the tank" for Barack Obama—and in ways that had never been seen before. Where in previous elections, the media bias was of the "read between the lines" sort, in 2008, there were few attempts at subtlety: Obamaphilia was omnipresent and over the top. Instead of cheerleading for their preferred candidate—and the Obama media coverage devolved into a sort of 24/7 cult of personality—CMM pundits and commentators blacked out news and commentary that cast their candidate in an unfavorable light. When forced to report news inconvenient to the Obama campaign, a healthy dose of attacking the messenger was required. Whoever had the audacity to report news contrary to the Democratic Party line was attacked.

The corporate media coverage of the 2008 presidential campaign didn't simply descend into incompetence or bias: It was starkly corrupt. Lest the reader believe this assessment is harsh or unfair, we present only a few of the most egregious examples for your edification.

Media Coverage Even a National Socialist Could Appreciate

Though Adolf Hitler is credited with the coining of the phrase "The Big Lie," the technique was perfected by one of his closest associates, Reich minister of propaganda in Nazi Germany, Joseph Goebbels. Sixteen years after Hitler's first use of the phrase "big lie" in *Mein Kampf*, Goebbels wrote about the English use of the media during World War II:

> The essential English leadership secret does not depend on particular intelligence. Rather, it depends on a remarkably stupid thick-headedness. The English follow the principle that when one lies, one should lie big, and stick to it. They keep up their lies, even at the risk of looking ridiculous.

A little thought experiment may be helpful at this point: Substitute the words "Corporate Mainstream Media coverage during the 2008 campaign" for "English" in the above paragraph. How fervently one supported Barack Obama during the 2008 election campaign will likely determine the degree to which one agrees with the resultant statement.

A few of the Big Lies about Barack Obama that the CMM pounded into the American electorate during the presidential election:

- **What Obama heard Reverend Jeremiah Wright say during his nearly twenty-year membership in Wright's Trinity United Church.** The evolution of what Obama claimed he heard and how closely he followed Reverend Wright's rants is a fascinating study in how the Obama campaign reacted to unpleasant revelations that threatened the carefully constructed Obama Narrative™. First came a denial of what Wright said. When videos of Wright in the pulpit shouting "God damn America" appeared, the campaign claimed—and the CMM dutifully reported as fact—that Obama had been absent whenever Wright had preached particularly controversial sermons. When proof appeared that Obama had been present on those days, the campaign claimed—and the CMM again reported as fact—that Obama couldn't recall those divisive words.

   Obama then gave his famous "A More Perfect Union" speech in Philadelphia on the subject of Reverend Wright and, more broadly, on race on March 18. A close inspection of the text of the speech raised more questions than were answered—but the CMM never asked the questions. Instead, it was too busy peddling the speech as one of almost legendary proportions, the sort of speech that would have been delivered if Martin Luther King, Gandhi, Frederick Douglass, and Buddha had been consulted beforehand. A representative sample of the reaction follows:

He did it. No other presidential candidate in the last forty years has managed to speak so much truth so eloquently at such a crucial juncture in his campaign as Barack Obama did today. And he did it by speaking about race, the most persistent source of hatred among us since America began. It turns out that a candidate for president with a white mother and a black father has a capacity that no one else has ever had before: he can articulate an equal understanding of black racism and white racism—and that makes it possible for him to condemn both of them with equal passion.

—Charles Kaiser, *Radar*

It was a moment that Obama made great through the seriousness, intelligence, eloquence, and courage of what he said. I don't recall another speech about race with as little pandering or posturing or shying from awkward points, and as much honest attempt to explain and connect, as this one.

—James Fallows, *The Atlantic*

Senator Obama on Tuesday morning responded to these recent fusses with a speech unlike any delivered by a major political figure in modern American history.

—David Corn, *Mother Jones*

But I do want to say that this searing, nuanced, gut-wrenching, loyal, and deeply, deeply Christian speech is the most honest speech on race in America in my adult lifetime. It is a speech we have all been waiting for for a generation. Its ability to embrace both the legitimate fears and resentments of whites and the understandable anger and dashed hopes of many blacks was, in my view, unique in recent American history.

—Andrew Sullivan, *The Atlantic*

It was a stirring speech that reached back to the founding in Philadelphia but then also challenged everyone to continue to move forward in the future. It was truly a transcendent speech and a remarkable piece of oratory.

—Donald F. Kettl, University of Pennsylvania

Wow. It was a speech that was not partisan. It was political with a small p and it was also philosophical. It was the most profound speech about race that I could recall in my lifetime.

—Jamal Simmons, unaffiliated Democratic strategist

While the media hailed the speech, not all voters were convinced that one speech trumped twenty years of Obama sitting in the pews of Trinity Church absorbing the sermons of Reverend Jeremiah Wright. Therefore, about five weeks later, Obama made a startling announcement: He was resigning from Trinity United Church of Christ. To the CMM, the Reverend Wright controversy—and all the questions it raised about how Barack Obama really felt about race, religion, and America—was now old news. Stories about Reverend Wright disappeared altogether from the CMM.

The Big Lie about Obama's relationship with Reverend Wright led to an even Bigger Lie: that Obama was a postracial uniter, a healer of racial strife. This was the verdict that news consumers of the CMM received from the media about Obama's involvement with Reverend Wright. Barack Obama was a transcendent figure standing above the divisive issue of race relations. It was this Big Lie that caused Sean Hannity to label 2008 as "the year journalism died."

- **The full extent of Obama's relationship with former domestic terrorist Bill Ayers.** This duty seemed to fall most heavily to the *New York Times*. The *Times* answered every revelation of Obama's chumminess with the former leader of the 1960s Weather Underground with Obama's claim that Ayers was "just some guy from the neighborhood." Instead of investigating the claims that Obama began his political career in the living room of Ayers's home, the paper responded with Obama campaign talking points. The Big Lie was that Ayers was someone Obama barely knew.

- **Obama: The Smartest Man Who Has Ever Lived™.** Regular followers of the CMM expect it to portray the Democratic presidential candidate as an incredibly intelligent individual (Bill Clinton did crossword puzzles—in ink!) and the Republican nominee as being so stupid as to hardly be able to dress himself. Ann Coulter has written extensively on the history of this CMM phenomenon, but 2008 surely set some sort of record for abject media brownnosing. Corporate media weren't merely a groveling collection of sniveling Obama yes-men; they were a veritable mob of yes-we-can-men.

If there existed a Nobel Prize for "Most Superlatives Used by the Media in the Description of One Man's Intellect," CBS, NBC, ABC, CNN, *Time, Newsweek*, the *New York Times*, most big-city newspapers, MSNBC, and the *Washington Post* would have jointly shared the award in 2008. Obama was not merely intelligent, he was otherworldly in his intelligence. Stories about Obama's intelligence continued unabated after the election. In October 2008, Gore Vidal told Joy Behar that Obama was "too intelligent for the job" and "too intelligent for America." But Vidal was hard-pressed to top *Newsweek*'s Evan Thomas, who told MSNBC's Chris Matthews that "I mean in a way Obama's standing above the country, above the world, he's sort of God."

- **The Obama Narrative™.** The single biggest lie told by the CMM depicted Barack Obama as a tabula rasa, a blank slate upon which the voters could write their hopes and aspirations, a man with nothing unsettling or extreme or disqualifying in his background. That was the marketing strategy used by the Obama campaign, which never could have been implemented without the wholehearted assistance of a compliant CMM.

How did a machine politician from the corrupt swampland that is Chicago, with little national experience, who had never been in charge of any significant undertaking; who had gained notoriety in the Illinois State Senate not by any accomplishments or by taking courageous stands but by the number of times he voted "present"; who counted among his important supporters a former terrorist, a race-baiting Black Liberation Theology preacher, and a corrupt slumlord; who claimed his first election victory by suing all of his opponents off the ballot; who had worked for Voter Fraud, Inc., otherwise known as ACORN; and whose run for state office in Illinois was endorsed by a Marxist third party become the Democratic Party nominee and, eventually, president of the United States of America?

The CMM not only failed to investigate and report this history, it actively engaged in ensuring that this news was suppressed. Then it ran interference whenever others *did* report it.

Sam Smith of *Undernews* nailed it in June 2007: "[The media] created the Barack Obama myth out of whole cloth. A political lightweight from the Chicago Democratic machine with a virtually non-existent record has been turned into JFK II."

Instead of the corporate media fulfilling its constitutionally protected job of vigorously vetting a candidate for president, it sabotaged those who tried. Rather than report the news—even with its traditional bias for progressive liberal Democrats—it engaged in content management. It wasn't a matter of incompetence or a bungling of duties, it was a concerted effort to circumvent the duties of a free press. In 2008, CMM "journalists" didn't suffer from a lack of will; they suffered from the delusion that they were wiser than the voters they were supposed to serve and inform. Theirs was a desire to shape the news, not report it. As November 4 neared, the CMM movers and shakers weren't afflicted with doubt about what was best for the country, they were afflicted with the conceit that Barack Hussein Obama was a once-in-a-lifetime political messiah for whom it was worth subverting the portion of the process they controlled.

And journalism be damned.

Herr Goebbels would have approved.

12

Campaign 2008: Rogue Democrat

On August 28, 2008, Barack Obama delivered his acceptance speech at the Democratic Party's National Convention in Denver, Colorado. In front of a set of massive Styrofoam Greek columns erected on the stage behind him, Obama opened with obligatory attacks on then-president George W. Bush's "broken policies." The newly designated Democratic presidential nominee recited a laundry list of all that was *wrong* with the country and all that was *right* with the Democratic Party, and finished with a plea to Americans attending the convention and watching at home on television to give him and his political party the chance to effect "change."

At least half a dozen times during his speech, Obama referred to Democrats, affirmed their viewpoints, and assured them that the policies he proposed to implement were ones with which they would agree. He finished by making an appeal for their support in the upcoming general election campaign for the White House. On November 4, 2008, many Democrats— and in particular, Democratic constituent groups, such as blacks and Hispanics—across the country responded positively to Obama's Denver appeal: The junior senator from Illinois became the forty-fourth president. By a large measure, Democrats supported Barack Obama in 2008.

But did Barack Obama support Democrats and the Democratic Party?

On September 24, a few weeks after Obama gave his speech in Denver, this writer noted the curious structure of the Obama campaign organization. Obama's campaign broke new ground in a number of ways (organizing via the Internet, declining federal matching funds, controlling personal information about the candidate's life and records, and restricting media access, to name but a few), but it was the structure of the Obama campaign itself that was most remarkable.

Like much that was remarkable about the 2008 Barack Obama campaign, this aspect was completely ignored by most media outlets. More curious yet, although it was grumbled about by local Democrats in some areas, the national Democratic Party remained absolutely silent on the matter. That silence continues today.

Election 2008 was the first time in history that a party's presidential candidate created hundreds of his own campaign offices that were totally independent from the offices of the candidate's own political party. Of course, these offices competed with Republicans, but they competed directly for money and manpower with local Democratic candidates as well in each locale where the separate Obama "Campaign for Change" offices were located. This writer conducted a little research at the time and found the following.

Obama Offices: Different, Separate, and Apart from Democrat Party Offices

Does the Obama campaign not trust the Democrats? Or is it the Clintons? Will Election 2008 be remembered as the first contest between Republicans and Obamacrats—or the first between the Obamacrats and the Democrats?

Senator Barack Obama has built a national organization separate and apart from the national Democratic Party apparatus—at least in any state where the outcome of the 2008 election was at all in doubt. In state after state, the Obama campaign, in a break with tradition, opened up its own offices— which largely pushed Barack Obama, and *only* Barack Obama— apart from the Democrat Party's own offices in those very same communities. The separate (vote Obama) but equal (to the Democratic Party) offices dotted a map of the USA.

Ohio had seventy Obama Campaign for Change regional offices—all of which were separate and apart from the Democratic Party. In Pennsylvania, there were sixty-three Campaign for Change offices. The list went on: Virginia, more than forty offices; Georgia, thirty-eight; North Carolina, thirty-six; Indiana, thirty-two; Colorado, thirty; Iowa, twenty-three; Minnesota, twelve; West Virginia, six. There were literally hundreds of these

Obama Only offices maintained by the Obama campaign; the exact number was hard to pin down, as many more offices were listed at the time as "pending," according to the Campaign for Change website.

In states where the outcome was already pretty much decided, Campaign for Change conserved its resources and operated few offices: one each in Texas and California, for example.

Did Obama trust the Democrats? Did the Democrats trust Obama? The Campaign for Change offices pushed one product and one product only: Barack Obama. In one weekend visit to Obama offices in several different states, it was found that local and state Democratic candidates did have a presence at the Campaign for Change offices—but not much of one.

Almost all of the usual campaign giveaways from local Democratic candidates were there: pencils, literature, stickers. They were all on a small table in the back of the large room at the Wheeling, West Virginia, Campaign for Change office.

That small table in the back of the room represented the presence of all of the local, district, and state Democratic candidates—combined. The rest of the spacious room was dedicated to Barack Obama. In almost every case, there was no mention of running mate Joe Biden.

Earlier in 2008, after Ohio governor Ted Strickland had turned down an Obama veep invitation, *Scared Monkeys* noted the difficulties Obama was having getting moderates in the Democratic Party to get in line behind him:

So much for gaining that candidate in an all-important must win battle ground state like Ohio. There will be no Obama-

Strickland ticket and Obama's chances of victory in Ohio just became more difficult. What is more interesting about this decision by Strickland is that he is a staunch Hillary Clinton supporter. What does that tell us about the Democratic party so-called coming together after the bitterly contested primary?

To add just a little bit more Democratic party unity, Democratic Representative Dan Boren of Oklahoma stated that Barack Obama is "the most liberal senator" in Congress and he has no intention of endorsing him for the White House. So much for support from moderate Democrats. As most had suspected, many moderate Democrats find Obama too liberal to endorse.

The Obama campaign and supporters would likely dismiss any protests about the separate offices as "smart thinking" and "targeting resources." But each office sucked up those resources: lease money, campaign materials, and manpower. The Campaign for Change offices were staffed by volunteers, but a volunteer who sat behind a CFC desk was a volunteer who did not knock on doors for the local Democratic candidate for state senate.

In this way, the Obama campaign was sure of one thing: The volunteer on the phone in a Des Moines Campaign for Change office would be talking about Barack Obama—not the local Democratic candidate for county commissioner.

The Obama campaign also apparently charged fellow Democrats for Obama campaign materials. At a Democrat-sponsored booth at an event in Wheeling, local Democratic Party volunteers who manned the location complained about this sign of Obamaization. The booth featured campaign materials from many local and state Democratic candidates, but not much Obama signage or literature.

"We had to pay for them," a lady complained. "They don't give us anything."

Even Obama supporters had to pay the campaign for everything in their offices. "Al," a local CFC volunteer at a local Obama campaign office, said he had to "pay for the lease out of my own pocket. All of the T-shirts, buttons, stickers here, I paid for." Still, "Al" didn't seem too put out by the admission.

So, if Obama volunteers were paying the campaign for all of the Obama materials in the Campaign for Change offices and picking up the tab for leases, wasn't this just good business sense for the Obama campaign? Seemingly so. Actually, this appeared to be financially brilliant for the Obama campaign. Each Campaign for Change office not only promoted the product of Brand Obama for President, it became a cash cow. It not only paid the freight for promoting Obama, it generated money for the national Obama organization by the purchase of Obama campaign materials.

Might there have been any other reasons for the Obama campaign to build this network dedicated to the election of Barack Obama outside normal Democrat Party channels? Perhaps so.

The Specter of Hillary Clinton

The Obama campaign may have set up all of those separate offices—in any state that might have been the least bit in play—

because of the woman Obama had beaten in the Democratic primaries: Hillary Clinton.

An Obama Campaign for Change office would certainly have been an office beyond any possible control of the Clintonistas. After a bruising primary battle, many Clinton supporters vowed never to support their party's nominee; a few contemporary headlines at PUMA (Party Unity My Ass) websites, which continued to support Hillary Clinton, bore this out:

**PSSST!! DID YOU KNOW OBAMA TAKES LOBBYIST MONEY,
EVEN THOUGH HE CLAIMS HE DOESN'T**

**IMPLOSION CONTINUES:
ET TU, NEW JERSEY?**

**GUESS WHO SAYS OBAMA HAS NO PLAN?
HARRY REID, THAT'S WHO . . .**

The preceding headlines came from the front page of *PUMA08.com*. They helped illustrate the rift between some supporters of Hillary Clinton and the candidate they claim was "selected, not elected" to represent the Democrats in November.

An AP-Yahoo News poll in September 2008 claimed that Democrats who backed Hillary Clinton in the primaries were not warming up to Barack Obama. Fifty-eight percent of Clinton supporters then backed Obama. That was the same percentage who said they backed Obama in June 2008, when Clinton called it quits and the PUMA movement was born.

The poll showed that while Obama had gained ground

among Clinton's supporters (69 percent viewed him favorably at that time, up nine percentage points from June), this had yet to translate into more of their actual support.

In part, this was because their positive views of Republican presidential nominee John McCain had also improved during this period. Those supporting McCain had also edged up, from 21 percent to 28 percent, with the number of undecided staying constant, the survey showed.

But the suspicions weren't a one-way street: Obama and many of his supporters hadn't warmed to the Clintons either. *Insight Analytical* claimed Obama didn't want Clinton Democrats and examined why:

> It's forty-four days until the General Election as I write this and after a long and hard fought primary season the Democratic Party, and the Obama campaign specifically, are still unable to get over their terminal case of CDS. I can't help but ask "Why?" For the uninitiated, CDS stands for Clinton Derangement Syndrome, usually defined as the uncontrollable impulse to rail against all things Clinton (Hillary, Bill, Chelsea, Hillary's supporters, and basically anything connected to centrist positions).
>
> Team Obama not only masterminded the overthrow of the Democratic Party to form the "New Democrats" (remember the May 31, 2008, coup when all semblance of the rules were overthrown at a behind-closed-doors meeting of the Rules and Bylaws Committee), they literally declared the nomination belonged to Obama despite the fact that:

Hillary Clinton won more of the popular vote than Obama (when the Florida and Michigan primaries are included as originally voted).

Automatic (also called super) delegates are unable to actually cast a vote until the national convention.

Obama did not actually have enough super delegates "locked in" to declare himself the winner when he did.

Hillary Clinton didn't contest the illegal theft of earned delegates in Michigan, despite her legal right to do so.

Bill Clinton was accused of having short coattails in the nineties, of being "good for Bill Clinton, bad for Democrats." It turned out that Obama had even shorter coattails. Bill Clinton campaigned for other Democrats while running for president—a lot, actually. In 2008, with some exceptions, Obama campaigned primarily for Barack Obama.

In September 2008 an outbreak of rumors concerning the supposed dumping of Joe Biden from the ticket was partly attributed to the "Obama only" syndrome. At the time, Will Bower, of *PUMA08.com*, didn't buy the "Dump Biden" rumors: "I believe that the 'Dump Biden' rumor is exactly that—a rumor."

Bower added, "I don't believe that Hillary would encourage Obama to do such a thing at this juncture. It would only serve to make him [accurately] look weak and indecisive."

Will Obama repeat his use of a national network of Campaign for Change offices separate from the local Democrat Party in 2012? Will Obama even run again in 2012?

Does it matter?

After all, Barack Obama—who has been described as having been in perpetual presidential campaign mode since 2007—has built his own network of volunteers, fund-raising, and organization. It is a network beholden to no one outside the Obama campaign. It's a network that's already in place and can be expanded upon in 2012 for a reelection run.

There were those who accused the Clintons of being only for the Clintons, but Bill and Hillary did not build a network of separate campaign offices that competed with other Democrats for money and volunteers—they worked within the framework already established by the Democratic Party.

Will the Obama organization supersede the Democratic Party? Or will the Clintons and their supporters be able to circumvent this looming obstacle at some point?

The year 2008 may be remembered as the beginning of a battle in which John McCain was only one opponent among many.

NOTE: Soon after the general election was over, talks began between Barack Obama's campaign and the Democratic National Committee, which was anxious to absorb parts of the Obama organization. In January 2009, it was announced that the DNC would assume control of Obama's web-based assets. According to *MSNBC.com*, "To build a wall between Obama's White House and the political organization he built, the mailing list and his Web site, BarackObama.com, are now maintained by the DNC."

There was no mention of Obama's Campaign for Change operation.

13

Campaign 2008:
The Human Gaffe Machine

Question: Suppose you're a reporter or commentator for a CMM organization that has pushed a Democratic Party candidate who has been running for the highest office in the land—one who had absolutely no relevant experience. What could you possibly write about said candidate that would persuade your readers to vote for him?

Answer: Why not write about how amazingly intelligent the candidate is? Of course, this has been the CMM boilerplate for Democratic Party presidential candidates for decades. Almost every corporate media article about the comparative intelligence of presidential candidates over the last thirty years has emphasized the scary smartness of the Democrat, while dismissing the Republican counterpart as dull, primitive, and stupid.

However, due to Barack Obama's total and complete lack of relevant experience, this strategy by itself might not have been persuasive enough to push BHO over the top. What other strategy might have been helpful?

Thus the narrative of "Barack Obama, World's Greatest Living Orator—Ever!"™ was born. Not only was the Democratic nominee so smart he could split atoms using only his mind, he was Demosthenes, Daniel Webster, John F. Kennedy, and Martin Luther King, Jr.—all rolled into one.

This theme of "Barack Obama, World's Greatest Living Orator—Ever!"™ dominated the media coverage of Barack Obama during the 2008 campaign. Very conveniently, a report that focused on "Obama as a modern-day reincarnation of Winston Churchill" did not discuss candidate Obama's lack of experience and other shortcomings—and the media could conduct only so many "Barack, what's your favorite color?" interviews.

One additional advantage (for the Obama campaign) of a media narrative obsessed with oratory: It's completely subjective. Who's to say what constitutes "greatness"? One man's Cicero is another man's Jerry Lewis. One doesn't know exactly how many speeches have been identified by the CMM as "Barack Obama's finest speech ever given" because in the corporate media's eyes, they all pretty much were cause to swoon.

However, a complete and objective reading of Obama's campaign pronouncements showed a different story. The difference between the media narrative of "Barack Obama, World's Greatest Living Orator—Ever!"™ and the reality of Barack Obama, Human Gaffe Machine, wasn't so much a gap as a yawning chasm, a Grand Canyon–like abyss that might have swallowed the various narratives and a candidate with so little else to offer. *If* the CMM had widely reported those verbal miscues.

For the skeptics, the following are some of the most egregious gaffes from the 2008 campaign. A few were outright fabrications by Barack Obama rather than bloopers. All were reported as they occurred by various Internet sites. Some got a few mentions in various other media. None were reported with the zeal that Sarah Palin miscues—both real and imagined—received.

These quotations are broken down into three broad categories: *gaffes,* which are unintentionally revealing truths that the speaker would prefer remain hidden; *howlers,* which are statements that make most nonpolitical people either laugh or do a double take; and *fabrications,* which are statements that are simply not true, or that require much "clarification" and spin doctoring in order to "explain" why the statement is not what it seems: a lie.

After reading the following quotations, the reader can then decide on the validity of the twin media narratives of Election 2008: Barack Obama, Genius, and Barack Obama, World's Greatest Living Orator—Ever!™

Gaffes

What I was suggesting—you're absolutely right that John McCain has not talked about my Muslim faith.

—Barack Obama interview with ABC's George

Stephanopoulos, who quickly corrected him: "Christian faith."

I think when you spread the wealth around, it's good for everybody.

> —Barack Obama defending his tax plan to
> Samuel Joseph "Joe the Plumber" Wurzelbacher,
> Toledo, Ohio, October 12, 2008.

Come on! I just answered, like, eight questions.

> —Obama's response when asked a question after a press
> conference, San Antonio, Texas, May 3, 2008. This statement
> would prove to be the epitome of President Obama's
> exasperation with any press event that wasn't highly
> managed after January 2009.

[Iran] doesn't pose a serious threat to us. Tiny countries with small defense budgets can't do us harm.

> —Obama campaign speech, Portland, Oregon, May 2008.

I've made it clear for years that the threat from Iran is grave.

> —Obama comment, the day after the previous quotation.
> Might also belong in the third category.

I've got two daughters. Nine years old and six years old. I am going to teach them first of all about values and morals. But, if they make a mistake, I don't want them punished with a baby.

> —Candidate Obama, Town Hall meeting,
> Johnstown, Pennsylvania, March 31, 2008.

We are the ones we've been waiting for.

> —Obama Super Tuesday speech, February 5, 2008.

You know, I don't understand when people are going around worrying about, "We need to have English only." They want to pass a law, "We want English only." . . . Instead of worrying about whether immigrants can learn English—they'll learn English—you need to make sure your child can speak Spanish.

—Campaign speech, Powder Springs, Georgia, July 8, 2008.

Obama himself reportedly does not speak Spanish, although "Fun Facts" that appeared in many newspapers worldwide around Inauguration Day reported that he did.

Of course, these same Fun Facts reported that Obama couldn't stand ice cream.

You know, it's embarrassing when Europeans come over here, they all speak English, they speak French, they speak German. And then we go over to Europe, and all we can say [is], "Merci beaucoup." Right?

—Campaign speech, Powder Springs, Georgia, July 8, 2008.

Obama himself does not speak French or German.

Howlers

This might be a good time to ask how friends, family, or coworkers would react if the reader had made these same statements.

On this Memorial Day, as our nation honors its unbroken line of fallen heroes—and I see many of them in the audience here today—our sense of patriotism is particularly strong.

—Barack Obama, 2008 Memorial Day commemoration,

Las Cruces, New Mexico.

I've now been in fifty-seven states—I think one left to go.

> —Obama 2008 campaign event,
> Beaverton, Oregon, May 9, 2008.

In case you missed it, this week, there was a tragedy in Kansas. Ten thousand people died—an entire town destroyed.

> —Barack Obama, 2007 campaign speech on a
> Kansas tornado that killed twelve people.

I didn't want to get into a Nancy Reagan thing about doing any séances.

> —Barack Obama, after saying he had spoken with all the
> living presidents as he prepared to take office, Washington,
> D.C., November 7, 2008. Obama later called Nancy Reagan
> to apologize.

I'm here with the Girardo family here in St. Louis.

> —Obama, to the Democratic National Convention via
> satellite from Kansas City, Missouri, August 25, 2008.

Just this past week, we passed out of the U.S. Senate Banking Committee— which is my committee—a bill to call for divestment from Iran as a way of ratcheting up the pressure to ensure that they don't obtain a nuclear weapon.

> —Barack Obama, Sderot, Israel, July 23, 2008.
> Obama was not on the Senate Banking Committee.

Senator Clinton, I think, is much better known, coming from a nearby state of Arkansas. So it's not surprising that she would have an advantage in some of those states in the middle.

> —Obama explaining in a telephone interview with McClatchy newspapers why he was trailing Hillary Clinton in Kentucky, May 16, 2008. Kentucky borders Obama's home state of Illinois; Arkansas does not.

We only have a certain number of them, and if they are all in Iraq, then it's harder for us to use them in Afghanistan.

> —Obama explaining a lack of translators in Afghanistan during a stop in Cape Girardeau, Missouri, May 2008. The real reason it's "harder for us to use them" in Afghanistan: The Afghanis speak Pashto, Farsi, or other non-Arabic languages. Iraqis speak Arabic or Kurdish.

How's it going, Sunshine?

> —Obama opening a campaign stop in Sunrise, Florida.

Fabrications

There was something stirring across the country because of what happened in Selma, Alabama, because some folks are willing to march across a bridge. So they got together and Barack Obama Jr. was born.

> —Obama explaining how he came to be, Selma, Alabama, March 2007. BHO was born in 1961. The Selma march took place in 1965. Obama spokesman Bill Burton later explained that Obama was "speaking metaphorically about the civil-rights movement as a whole." Yeah, that's the ticket, "metaphorically."

Here's something that you will rarely hear from a politician, and that is that I'm not familiar with the Hanford, uuuuhh, site, so I don't know exactly what's going on there. [Applause.] Now, having said that, I promise you I'll learn about it by the time I leave here on the ride back to the airport.

> —Obama Oregon campaign appearance, May 2008.
> Obama voted on at least one defense-authorization bill
> that addressed the "costs, schedules, and technical issues"
> dealing with the Hanford facility.

I was a constitutional law professor, which means unlike the current president I actually respect the Constitution.

> —Obama to an audience at a campaign fund-raiser, March 30,
> 2007, AP. According to the University of Chicago website on
> the same day, Obama was listed as a "Senior Lecturer In Law
> (On Leave Of Absence)." There is a great difference between
> this and being a "constitutional law professor," which became
> more than evident after the passage of ObamaCare. A dozen
> states have challenged its mandate to force Americans to buy
> insurance on the ground that it's unconstitutional.

It might have been an Ebony *or it might have been . . . who knows what it was?*

> —Barack Obama wrote in his autobiography, *Dreams from*
> *My Father*, that he was "deeply affected" at age nine by a
> *Life* magazine article that contained two accompanying
> photographs of an African-American man physically and
> mentally scarred by his efforts to lighten his skin. Obama
> wrote that the photo triggered his "racial awakening." The

Life article and the photographs don't exist, say the magazine's
historians. Obama offered the above quotation as an
alternative explanation when a *Chicago Tribune*
reporter pointed out that no such *Life* article existed.
A search of *Ebony* also turned up empty.
Chicago Tribune, March 25, 2007.

*My father served in World War II, and when he came home, he
got the services that he needed.*

—Obama, August 2008 campaign speech. At the end of
World War II, Obama's father was ten years old.

*I had a uncle who was one of the, who was part of the first
American troops to go into Auschwitz and liberate the con-
centration camps. And the story in my family is that when he
came home, he just went into the attic, and he didn't leave
the house for six months. All right? Now, obviously something
had affected him deeply, but at the time, there just weren't the
kinds of facilities to help somebody work through that kind of
pain.*

—Obama campaign speech, Las Cruces, New Mexico, May
26, 2008. It was Russian, not American, troops who liberated
Auschwitz. The Obama campaign later "clarified" Obama's
quotation, stating that it was his great-uncle and he really
meant Buchenwald instead of Auschwitz.

You're likable enough, Hillary.

—Obama, to Senator Hillary Clinton, during
New Hampshire debate, January 2008.

This is not a complete list of Obama verbal miscues during the 2008 election campaign, but it is a representative list. Was the reader familiar with all of these quotations? If not, why? Were they not newsworthy? Would it have made a difference in how voters perceived Barack Obama if they had been widely reported?

Taken as a whole—and there are many more; a quick Google search of "Barack Obama gaffes" returns almost 200,000 results—they effectively put the lie to the way the CMM presented candidate Barack Obama to the American electorate during the 2008 election: "Barack Obama, World's Greatest Living Orator—Ever!™"

14

Our Very First President of Self-Esteem

Who is Barack Hussein Obama?

Sometime in Barack Obama's second year in office, the media transformed Obama into our very first President of Self-Esteem. Americans paid higher taxes, dealt with more regulations, alienated allies, comforted enemies, dithered on national security, gave more rights to terrorists—but were told by the CMM, "Don't worry. Really, you're all winners!"

Welcome to the Obama presidency and America's first self-esteem president.

At some point in the 1960s, the idea that "competition is bad" got added to the educational establishment equation and seeped into grade schools. Games were invented (Frisbee,

Earthball) that ensured that no one would have to suffer the agony of being on the losing side of a game. There were no winners, there were no losers: There were only players. Since there was no score, every single child was assured that he or she was a winner.

This accompanied another contemporary practice in education: the end of grouping children by achievement level. Grouping, the educators assured parents, was wrong; there really were no differences in children's innate abilities, only differences in how those abilities were developed. Of course, the end of grouping didn't fool the children: They all still knew which of their classmates was the funniest, which could run the fastest, who was the strongest, the smartest, and so on.

Activities involving friendly competition were replaced by activities that killed time. Books appeared with titles like *Everybody Wins: 393 Non-Competitive Games for Young Children*. It was the perfect book for a noncompetitive age. Instead of dodgeball, basketball, and baseball, a variety of games were introduced that recreated all of the magic and satisfaction of winning a game of Solitaire. But it didn't matter because Everyone was a Winner!

Really.

Generations of kids quit trying and learned instead to ask, "Who are you to judge?" Many of these, weaned on this philosophy of noncompetitive games, grew up to become reporters and commentators at Corporate Mainstream Media news organizations that covered the 2008 presidential election and, later, the Obama White House.

Obama said there were fifty-seven states? Misspelled common words on TV? No problem, the word from the press was, "He's a genius."

BHO threw like a girl? Bowled like a—well, the president said a Special Olympian; he apologized for that remark later, so let's just skip it.

Obama said he's a "huge White Sox fan" but couldn't name even one player who ever played for the Chicago team. Once more, no problem: this president was a genuine Sports Monster.

We were told that Obama was a "gifted" and "masterful" orator. The corporate media hammered that meme until it became a cliché. However, a steady stream of *YouTube* videos provided ample evidence that whenever BHO went off teleprompter, his true gift was for gaffes.

Increasingly, the president was not believed and not trusted. This had to do with people having gained the ability to check his claims for themselves. They no longer had to get their facts from a big-city daily newspaper or a talking head at an alphabet network or cable newscast.

The CMM could hide who Barack Obama was and what he stood for during the months of the election season. Obama could make outrageous statements ("I won't raise taxes on anyone making under $250,000") despite evidence that clearly indicated he was quite likely to do otherwise, and there was no way to contradict him—he'd sponsored very few bills and the CMM didn't talk about his extreme-liberal voting record during Obama's short time in the U.S. Senate. After months of having been required to actually govern, Barack Obama has painted his own picture of who he is and what he stands for. The media can no longer spin gold from dirt.

The result of the ObamaCare fiasco is that everyone in America will soon be awarded a prize that few want. Obama-Care is like a toxic blue ribbon that gathers dust in a box in the attic until it's finally tossed out. Only the ObamaCare ribbon can't be tossed out. Every April 15, the IRS will check on your "award," reminding Americans that they've "won."

Really.

Americans are looking at the results of Obama's term in office. Obama is failing, yet the media continue their tired line that "Obama's a winner—and so are you!" We can feel the slide backward, feel the insecurity. Our allies are worried, our enemies, not so much. But all of this is of no concern: In Obama's America, as the country struggles under the governance of our first Self-Esteem President, there are no losers, only winners.

Really.

15

The Obama Enemies List

Barack Obama got an early start on his presidential enemies list. Unlike liberal nemesis Richard Nixon, Obama not only started his enemies list during the 2008 election campaign—he published it on the campaign website dedicated to propagating the official Obama Narrative™: *Fightthesmears.com.* The more the candidate called for "Change," the more he resorted to Nixonian politics of the past.

Barack Obama—who had repackaged failed liberal ideas in a shiny rhetorical package, sold this gag gift to the young and historically ignorant, and parlayed it into the Democrat presidential nomination—used his *Fightthesmears.com* (FTS) campaign website to publish his first enemies list and attack those who disagreed with his prime objective: winning the presidency.

FTS labeled conservative activists as part of a "smear." Their offense? Basically, it was working against the Obama campaign. *FTS* redefined the word "smear" to mean "those who do not agree with Barack Obama." Obama's site didn't propose that the activities the activists engaged in were illegal, immoral (to anyone other than rabid liberals), or untrue—it just implied it. In short, it was a smear by *Fightthesmears.*

Dubbed "Smear Inc.," the list at *FTS* was composed of several people who were involved in conservative causes. The list was included in a post titled "Behind the Smears" and was the first time that a presidential candidate had ever publicly published an enemies list. Who made the cut on the first version of Obama's enemies list?

David Bossie

His crime? According to FTS:

> Bossie runs Citizens United, has paired with Floyd Brown for years. Bossie and Brown harassed the Clintons throughout Bill Clinton's administration, with even George H. W. Bush calling his behavior in the 1992 presidential election (which included harassing the family of a recent suicide victim) "filthy campaign tactics." After writing a 2000 book about Al Gore that went little-noticed, in 2004, Bossie and Floyd Brown, working as the group Citizens United, made a movie called *Celsius 41.11* and ran television ads attacking John Kerry.

Floyd Brown

Brown, "the leader of the National Campaign Fund, the Legacy Committee, Citizens for a Safe and Prosperous America, and the Policy Issues Institute, once bragged he was part of 'the heart and soul of the right-wing conspiracy' and has a history of surfacing every four years to make right-wing attacks against Democrats in presidential elections. Most infamously, Brown was responsible for the 1988 'Willie Horton' ad against Michael Dukakis."

Bob Perry

Perry "is one of the biggest Republican donors in the country and was the main financier of the Swift Boat Veterans for Truth in 2004, giving $4.5 million. The ads produced by the Swift Boat effort were so disingenuous that John McCain himself denounced them as 'dishonest and dishonorable.'"

Craig Shirley

"Shirley, who runs Stop-Him-Now.com, was a McCain campaign consultant and endorser until the campaign was faced with the possible illegal arrangement. Shirley, another member of the team that produced the Willie Horton ads in 1988, harassed the Clinton administration for years, staging the press conference where Paula Jones was introduced."

• • •

Others making the Obama honor roll were: "Bruce Hawkins, the Executive Director of the National Campaign Fund, has been involved in Republican campaigns for twenty years."

The *FTS* website claimed that "Hawkins was disbarred by the State of Washington" for a business-gone-bad (our words).

Also meriting mention by *FTS*: "James Lacy is the treasurer and general counsel of the National Campaign Fund. He was the treasurer for the Legacy Committee; is the contact for the Policy Issues Institute; and is the treasurer for Citizens for a Safe and Prosperous America. Lacy is a 'long-time conservative activist' and a 'soldier in the conservative movement for many, many years. Lacy, who served as a lawyer for the Minutemen, once said he was willing to do whatever it takes to preserve the Minuteman Project.'"

At least Nixon waited until he was actually elected before compiling his enemies list. Jake Tapper of ABC News had a revealing observation at the time: "Interestingly, the Obama campaign fails to connect any of the 'Smears' it disproves to any of these charter members of Smears Inc."

What was ironic, Orwellian, or hilarious—depending on how one viewed it—was the quotation featured at the top of *FTS*: "What you won't hear from this campaign or this party is the kind of politics that uses religion as a wedge, and patriotism as a bludgeon that sees our opponents not as competitors to challenge, but enemies to demonize." The statement was made by Barack Obama on June 3, 2008.

What made this quotation hilarious were the actions of the Obama White House fifteen months later. By October 2009, the administration had "declared war" against a number of opponents, including Fox News and the U.S. Chamber of Commerce. The White House attempted to marginalize opponents by denying that they had legitimate differences.

Another example was the administration's contention that Fox News was not really a "news organization." The White House tried hard to put some muscle behind its rhetoric by blacklisting Fox News from a round of interviews with "pay czar" Kenneth Feinberg, but relented after other news organizations threatened to boycott the event if Fox wasn't included.

Here's a partial Obama Enemies List. The list was compiled from media accounts that reported White House attempts to "demonize," "marginalize," or "declare war on" the named person, group, or organization:

- Fox News.
- Medical doctors—during the ObamaCare debate for chopping off feet and yanking tonsils for the money they could make.
- All opponents of ObamaCare, including the Tea Party and private companies that cut back on employee health insurance after its passage into law.
- Rush Limbaugh—for his daily radio show comments critical of Obama.
- The insurance industry—for opposing ObamaCare.
- Glenn Beck—for his relentless exposés of administration officials.
- Chrysler's debt holders—for refusing to relinquish their rights when the government took over the auto company.

THE SECRET LIFE OF BARACK HUSSEIN OBAMA

In addition, David Limbaugh compiled his own handy list for *Newsmax,* which included the following Obama "enemies." These were attacked either in print by members of his administration or by Barack Obama himself:

> He [Obama] has demonized "big oil" and other energy producers, free-market capitalists, corporate executives, pharmaceutical companies, Republicans who oppose his healthcare plan as dishonest and partisan, the wealthy, municipal policemen who dared arrest his Ivy League professor friend for disturbing the peace, pro-lifers, global-warming skeptics, the CIA, the military, the best healthcare system in the world, and George W. Bush every time he needs cover for the inevitably negative consequences of his policies.

Limbaugh also included small-town Americans, opponents of amnesty for illegal aliens, who were condemned as "demagogues," and the Tea Party, which Obama likened to an "angry mob" and to "potential terrorists."

As with any enemies list, the expectation should be that the list will grow longer as more groups and individuals differ with the Obama administration's agenda. The rule of thumb for such things is the same as that for eating that first salted peanut: Once you start, it's hard to stop.

16

The Complete Guide to
Obama Creepiness

Creepy: *adj* \\'krē-pē\\ **1** : producing a nervous shivery
apprehension
2 : of, relating to, or being a creep : annoyingly unpleasant.

One doesn't want to make the claim that there has been a lot
of creepy stuff associated with Barack Obama, but . . . the
enterprising sort—with a lot of time, a little inclination, and
access to the Internet—might well put together a pretty impressive "Today in Creepy Obama" calendar. Might even make
a few bucks, if the budding entrepreneur is one of the teeming
masses unlucky enough to have been steamrolled by the continuing miracle that is the "Obama Economy." Throw in all of
the creepy stuff that has come out of the president's mouth, and
there might even be enough material for a whole chapter in a
book.

No doubt about it, there's a lot of annoyingly unpleasant information available on Barack Obama for any individual who has had the time and wherewithal to pursue it. A further requirement in this line of inquiry is that the researcher should not be in the employ of the Corporate Mainstream Media, one of the prerequisites of CMM reporters being an utter and complete lack of curiosity about all things Barack Obama.

However, after categorizing the immense amount of forbidden Obamalania, there still remains an odd lot of facts and figures about Barack Obama that defy pigeonholing. They are of a particular sort: eerie, haunting, spooky, uncanny, unearthly, weird. In a word: creepy. Those have been collected in this chapter and presented, sometimes with comment and sometimes "as is."

NOTE: This chapter is limited to events before January 11, 2011. Therefore, the chapter's description of it as "complete" is a bit of literary license. Besides, when chronicling the adventures, creepy or otherwise, of the forty-fourth president of the United States of America—a man who has gone to great pains to carefully craft the information that the world receives about him— who knows where all of the rocks are, let alone has the time to turn them all over?

Branding a Massacre. In the aftermath of the Tucson shooting of Representative Gabrielle Giffords in January 2011, President Obama traveled to the University of Arizona to deliver a speech at what was billed as a "memorial service." It was as if they held a funeral and a pep rally broke out. Obama's speech itself was fairly pedestrian stuff. The only eyebrow-raising part of the speech occurred when the president said that he was in the congresswoman's hospital room and "Gabby opened her eyes, I can tell you." Several commentators remarked that it was as if "Obama walked into the room and she [Giffords] could see again." That's a bit ungracious.

However, the mood of what was supposed to be a service for remembering the victims of a mentally disturbed gunman was, from its opening moments, if not exactly creepy, then surreal. Political figures such as House Minority Leader Nancy Pelosi received cheers and applause upon their arrival. Other memorial messages by the speakers were repeatedly interrupted by hoots and cheers. The entire affair reminded many of an Obama political pep rally. Truth in labeling might have required that the event be promoted as the "Tucson Meme-orial."

In what was perhaps the tackiest (creepiest?) touch, free T-shirts were given to each of the attendees of the service—on which the logo and inscription "Tucson—Together We Thrive" was emblazoned. Perhaps the tired "I attended a memorial service and all I got was this lousy T-shirt" was not exciting enough. If not a moment of Obama high creepiness, the entire affair had an unreal, rather intense irrationality to it.

When you can't send roses. In September 2009, President Obama canceled a Bush-era deal that would have placed a missile-defense system in the Czech Republic and Poland. Both the Poles and the Czechs took the news fairly hard—though graciously—which anyone who has read much history could understand. But what made the action particularly hard to swallow for the Poles was the timing of the cancellation announcement.

Grand student of history that our Diplomat in Chief is, President Obama announced his reneging on the deal on September 17, 2009—which just happened to be the seventieth anniversary of the Soviet invasion of Poland at the beginning of World War II, when the Soviet Union was an ally of Adolf Hitler's Nazi Germany. The timing of the announcement, which came after Russian pressure on the Obama administration to scrap the deal, was decidedly creepy, especially if you were a Pole.

To add insult to insult, when the president of Poland died in April 2010, President Obama skipped the funeral "due to volcanic ash."

When Obama was "president-elect." It can be argued that no one in the history of the United States has ever tried harder to "look presidential" than Barack Obama. Before Barack Obama took the oath of office, his campaign team was obsessed with deploying symbols and logos. It began with the replacement of the American flag painted on the tail of the Obama campaign plane with the infamous Seal of Obama before he jetted overseas on his "I'm Here!" tour, one of the seemingly endless succession of flags, logos, songs, or chants used to help initiate outsiders into the Obama cult of personality. Obama's acceptance speech at the Democratic National Convention in front of two huge, fake Styrofoam Greek columns was another example. Team Obama was all about the optics, obsessed with controlling the setting in which their brand-name candidate appeared. If an official-looking fake seal contributed to Obama's "presidential" look, chances are it was used.

It's easy to understand why: Team Obama successfully elected a little-known man with no experience almost solely based on their astute use of such symbols—and a never-ending torrent of cash that poured into Obama Central. Still, the best official-looking fake seal from those days before January 21, 2009, had to be the seal of the Office of the President-Elect.

Immediately after the election, Obama appeared on a stage festooned with American flags sporting a lone podium to which was affixed a large, powder-blue circle with the words "Office of the President-Elect" on it. Technically, Obama did not even become the president-elect until the Electoral College convened and cast their votes based on the results of the November 4 general election, as stated in the Constitution. That didn't occur until December 15, 2008. Congress then officially counted the electoral votes on January 6, 2009. Obama supporters pointed to wording in a transition-of-power law covering outgoing and incoming administrations as justification for the display of the really impressive fake seal.

Obama supporters missed the point. Their defensiveness was unnecessary: Of course it was *legal*. It being America, Obama was free to stand behind any symbol of his choice—including a life-size statue of Pinocchio or the entire assembled Mormon Tabernacle Choir—no matter how odd or ridiculous it appeared to those viewing it from outside their ranks. It was like showing up in court and seeing a bank robber and his attorney seated at a "Table of the Accused" complete with logo. It would most likely be legal, but it offended tradition—and part of the power of the presidency is tradition. Like the whole Obama cult of 2008, it was just a bit creepy.

Scrub-a-dub-dub. After Obama was elected president, the Obama campaign team continued their designer branding of everything they came in contact with by christening a new government website: *Change.gov.* Yes, it all seems silly a few years later, but back in 2008, it was "cutting-edge Obama."

Change.gov was announced as the place to go for the latest announcements from the Office of the President-Elect. If it was anything, *Change.gov* was all about changes—as in "Oops! We'd better change that!" There were several stories that appeared on the site and then, after several hours of unwanted publicity, disappeared. The site was scrubbed. At *Change.gov*, change came quickly indeed!

The entire *Change.gov* episode was creepy for any number of reasons. First, when you have the word "Change" alongside the "gov," it seems likely that Change is not so much a suggestion as a command. Second, there were only seventy-seven days between the day that Senator Obama became President-Elect Obama and the day the Oath of Office was administered. Until that day, Obama was still a senator. Still, that wasn't good enough; so for seventy-seven days, Barack Obama stood in front of a podium declaring himself to be the President-Elect. Then came "America Serves."

With problems besetting the United States on any number of fronts, one of the first items posted at *Change.gov* announced that students would be required to perform community service. Not asked, not presented with a choice so parents could make a decision, but *required*. This was a bit disturbing to those who still took the whole "Land of the Free" thing seriously. It was creepy because just three days after the 2008 election, one of the things most prominent on the incoming administration's agenda was requiring students to "serve" and perform "community service." Here's what was posted:

> The Obama Administration will call on Americans to serve in order to meet the nation's challenges. President-Elect Obama will expand national service programs like AmeriCorps and Peace Corps and will create a new Classroom Corps to help teachers in under-served schools, as well as a new Health Corps, Clean Energy Corps, and Veterans Corps.
>
> Obama will call on citizens of all ages to serve America, by developing a plan to require 50 hours of community service in middle school and high school and 100 hours of community service in college every year.
>
> Obama will encourage retiring Americans to serve by improving programs available for individuals over age 55, while at the same time promoting youth programs such as Youth Build and Head Start.

Within hours, a number of bloggers had noticed the posting and started writing about it, including this author. The reviews for Barack Obama's "America Serves" weren't good, to say the least. Within hours after the critical reviews appeared, *Change .gov* changed the wording on its "America Serves" post. In particular, it changed "required" to "set a goal"—which changed the entire meaning of the post.

The site made no acknowledgment of the changes. That's creepy in an Orwellian way, but what was even creepier was that within minutes, a small army of Obamabots appeared at sites around the Internet wherever posts had been published that criticized "America Serves," casting aspersions on the pieces. Most of these comments were of the "The word 'require' isn't in the quote; it's crap like this that has destroyed the conservative movement in America" variety.

The sudden influx of readers who had read the changed version of "America Serves" *and* happened to continue to those websites that had criticized the original wording of the piece the day before might have been just a coincidence. However, the uniformity of thought and the speed at which the commenters appeared made that theory suspect. Three notes about the layers of creepy contained in this incident:

1. Creepy subject matter using creepy doublespeak (compulsory volunteerism) on a creepy government website.
2. Creepy changing of the offending wording without noting that it had been done.
3. Sending out minions in the guise of disinterested readers to make those who had written about the subject look as if they were fabricating the entire issue.

This won for the entire episode the Triple Crown of Creepy.

There were two things for which to be thankful: that enterprising bloggers had captured screenshots of the original wording on the site and had visual proof of what the president-elect's team had originally posted, and that Americans only had to put up with the puffery of the Office of the President-Elect for seventy-seven days.

Another of the changes that were scrubbed had to do with the administration-elect's immigration plan.

The time to fix our broken immigration system is now. . . .
We need stronger enforcement on the border and at the
workplace. . . . But for reform to work, we also must respond to
what pulls people to America. . . . Where we can reunite fami-
lies, we should. Where we can bring in more foreign-born work-
ers with the skills our economy needs, we should.

—Barack Obama, statement on
U.S. Senate floor, May 23, 2007.

Dan Amato, writing at his immigration website, *Digger's
Realm*, noted, "Included in this was their agenda on immigration,
which I was planning on posting an article about, but when I went
back today it was mysteriously deleted. It seems that the website
has lived up to the name of 'Change.' However, I managed to grab
a screenshot of the immigration page prior to its deletion."

Just another day at the Obama Ministry of Truth.

A few days later, Obama supporters began agitating for a
national holiday to honor their hero. A local chapter of Obam-
aphiliacs titled "Yes We Can" announced their plans to hold
meetings in a Kansas McDonald's to plot strategy for a national
holiday honoring a man who had not yet served a day as president. There was no word whether "Yes We Can" served Kool-
Aid at its meetings.

It should be noted that Barack Obama did have a list of
accomplishments in those heady days. They consisted of:

- He had headed up a presidential campaign.
- He had named two people to important posts in his upcoming administration.

- He had garnered 52 percent of the country's support in the just-completed election.
- He had authored two memoirs.
- He had been a member of the U.S. Senate for almost four whole years.
- He had excited supporters.
- He had put together a team that came up with a variety of nifty prepresidential seals that featured the words "Obama" or "Change" or both.

After January 2009, fortunately, the news cycle reset.

The civilian military force. One of the creepiest statements that Barack Obama made got scrubbed by the Corporate Mainstream Media almost immediately. On July 2, 2008, at an appearance in Colorado Springs, candidate Obama called for a civilian military force.

The speech itself was standard fare. Obama talked about his plans to double the size of the Peace Corps and quadruple the size of AmeriCorps and the size of the nation's military services. Then he made what *World Net Daily* founder Joseph Farah called a "shocking pledge": "We cannot continue to rely on our military in order to achieve the national security objectives we've set. We've got to have a civilian national security force that's just as powerful, just as strong, just as well-funded."

Outside Colorado Springs, no one heard Obama make that pledge; the media didn't include that remark in the published transcript. What's extra creepy—besides the call for a civilian army, which is creepy enough—was the total news blackout of those two particular sentences. The CMM is thought to be almost monolithic in its progressive liberalism, but the *Wall Street Journal* was among those that didn't publish those interesting remarks. The Obama website also failed to post—perhaps one of the few times ever—a transcript of the Obama speech.

World Net Daily has been no stranger to controversy; it has tackled several stories that both the progressives and the conservative press have largely ignored. This time was no different; it produced an unedited videotape of the Colorado Springs speech. Obama clearly said those two sentences, but they were "airbrushed" out of the speech by the press.

There was no discussion on this controversial proposal because the CMM refused to report it. As had happened so many other times during Campaign 2008, the national press simply failed: Americans were deliberately kept in the dark due to decisions made by the CMM. Again.

The only organization that publicly requested an explanation from Barack Obama was *World Net Daily.* Despite repeated requests, it was ignored. Team Obama was able to ignore the request of one entity; it would never have done so if others in the press had repeated that request. The Corporate Mainstream Media Narrative™ had become indistinguishable from its Obama counterpart: Both were composed of fanciful tales from a glorious and heroic past. When Obama became president, he never elaborated on his plan for a civilian military force.

Before Obama was inaugurated, "Service" was one of the first themes picked up by the Hollywood left and the other celebrities who mobilized to make the idea of service sound "cool." Ashton Kutcher, Demi Moore, and several other celebrities put out a particularly creepy video entitled *I Serve.*

Among the celebrities' pledges were:

- Drinking less bottled water
- Being a better mom
- Advance stem cell research
- To not flush the toilet after urinating
- To never give anyone the finger when I'm driving again
- To be of service to Barack Obama
- To sell my obnoxious car and buy a hybrid
- Former New York Giant Michael Strahan, who is black, pledged "to consider myself an American, not an African-American"
- Anthony Kiedis of the band Red Hot Chili Peppers picked up the MVP—Most Vacuous Pledge—Award: "I pledge allegiance to the funk, to the United Funk of Funkadelica"; Kiedis later kissed his own biceps, while promising, "I pledge to be of service [kiss] to Barack Obama [kiss]"

The video was immediately branded "creepy," and not just because of the robotlike way the actors recited their lines about "why I serve." The idea of personally pledging allegiance to an individual president rankled many writers, especially on the Internet—particularly the line "I pledge to be of service to Barack Obama."

Someone by the name of William Charles Edwards, Jr., started a *Facebook* page titled "Ashton Kutcher & Demi Moore pledge to serve Obama." It was linked to a *Facebook* group, "Stop Barack Obama (One Million Strong and Growing)." Edwards started his page with the following observation:

In an eruption of creepiness, Ashton and Demi pledge servility to Barack Obama. These are the closing remarks to a four minute video showing dozens of celebrities making pledges of all different kinds which build up to this stunning finale. I understand that this has already been shown to some kids.

The video was the epitome of creepiness—and numerous pieces placed "I Pledge" and some variation of "creepy" in their headlines. After a hailstorm of protest from parents whose children had been shown the video in their classes as a part of Barack Obama's address to the nation's schoolchildren, the video passed into history.

On March 19, 2009, the U.S. House of Representatives approved a plan to set up a new "volunteer corps," which would consider the question of a "fair and reasonable mandatory service requirement for all able young people." A "public service academy" to train these future "leaders" was also something the bill, which allocated $6 billion to its implementation, promised to consider.

On April 21, 2009, the "Serve America Act" became Public Law No. 111-13, after being passed by the Senate on March 9, 2009, and signed into law by Barack Obama.

The idea of "service" lay dormant for almost two years until a letter under the signature of the First Lady was sent out by the Obama website *Organizing for America* in time for Martin Luther King Day 2011. The email tied the idea of service to the civil-rights leader:

Friend—

The Reverend Martin Luther King, Jr., is usually remembered for his heroic leadership of the civil rights movement—he led the successful Montgomery bus boycott, delivered the "I Have A Dream" speech at a time when such words were still controversial, and ultimately gave his own life to the cause of equality.

But Dr. King was much more than a civil rights champion—he was a man who lived his entire life in service to others, speaking out against poverty, economic injustice, and violence. Wherever he saw suffering, he did what he could to help, no matter who it was that needed him or why they were in pain. Through his leadership, he showed us what we can accomplish when we stand together.

Each January, we remember Dr. King on his own holiday— and one of the best ways to preserve his legacy is to engage in service ourselves. As Dr. King told us, "Life's most persistent and urgent question is: 'What are you doing for others?'"

That's why this Monday, January 17th, Organizing for America volunteers will be participating in service projects all across the country in Dr. King's honor. There will be food drives, neighborhood clean-ups, education projects, blood drives, and more.

Will you find and sign up for an event in your area, and help make this country an even better place?

This movement is about so much more than politics—it is about coming together through progress, change, and community. Lifting each other up in dedication and service is

one of the best ways not only to honor Dr. King, but to honor
each other. By giving service a new role in this country, we can
establish a new foundation for our economy and a brighter
future for our children.

That is why service is key to achieving our national
priorities, and why Barack recently helped out at a Boys and
Girls Club service event. Since moving to Washington, D.C.,
two years ago, he and I have gotten to know the community
through similar service projects, including past Martin Luther
King Day events. I treasure those opportunities, and I look
forward to another one next week. Every time we pitch in, we
get so much back, and always learn amazing things from our
neighbors.

All of us have something to contribute, and all of us can
make a meaningful difference in someone's life. It's a great way
to remind others that they are not forgotten, and to remind
ourselves that there are always things we can do.

Please help Barack and me honor the legacy of Dr. King,
and join us in service to our country once again this year.
http://my.barackobama.com/MLKday

Thanks,
Michelle

Random Creepiness

Let's get this party started. Obama instructed his aides
to begin preparing for the transition of power in July 2008, a
month after his bruising Democratic primary battle with Hillary

Clinton and a month before he gave his acceptance speech in front of two twenty-foot-high fake Greek columns.

Fire from the left. Progressive-liberal cartoonist/journalist Ted Rall, May 29, 2009: "Obama is cute. He is charming. But there is something rotten inside him. . . . Obama has revealed himself. He is a monster, and he should remove himself from power." While conservatives have had their disagreements with Rall's politics, there was no disagreement over Rall's powers of observation in this instance.

Fundamentally changing the holiday season. As 2009 drew to a close, guess whose face ended up on a Christmas ornament hanging from the Obama White House Christmas tree? Mao Zedong!

While the president was battling to transform his Obama-Care legislation into law—despite a majority of the country disapproving and 80-plus percent who were satisfied with their health care—perhaps the president took inspiration from the following observation from Mao:

> Revolution is not a dinner party, nor an essay, nor a painting, nor a piece of embroidery; it cannot be advanced softly, gradually, carefully, considerately, respectfully, politely, plainly, and modestly. A revolution is an insurrection, an act of violence by which one class overthrows another.

Che is so passé. Che Guevara iconography has always been a big hit among Obama supporters. During 2008, a week didn't go by when a photo or videotape didn't surface that featured some local official endorsing Barack Obama—with a picture of the Communist Cuban murderer in the background somewhere. "Spot Che!" became something of a pasttime in certain corners of the Internet. The night Obama won the election, a crowd gathered on the White House lawn in celebration while some of them waved the Soviet flag.

Who knows? Obama had a meeting with big bankers in March 2009. Banking and finance has been one industry with which Barack Obama has been cozy since he became president, taking their money and installing numerous big bankers as members of his administration. The actions of Barack Obama have clearly been different from the words of the much-publicized quotation that happened to "leak" from the meeting: "Be careful how you make those statements, gentlemen. The public isn't buying that. My administration is the only thing between you and the pitchforks."

Commentators on both the left and the right responded by claiming that "Obama is threatening the nations' bankers!" Threatening? By accepting more of their money? Is that what passed for a presidential threat in 2009? The get-tough quotation was more than a year old before Barack Obama made his bid to become Captain Kick-Ass during the oil spill that resulted from the explosion of BP's Deepwater Horizon platform in the Gulf of Mexico.

Obama told NBC's Matt Lauer that he was taking his time directing aid to the Gulf, "so I know whose ass to kick." Obama has tried very hard at times to project a macho image by using tough talk. One suspects he'd have an easier time pulling that off if he would stop being photographed riding a girls' bicycle.

The shout-out after the Fort Hood massacre. One

of Obama's creepiest moments came at his surreal press conference that followed the murder of thirteen servicemen and women and the wounding of thirty others at Fort Hood, Texas, on November 5, 2009. The national TV and cable news networks interrupted their programs and switched to the president, who was beginning to deliver a speech at the Tribal Nations Conference for America. Anyone who watched the president live on television at the time had a once-in-a-lifetime chance to see tone deafness at its finest.

> Please, everybody, have a seat. Let me first of all just thank Ken and the entire Department of the Interior staff for organizing just an extraordinary conference. I want to thank my Cabinet members and senior administration officials who participated today. I hear that Dr. Joe Medicine Crow was around, and so I want to give a shout out to that Congressional Medal of Honor winner. It's good to see you.

After a few more remarks about how "hard his team would work," the president got into the reason for the TV face time:

> Now, I have to say, though, that beyond that, I had planned to make some broader remarks about the challenges that lay ahead for Native Americans as well as collaboration with our administration.
>
> But as some of you might have heard, there has been a tragic shooting at the Fort Hood Army base in Texas. We don't yet know all the details at this moment. We will share them as we get them.

After three minutes of small talk conducted before a national TV audience, the president finally commented on the victims of Major Nidal Malik Hasan, a U.S. Army major who was serving as a psychiatrist. It was very bizarre to watch and still a creepy piece of Obamalania about which to write.

The men and women who died at Fort Hood were reported to have been shot "execution-style." RIP.

Spc. Frederick Greene, 29

Pfc. Aaron Nemelka, 19

Pfc. Michael Pearson, 22

Spc. Kham Xiong, 23

Pvt. Francheska Velez, 21, and her unborn child

Mr. Michael Cahill, 62

Lt. Col. Juanita L. Warman, 55

Maj. Libardo Caraveo, 52

Capt. John P. Gaffaney, 54

Capt. Russell Seager, 41

Staff Sgt. Justin Decrow, 32

Sgt. Amy Krueger, 29

Spc. Jason Hunt, 22

Michelle Obama's fabulous let-them-eat-cake Spanish getaway. While not about Barack Obama per se, the spectacle of the First Lady embarking on what was described as a "Marie Antoinette–like" trip to Spain while much of the United States was gripped by high unemployment and low job creation was so politically tone deaf, it reminded one of the president.

As usual, no matter how eerie or otherworldly the news coming from the Obama administration, the coverage in the CMM managed to top it on the Creep-O-Meter. The *Washington Post's* Kathleen Parker—no stranger to tone deafness herself—begged readers, "Give the lady a break. She deserves a vacation." Parker was clearly in the minority on that subject—though perhaps not in the swanky circles she frequented. Parker also contributed this bit of hilarity, attributing the dustup over the trip's outlandish details and enormous costs to "bloggers suffering from boredom."

"How better to pass the time than by wondering how the more fortunate are living?"

Various estimates of the trip's cost to U.S. taxpayers were reported, but were never confirmed by the White House. At the end of the day, even such a defender of Beltway excess as Kathleen Parker had to admit that the trip was "out of step" because many Americans were worried about "the stagnant job market, the depleted fortunes of the middle class, millions of lost homes and, for many, the prospect of an insecure financial future."

Michelle Obama's vacation time during March–August 2010 included a March visit to New York City with friends where she took in some Broadway shows; a weekend trip home to Chicago over Memorial Day; a jaunt to Los Angeles for some sightseeing, accompanied by members of her family; a visit to Camp David; a July weekend in Maine; her August sojourn on the Spanish beaches; and an overnighter on the Florida Gulf coast in the wake of the BP disaster. Immediately after participating in a few photo ops on the Gulf, the Obamas escaped to the confines of Martha's Vineyard for the rest of their vacation time.

Continuing a tradition started in 2009, the Obamas wound up in Hawaii for Christmas vacation 2010, a locale where, according to reports, they previously had never taken a Christmas vacation. Until the federal government started picking up the tab.

Doc zombies. On July 22, 2009, during the ObamaCare debate, the president went on TV to try to drum up support. Instead, he left everyone talking about this strange piece of oratory. Describing a parent who brings in a child with a sore throat, Obama claimed, "Right now, doctors a lot of times are forced to make decisions based on the fee payment schedule that's out there. . . . The doctor may look at the reimbursement system and say to himself, 'You know what? I make a lot more money if I take this kid's tonsils out.'"

The Evil Doc Zombie Tonsil Yankers were joined three weeks later in the Obama rhetorical museum by their companions, the Evil Doc Zombie Foot Choppers: "All I'm saying is, let's take the example of something like diabetes, a disease that's skyrocketing partly because of obesity. Partly because it's not treated as effectively as it could be. Right now if we paid a family—if a family care physician works with his or her patient to help them lose weight, modify diet, monitors whether they are taking their medications in a timely fashion, they might get reimbursed a pittance. But if that same doctor ends up getting their foot amputated, that's $30,000, $40,000, $50,000. Immediately the surgeon is reimbursed."

What word would readers use to describe the two previous examples of Obama oratory? Is "creepy" too harsh? Obama had scored twice in the "Doctors cut off their patients' body parts to make money" rhetorical department, an unprecedented achievement. But then, it was a historic accomplishment the first time.

Android in chief. One of the finest displays of presidential creepiness occurred on September 23, 2009. While in New York City for an appearance at the United Nations, Obama hosted a reception at the Metropolitan Museum of Art. During this event, he stood for 135 separate photographs with visiting foreign dignitaries who were in town for the U.N. meeting. A rapid-fire slide show from Eric Spiegelman soon made its appearance on the Internet that showcased Barack Obama with exactly the same smile in every shot. Spiegelman titled this remarkable compilation "Barack Obama's amazingly consistent smile." This author posted that compilation, which is easily the most eerie Obama viewing experience he'd ever watched, under the headline "Obama at the U.N.: The Android-in-Chief."

It's no exaggeration to say the face that was frozen in 135 separate photographs was exactly the same. Not almost the same, not nearly the same, it was the exact, same face. Readers unfamiliar with the slide show may check for themselves by performing a Google search for "Barack Obama amazingly consistent smile."

Kinda funny. Reuters reported on May 10, 2009, that Obama joked, "Finally, I believe that my next one hundred days will be so successful that I will be able to complete them in seventy-two days. And, on the seventy-third day, I will rest."

On his seventy-second day, Obama completed the G-8 summit by meeting with the pope.

The little book that could. In January 2009 when Obama took office, online retail giant Amazon offered customers the

Pocket Obama and compared it to Mao's *Little Red Book*—which the Chinese Communists required every Chinese citizen to own, read, and carry with them at all times. Amazon's sales review alluded to this history with a particular bit of creepiness that foreshadowed the administration's exhibition of Maophilia in the months to come:

> Printed in a size that easily fits into pocket or purse, this book is an anthology of quotations borrowed from Barack Obama's speeches and writings. *POCKET OBAMA* serves as a reminder of the amazing power of oratory and the remarkable ability of this man to move people with his words.
>
> His superb and captivating oratory style has earned comparisons to John F. Kennedy and Martin Luther King, and this collection presents words that catapulted his remarkable rise to the American Presidency. Includes themes of democracy, politics, war, terrorism, race, community, jurisprudence, faith, personal responsibility, national identity, and above all, his hoped-for vision of a new America.
>
> This book is truly a primer for readers who want to examine the substance of his thought and reflect on the next great chapter in the American story. **It is an unofficial requirement for every citizen to own, to read, and to carry this book at all times.**

The *Pocket Obama* was the perfect way to enable Americans to carry a little bit of creepiness around with them at all times.

A cult so creepy even the CMM couldn't ignore it. Evan Thomas of *Newsweek*, which battled *Time* for the title of

"Most Unctuous Obama Suck-up, Newsweekly Division," had the perfect ending comment for this section.

Speaking on PBS's *Charlie Rose* show the day after the 2008 election, Thomas admitted, "There is a slightly creepy cult of personality about all of this." Thomas's editor at *Newsweek*, Jon Meacham, also had some thoughts on the creepy cult that the CMM ignored prior to election day 2008:

> Have you ever seen a victory speech where there was no one else on stage? No adoring wife, no cute kid—he is the message.
>
> —*Newsweek* editor Jon Meacham,
> *Charlie Rose*, November 5, 2008.

For the record, Thomas's full quotation follows:

> There is a slightly creepy cult of personality about all of this. I'm a little uneasy that he's so singular. He's clearly managing his own spectacle. He knows how to do it. He's a—I think, a deeply manipulative guy.

Of course, when it mattered most whether *Newsweek* readers got the complete story on Barack Obama, Thomas and Meacham both kept an absolute, monklike silence.

17

D.C. Scuttlebutt:
Dirty Filthy Obama Gossip

For months a hero-worshipping CMM practiced a sort of pretend journalism: It pretended to ask relevant questions of President Obama and he pretended to answer them. ObamaCare infomercials were substituted for televised interviews while new ways were found to shower superlatives on a president whose poll numbers steadily plummeted monthly throughout 2010.

However, at last it happened: In September 2010, juicy Obama gossip finally bubbled to the surface—percolating mostly on the Internet, but in the pages of more mainstream publications as well, if one read between the lines. These first signs of presidential mortality were of the usual type for the genre: unnamed insiders with supposed news of the inner workings of the White House leaking it to whoever was writing.

This writer received one of the first batches of scuttlebutt in an email from an unusually reliable source, "Dossier." "Dossier" had a knack for discovering information that was under wraps and had an almost 100 percent record of reliability for tips. His information was published at *DBKP—Death By 1000 Papercuts* under the title of "D.C. Scuttlebutt: Obama a 'Chainsmoking, Nervous Wreck'":

> Spoke with a friend of mine in D.C. who is in very well-connected politically on the Dem side and I asked him about the mood in D.C. He advised me Obama is a shell of a man, second guessing himself non-stop, reeking of cigarettes and consumed with the color of his rapidly-graying hair. Our informer goes on to say that they realize it's "second party hearsay" but that it is "consistent with other reports I've heard."

Also featured in the post were photos of "old Obama" and "new Obama" comparing his hair color. As the email had claimed, in some of them his hair had visibly grayed. The presidency is a tough job for anyone. Also admitted in the post: "We don't know if it's true. But it is interesting."

The item about the "color of his rapidly-graying hair" provoked much discussion in September 2010. A number of pictures appeared on sites that commented on the article, with the argument centering on whether Barack Obama was indeed going gray. All doubt was removed four months later. A close-up of the president speaking at the Tucson memorial service was posted to the DNC's Organizing for America website: it showed a Barack Obama who was almost totally gray.

The very next day, another Internet item appeared elsewhere that seemed to back up some of the whispers "Dossier" had heard. It was titled "White House Insider On Obama: President Losing It." Posted by "Ulterman" at a website by the name of *NewsFlavor,* it hit the web on September 7, 2010. After months of subsisting on the thin gruel of the CMM's superhero version of Barack Obama, here was the second helping of the rich soup of tasty, flavorful gossip!

The second report had many more salacious details attributed to a "White House insider" who had "been a participant with three previous presidential hopefuls." Any enterprising reporter could, if he had wanted to ascertain the identity of the supposed "insider," have compiled a fairly short list of operatives, based on clues the article contained. As with most items of this sort, *what* was said seems more important than *who* exactly was supposed to have said it.

The leaker—let's call him "Mr. X"—suggested that he admired Barack Obama. Some of his revelations were numbingly mundane to the point of unintended hilarity. Example: his answer about whether the CMM had assisted Obama during the election (supposedly revealed "with a sly smile"):

> Sure—we definitely had people in the media on our side. Absolutely. We went so far as to give them specific ideas for coverage. The ones who took that advice from the campaign were granted better access, and Obama was the biggest story in 2008, so yeah, that gave us a lot of leverage.

Maybe the "sly smile" had really been a "convulsing belly laugh." One didn't have to be a "political insider" to reach

Mr. X's conclusion. Other less-than-earthshaking revelations included:

- Barack Obama was obsessed with Fox News and "incredibly thin-skinned."
- Obama didn't work much once the campaign was over.
- Obama "despised" Joe Biden. The president's attitude was supposedly "Give Joe a job and get him the hell out of my hair."
- Hillary Clinton frightened BHO. He was "scared to death of Hillary"—oh, and he didn't trust her.
- Bill Clinton doesn't like Barack Obama.
- The president lacked "focus" and would rather watch ESPN.
- Barack Obama was not an intellectual giant. "He just doesn't strike me as particularly smart."

None of these "revelations" was particularly eyebrow-raising. Some actually qualified as "disinformation"—such as Mr. X's comment that Big Bankers hated Obama. A few more of those revelations:

- Infighting at the Obama White House—as in every White House dating back to probably George Washington—was present. In fact, it was "off the charts."
- The Obamas had marriage issues, which was why the president was so detached.
- The president was "losing it," which didn't mean going crazy, just becoming more detached. Detachment was a big theme with this "insider."

- The "insider" stated that he saw Barack Obama "yelling at a staffer" while "throwing a tantrum" that was reminiscent of a "spoiled child."
- The president was upset at the banking system and thought the banks were out to get him because of his tough regulatory stance.

This last "scoop" was so utterly unbelievable, it cast doubt on the entire piece. The idea of Barack Obama being hated by Big Bankers is a total fiction belied not only by money that poured into his campaign but also by the sheer number of ex–Big Bankers in the employ of the Obama administration. Oh, well. A few more before moving on:

- "As a president, Obama has many flaws, but as a candidate, he is near flawless." Really? Perhaps Mr. X had never seen the video of candidate Obama telling a crowd in Oregon about his swing through the "fifty-seven states." Totally flawless.
- "Obama is lazy. He really is. And it is getting worse and worse. Everything was handed to him." Conservative readers of the piece no doubt nodded their heads.

Only a few items clearly qualified as "insider whispers" that rang true. These included:

- The only reason Obama would run again in 2012 is that "he just loves it [campaigning] so much."
- One sweet piece of gossip—whether real or imagined—was the following observation: "When you take away the

crowds, Obama gets noticeably smaller. He shrinks up inside of himself." Nice.

- Democratic Party insiders don't think that Barack Obama is up to the job of president and don't want him to run again in 2012.

One take: This multipage report, which got reprinted at a number of conservative blogs, had the ring of being manufactured—clever, but still a piece that could have been written by anyone who was paying attention to the headlines of the previous two years and had the imagination to put into the mouth of a mysterious "Mr. X" the words that were being written by Obama's many observant opponents.

Still, it was convenient for the author to use the "Mr. X" piece to "confirm" what he'd originally written about Obama's being a nervous, chain-smoking wreck—with the following caveats:

There was lot of information—or misinformation, depending upon the individual reader's take—in the article. Also, lots of questions, but the questions depend upon the individual reader's viewpoint prior to reading. Is this information correct?

Is this planted by Pro-Obama people to garner sympathy for the president or try to explain some of his actions? Is this an attempt to make him appear more "human"? Or does this information come from a Pro-Clinton source? Is it to try and make the president appear like he's in over his head? Nothing in the article was made to make Bill or Hillary Clinton out to be anything but stand-up people, so that's a distinct possibility.

Or is this just talk? Just the idle chit chat between someone who's talking about their honest impressions and has no ax to grind? Or, is this just someone blowing up his own self-importance? Is it just a figment of someone's imagination?

The reader might remember that Obama gossip at this time was at a premium; there simply wasn't much available and beggars can't be choosy. Even the *National Enquirer* had made only one foray into the Obama Gossip arena. What was a bit more surprising, even the lower-level tabloids—always a fertile ground for lightly sourced, so-called insider information—had steered clear of Obama whispers. This situation was a sharp contrast with Obama's predecessor, George W. Bush. During Bush's two terms, the tabloids were awash with scandalous Bush info: pieces in which Bush had fallen off the wagon, was drinking again, or the upcoming specter of a messy divorce were regular features of the tabloids from 2001 to 2008.

All was quiet on the Obama tabloid trash front for several weeks. Then, in early November 2010, "Dossier" sent another email, alerting me to some information published by investigative journalist/muckraker/former member of the intelligence community/syndicated columnist Wayne Madsen. The piece was published at *DBKP—Death By 1000 Papercuts* as "Obama's Increasingly Bizarre Behavior: D.C. Scuttlebutt":

More trashy gossip from D.C.: More trashy gossip about the supposed bizarre behaviors of our 44th president. More D.C.

scuttlebutt about Barack Obama. Our take? As long as there are powerful people, others will whisper about them.

About two months ago, we published a bit of filthy, gossipy hearsay ["D.C. Scuttlebutt: Obama a 'Chainsmoking, Nervous Wreck'"]. We then followed that up with a confirmation of sorts a few weeks later. Now there's more: this time, from investigative journalist/muckraker, Wayne Madsen's "White House: Obama Conducting Reign of Terror."

"President Obama was urged by the few White House insiders from whom he still takes advice to leave the country on his ten-day Asian trip, his longest trip abroad since becoming president, in order to not inflict any more damage to the Democratic Party in the wake of one of the worst electoral defeats for the party of an incumbent president in recent history.

"According to sources close to the White House, who put themselves in great danger by even talking to members of the media, the plans to have Obama leave for a visit to India, Pakistan, Indonesia, South Korea, and Japan are an attempt to get Obama out of the country while top Democrats can sort through the political disaster created for the party by Obama's increasingly detached-from-reality presidency."

Of course, Mr. Obama was not greeted by everyone in India with open arms—as we reported in "Obama Effigy Burned by Students in India, Small Protest in Mumbai."

Among the claims in the Madsen piece are several interesting ones, such as:

- Virtual political guerrilla warfare has broken out between Obama's inner circle on one hand and senior Democratic officials, including outgoing House Speaker Nancy Pelosi, Democratic Party strategist James Carville, former Demcratic National Committee chairman Howard Dean, and, behind the scenes, Vice President Joe Biden and former president Bill Clinton, on the other.

- Obama's bizarre behavior spills over into a Democratic fundraiser: "Obama briefly appeared at the fundraiser at Brown University, where Democratic loyalists paid $7500 to hear Obama speak, but departed after only twenty minutes, telling the assembled guests that he had to go back to the White House to 'tuck in my daughters, walk the dog, and scoop the poop.'"

The widely-reported story from Obama's time in Rhode Island was his non-endorsement of the Democratic nominee for governor, Frank Caprio—and Caprio's response that the president "could take his endorsement and really shove it as far as I'm concerned."

The piece further reported a few more revelations by Madsen, including the eye-opener that Obama was taking "prescription anxiety medication." The report finished with a standard caveat when dealing with information of this genre:

We'll just note that all this trashy gossip only contributes to our theory, first proposed in September, that there will be no Hillary–Obama 2010 Rematch: Not Going to Happen—because Barack Obama will not be running for re-election.

Expect more of these types of stories from a once-adoring press: Obama isolated ahead of 2012. A Mouthpiece Media that squashed all news that didn't help the 2008 Obama campaign will increasingly target a wounded president ahead of decision time 2012, as the MPM attempts to pimp for a stronger candidate.

Madsen's original report contained much more "insider dish," including the whisper that "several top Democrats consider Obama's chances to keep the White House in 2012 as slim." The most shocking information to come out of Madsen's piece might have been the claim that "a team of ex-CIA officers are traveling the globe assembling a dossier of documents on Obama's past, including his education, passport, travel, and residency records." Reportedly, this team had already been to Indonesia, Kenya, Pakistan, and other countries, "collecting documents that are not already maintained in the CIA's own files on Obama's past."

While some dismissed Wayne Madsen as a gadfly, he had some hefty credentials, having appeared as a national security commentator on Fox News, as well as on ABC, NBC, CBS, PBS, CNN, BBC, Al Jazeera, and MSNBC. Madsen also had been "invited to testify as a witness before the U.S. House of Representatives, the U.N. Criminal Tribunal for Rwanda, and a terrorism investigation panel of the French government."

Gossip is gossip, but gossip from a source such as Madsen is better sourced than, say, the *Globe*'s standard fare. The take from all of the preceding? After months of sanitized reporting on the doings and personal life of Barack Obama, accounts of a

less-than-hagiographic nature were finally beginning to be published in September 2010. As happens with such things, the
reader is reminded of different phrases. One might be "When it
rains, it pours."

This writer is also reminded of Louis XV. Louis XV (February 15, 1710–May 10, 1774) was king of France from 1715
until his death in 1774. At the beginning of his reign, Louis en-
joyed favorable popular opinion. However, over time, his lack of
morals, his inability to reform the system, his foreign policy, and
several unpopular policies lost him the support of France.

Louis failed to solve France's serious financial problems because he couldn't say no to his cronies. The king also suffered
from boredom, and though he was aware of the forces threatening his family's rule, he failed to do anything to lessen their impact. Legend has it that Louis said, *"Après moi, le déluge"* ("After
me, the flood"—which basically means "After I'm gone, this
place is going to hell"). Louis died one of the most unpopular
kings in French history.

That's a fair description of what comes to this writer's mind
after reading the latest D.C. scuttlebutt about Barack Hussein
Obama.

Two additions to the above should be noted.

The Larry Sinclair Claims

Larry Sinclair was a gay former felon, who appeared in a home-
made *YouTube* video that "went viral" in February 2008. In his
video, Sinclair claimed that in 1999 he'd shared drugs and gay
sex in the backseat of a rented limo with then–Illinois state sen-

ator Barack Obama. He also claimed that later the same evening, Obama showed up at Sinclair's room at a motor lodge in Gurnee, Illinois, for more of the same.

Sinclair was something of an Internet sensation, but his claims never quite made it into the CMM. He was featured in an issue of the supermarket tabloid the *Globe*. Sinclair also rented a room at the National Press Club for a press conference—at the conclusion of which he was arrested on an outstanding warrant from Delaware. Sinclair also submitted to a polygraph, which basically found that "the subject was deceptive."

DBKP—Death By 1000 Papercuts initially gave Sinclair's claims a fair hearing during the four months following his debut on *YouTube*. While his background, propensity for using his newfound fame to hold a series of "fundraisers," and zeal for filing lawsuits against those who disputed his accounts were not held against him, the evolution of the basic facets of his story was.

DBKP's Elaine Marlow spent hours transcribing every word spoken by Sinclair from video and radio interviews as well as interviews in print and on the Internet. She then constructed a detailed timeline that logged his various claims and the dates on which Sinclair claimed events occurred. She published her findings in a three-part series entitled "Debunking Larry Sinclair."

Wayne Madsen's later scuttlebutt that "Barack Obama frequented a gay Chicago bathhouse" may at some point lead to a revisiting of Sinclair's claims. If Madsen's claims were true, a conspiracy theorist might wonder if Sinclair wasn't just an easily debunked plant. Of course, such speculation is how rumors get started.

The Vera Baker Story

The *National Enquirer* published a few pieces on the claims of a limo driver who had dropped an Obama associate off at a D.C. hotel several years before the 2008 election. The hotel was one where Barack Obama was staying at the time. The associate's name was Vera Baker. The limo driver maintained that Baker and Obama spent the night together. No corroborating evidence for the limo driver's claims could be found—though that wasn't due to a lack of effort on the *National Enquirer*'s part.

Baker subsequently played a part in Obama's political network, though she kept an ultralow profile. During the 2008 campaign, Baker suddenly moved to the Caribbean, where it was whispered that she was involved in overseeing a mysterious fund-raising apparatus.

18

One All-Purpose Positive Chapter
about Barack Obama

"All doom and gloom!"

"From cover to cover, a hate-filled screed!"

"Not one positive word written about our country's first biracial president."

Those who have read the previous chapters can be excused for thinking that this volume contains nothing but negative information about Barack Hussein Obama. While there was no effort made to concentrate on or exclusively catalog negative material, the purpose of this project was to include underreported and unreported information about our forty-fourth president. Since the Corporate Mainstream Media has chosen to report overwhelmingly positive news, much of what was left that flew "under the radar" happened to be perceived as "negative."

In order to counter this, it was decided to include one chapter containing nothing but positive information about our beloved forty-fourth president, Barack Hussein Obama.

Four Reasons That Barack Obama Cannot Be the Antichrist

This is an opportunity to defend President Obama from the somewhat baseless charge that he is the "lawless one" foretold in the Bible. There are literally dozens of websites dedicated to the proposition that "Barack Obama is the Antichrist." We hate to be the one to spoil this particular party; however, here are some reasons Barack Obama is *not* the Antichrist.

1. *He will oppress the saints and be successful for three and a half years* (Daniel 7:25; Revelation 13:7).

Whether one's political leanings are left or right, anyone who has closely followed the presidency of Barack Obama would be hard-pressed to convincingly argue he's had six successful months during his entire term—let alone three and a half years.

2. *His name will be related to the number 666—but not necessarily in an obvious fashion* (Revelation 13:17–18).

There are a couple of numbers associated with Barack Obama but none of them apparently involves 666—other than that Illinois lottery number the day after he was elected. One number that is never far from Obama's mind is one, as in "I'm

Number One!" Another is 132, the number of times Obama famously referred to himself in one speech in Ohio on January 26, 2010.

3. *He will be worshipped by many people* (Revelation 13:8).

While many young followers of Barack Obama certainly exhibited an almost cultlike behavior during the election campaign of 2008 (as chronicled in Jason Matera's book, *Obama Zombies*), time and circumstance have forced many Obama adherents to fall by the wayside. As this is being written, Obama's poll numbers hover in the high 30 percent to low 40 percent approval range—and have plummeted steadily over the first two years of his term.

If his poll numbers continue their downward slide, it's likely that soon there will be twice as many people who strongly disapprove of Barack Obama as approve. Not nearly enough to qualify as "worship."

4. *His arrival on the world scene will be accompanied by miracles, signs, and wonders* (2 Thessalonians 2:9).

Early campaign stops of Barack Obama reported a number of "fainting women"—in fact, *US News* reported that "women are dropping like flies at his rallies." Basically, the story was that these were women so overcome by the magic of being in the presence of Candidate Obama that they fainted. There was some discussion about whether these women were overcome by the sheer magnitude of being in Obama's presence or, like shills at Elmer Gantry's tent revivals, were merely supporters who staged their fainting for the rubes.

While swooning supporters make for great political theater, they're hardly the stuff of "miracles, signs, and wonders" that signal the appearance of the Antichrist.

For those interested in biblical prophecies, there are twenty-five to thirty characteristics by which one can tell the real-deal Antichrist. Barack Obama seems to exhibit no more than three or four of these characteristics. Therefore, this writer feels confident going on record to state that Barack Obama is not *the* Antichrist.

Barack Obama Is the Only U.S. President to Have a Brand of Cigarettes Named after Him

According to reports, our forty-fourth president is the inspiration behind Bama brand cigarettes, a product one of its creators called "edgy." The brand, which is sold in five states, was created in May 2010 by Rob Klotzback and two other men. Barack Obama thus joined such icons as camels, Winston Churchill's ancestor (John Churchill, the first duke of Marlborough, after which Great Marlborough Street was named; Marlboro brand cigarettes took their name from this London street), and a very upscale street in the West End of London (Pall Mall) as places and things that have had cigarette brands named after them.

In addition to Bama brand cigarettes, other items named after Barack Obama include streets and schools (including two in Kenya, the Senator Obama Primary School and Senator

Obama Secondary School), as well as Mount Obama in Antigua and Barbuda.

Barack Obama Raises the Dead

Barack Obama reinvigorated a moribund political party. Unfortunately for the president, that political party was the Republican Party. Despite many GOP obituaries in the mainstream press after the 2008 general election (John Lund, writing in *Time*, began one May 2009 piece, "These days, Republicans have the desperate aura of an endangered species"), twenty-four months later Barack Obama, through his actions and his policies, had brought the Republicans back from the dead.

The GOP made historic gains in the midterm elections of 2010, as voters went to the polls to register their disapproval of or disappointment with the president. Enthusiasm among Republican voters reached never-before-seen highs in such polls as Gallup and Pew in the days before the 2010 election, with respondents naming Obama and his policies as the reason GOP voters couldn't wait to cast their ballots.

Obama Actually Struck a Blow for Transparency—On His First Day in Office

A funny thing: When George W. Bush took office in January 2001, the presidential papers of both Ronald Reagan and Bush's father, George H. W. Bush, were slated to be made public. George W. Bush kept delaying the release date of those papers until November 1, 2001, when he signed Executive Order

13233, which limited access to the records of former U.S. presidents. EO 13233 also limited access to the papers and records of former vice presidents—which, coincidentally, also covered George H. W. Bush. EO 13233 clearly violated existing U.S. laws and severely cut back on public access to presidential records.

One of Barack Obama's first actions upon taking office was to revoke EO 13233. This struck a blow for transparency in government. It's too bad many people feel that Obama became less interested in transparency when it came to his own presidency—as with his oft-repeated promise (on eight separate occasions) to televise "on C-SPAN" the workings of the Obama-Care health-care negotiations.

Obama Cheered for the Right Team in at Least One Super Bowl

A positive item is in the eye of the beholder.

Since this writer comes from the Pittsburgh area, Barack Obama's cheering for the Steelers to win the 2009 Super Bowl (which they did for an NFL record sixth time) is one of his positive accomplishments. No one, of course, knows if the president's cheering helped the Steelers on to victory, but at least his heart was in the right place—at least in the opinion of fans of Steeler Nation.

This chapter will most likely do nothing to stem possible accusations that this book is one-sided. However, no one can accurately make the charge that it is *completely* one-sided.

19

Welcome to the Barackalypse, Baby! Snapshots from Obama's America

Barack Hussein Obama's America: The way things have worked out, it might just be the political equivalent of the Zombie Apocalypse. While no sightings of the undead have been reported—outside of a few Obama rallies—trial, tribulation, and high anxiety have blanketed the United States.

Trillion-dollar-plus deficits every year; Social Security out of money years before the "experts" predicted; millions of houses lost in an automated roboforeclosure system; billions for cronies who traffic in make-believe jobs "saved or created"; real jobs that disappeared, some never to return; food and energy prices on the rise; the IRS empowered to ensure that every American has approved health insurance; crackdowns on Internet freedoms; a war against contrary thought; billions of dollars to help

Brazilian and Chinese energy companies while the extraction and production of American-based energy are stifled—and the list goes on.

The long-term consequences have become so apparent that "Miss Me Yet?" billboards, a sign of nostalgia for the "good old days" of George W. Bush, have sprung up around the country. Every speech delivered by Barack Obama is still his "greatest speech ever!" in the reports of a drooling CMM. An ever-skeptical public hasn't been convinced and is tuning out the constant drone of the CMM noise machine.

Life is lived not in the pages or sets of the CMM, but out in the real-world America that has resulted from the policies and rhetoric of Barack Obama and his administration. The Barackalypse is already upon us. Gathered here are twelve signs of this event, taken from the headlines of today's media reports. Some were culled from *Instapundit*, others from *Drudge*; a few were seen at various websites around the Internet.

The damage already done may be fixed by future elections, but it's not going away any time soon. At the earliest, its effects won't be nullified until 2012—if ever.

Welcome to the Barackalypse, baby!

1. The Fabulous Obama Money Pit

In the first two years of Barack Obama's term, America plunged deeper into debt—a lot deeper.

In the first nineteen months of the Obama administration, the federal debt held by the public increased by $2.5260 trillion, which is more than the cumulative total of the national debt held by the public that was amassed by all U.S. presidents from George Washington through Ronald Reagan.

According to the Congressional Budget Office (CBO), at the end of fiscal year 1989, which ended eight months after President Reagan left office, the total federal debt was $2.1907 trillion. According to the Cato Institute, "That means all U.S. presidents from George Washington through Ronald Reagan had accumulated only that much publicly held debt on behalf of American taxpayers. That is $335.3 billion less than the $2.5260 trillion that was added to the federal debt held by the public just between January 20, 2009, when President Obama was inaugurated, and August 20, 2010, the nineteen month anniversary of Obama's inauguration."

By contrast, President Reagan—who was relentlessly pilloried by the CMM and the Democrats for "busting the budget with military spending"—increased the public debt during his two terms by $1.4788 trillion. That is a trillion dollars less than the $2.5260 trillion increase in the debt held by the public during Obama's first nineteen months.

"When President Barack Obama took the oath of office on January 20, 2009, the total federal debt held by the public stood at $6.3073 trillion, according to the Bureau of the Public Debt, a division of the U.S. Treasury Department. As of August 20, 2010, after the first nineteen months of President Obama's forty-eight-month term, the total federal debt held by the public had grown to a total of $8.8333 trillion, an increase of $2.5260 trillion," again according to Cato.

In just the last four months of that period (May through August 2010), according to the CBO, the Obama administration ran cumulative deficits of $464 billion, more than the $458 billion deficit the Bush administration ran through the entirety of fiscal 2008.

The CBO's predicted annual budget deficit for fiscal 2010 is in excess of $1.3 trillion: "The first two fiscal years in which Obama has served will see the two biggest federal deficits as a percentage of Gross Domestic Product since the end of World War II."

Barack Obama: decidedly mediocre when it came to solving the nation's problems—but absolutely historic when the subject turns to spending money that the nation doesn't have.

2. Making America Safe for the Communists

The election of Barack Obama was only sixty years after the heyday of the House Un-American Activities Committee, an era vilified by progressives. It only required sixty years for Democrats in Congress to go from investigating Communists to making them a part of their get-out-the-vote machinery.

From the Communist Party USA website, twelve days before the 2010 midterm elections:

> 12 days to go: The election depends on you!
>
> If the grand alliance that elected Barack Obama comes out in full force to vote we can stop the Tea Party/Republican takeover, continue moving forward, and push further for green jobs, union rights, health care, and the safety net for the common good.
>
> If voters fail to turn out, the Tea Party/Republican "Prom-

ise to America" alternative is clear: continued tax breaks for the top richest two percent which will increase the deficit, privatization of social security, repeal of health care and financial reform, no extension of unemployment compensation, outsourced jobs, increased racism, and severe limits to democratic rights.

Everyone can make a difference. If you are not already connected, plug into one of the opportunities listed below, or find something in your own neighborhood to make your voice heard with door knocking, phone banking, and helping line up others to volunteer as well.

The Communists listed the following "Resources to help get out the vote," which just happened to be a laundry list of Democratic Party support groups:

AFL-CIO Labor 2010
One Nation Working Together—Events
MoveOn—Stop the Takeover
Barack Obama's Organizing for America Call for Change
Hip Hop Caucus—Respect My Vote
MTV's Rock the Vote / Register to Vote
Election Protection . . . Right to Vote
NCLR—Vote for Respect

An article at *Hot Air* that displayed photos of CPUSA members signing up volunteers—and featured a cardboard ballot box with Obama's "O" symbol displayed prominently on the front— caused writer Doug Ross to observe, "They're not even trying to hide it anymore! Just wondering: when did it become accept-able among Democrats to openly collaborate with Communists, whose stated goal is the destruction of the American economy?"

Ross continued: "Socialism, Communism, and any other branch of Marxism is completely incompatible with the United States Constitution. And any Democrats who sympathize with these philosophies have automatically disqualified themselves from holding office. Because they simply can't honestly take an oath to uphold that which they despise."

Just another sign of the Barackalypse: The Communist Party USA, which has pledged to destroy the American economy, has come out into the open. Instead of doing this work subversively as in decades past, they worked hand in hand to secure victory for their allies, the Democratic Party.

3. I Think I Feel a Draft

Another sign of the Barackalypse is the attempted return of government-sponsored indentured servitude: first, in the guise of "service" in the various Obama civilian services; and second, in the form of Charlie Rangel's proposal to force Americans into a draft for Obama's national security force for "homeland security."

Rangel faced ethics charges in the House at the time he in-troduced his proposal, the Universal National Service Act. The act would require "all persons" from ages eighteen to forty-two "to perform national service, either as a member of the uni-formed services or in civilian service in furtherance of the na-tional defense and homeland security."

Rangel's plan authorized "the induction of persons in the uniformed services during wartime to meet end-strength requirements of the uniformed services, and for other purposes."

When Barack Obama campaigned for president in 2008, he said he wanted to create a "civilian national security force" as big and well-funded as the $650 billion–plus U.S. military, a mysterious campaign promise ignored by virtually the entire media except *World Net Daily.* The idea then lay dormant for nearly eighteen months—until Rangel's proposal.

Why does the United States need such an internal security force? Why has there been no discussion of such a proposed force in the CMM? Why has not one member of our constitutionally protected press raised a question about this force? Where was the outcry from progressives, who are usually quick to condemn any action to expand the military? Why have such supposedly "conservative" outlets as Fox News and the *Wall Street Journal* ignored this story? Though the proposal was Charlie Rangel's, the media failure has been bipartisan.

4. Isn't Anyone Up for Buying Some More American Debt?

The decrease in the number of foreign countries lined up to purchase a part of the United States' spiraling debt is another sign of the Barackalypse. Communist China, the largest owner of U.S. debt, has not been shy the last couple of years in voicing its displeasure at U.S. policies that devalued the dollar. These policies have cheated the Chinese out of billions of dollars— and they have been well aware of it.

Fortunately, United States Treasury bonds are still one of the safest places to park money. One of the reasons U.S. bonds are so safe is the strong economy built up over the last two hundred years using the free market. That would be the same free market that Communists—including those operating in the United States—have worked to destroy or "fundamentally transform."

5. It's a SNAP to Set a Food Stamp Record

More debt plus fewer jobs equals more food stamps used by a record number of Americans. The number of people on food stamps hit a new all-time high in September 2010 when nearly 43 million people enrolled in the program. The previous record was set in May 2010 when 40.8 million Americans signed up for the food assistance program.

Many individual states set records as well in 2010. In December, Barack Obama's home state of Illinois set a record when 857,282 households were enrolled in the Supplemental Nutrition Assistance Program—commonly known as food stamps—a figure up 12.7 percent from 2009.

"What we're seeing this time is quite a few people who are new to the program, who never before in their lifetime expected to take advantage of any government program," said Jean Daniel, a spokeswoman for the government agency that oversees the food-stamp program.

6. Let's Eat: Less Food for More Money

In 1928, Herbert Hoover ran on the slogan "A chicken in every pot and a car in every garage." Eighty-odd years later, Obama might want to dust that slogan off for use in some future speech—with a few minor changes. "Ramen noodles in every pot and your car's in the garage—because who can afford gas?" Over the first two years of his term, President Obama and his administration have worked tirelessly to make that imagined slogan a reality.

Commodity prices rose all over the world, particularly those valued in U.S. dollars. World wheat and maize prices rose 57 percent, rice 45 percent, and sugar 55 percent over the last six months of 2010. By the end of 2010, soybeans had risen as well, to their highest price in eighteen months.

The U.N. blamed the 2010 food price increases on a combination of environmental degradation, urbanization, and large-scale land acquisitions by foreign investors for biofuels—that's ethanol. In the United States, ethanol is documented to be inefficient, subsidized by the government, and destructive to most internal combustion engines over time. Is there nothing it can't do? The ethanol program continues because congressional representatives rake in millions in contributions (bribes) from its corporate lobbyists.

Under Obama, thousands of acres of America's most productive California farmland have been devastated due to a government shutoff of water. Fishing and shrimping in the Gulf of Mexico have also seen production decline as the entire Gulf region has suffered, not only from the BP Deepwater Horizon explosion but from the Obama administration's comfy cronyism with the culprits.

So while the delta smelt and the EPA wiped out thousands of acres of California's best farmland and disrupted fishing, the BP oil spill was disrupting food production in another part of the United States. Less food for more money is another sign of the Barackalypse. On the bright side, schoolkids will likely be slimmer.

As January 2011 dawned, so did the spiraling of gas prices, pushed higher by the Federal Reserve's policy of "Inflation Now for All Americans," otherwise known as QE2. Some analysts speculate that gasoline will cost between four and five dollars per gallon by the end of 2011. This author happens to think gas will cost five to seven dollars.

Hope, Change, Ouch!

7. Congress Loots Food-Stamp Funds

Record numbers of Americans were on food stamps and food costs were soaring: What better time to cut food stamps? In December 2010, Barack Obama took time to sign his wife's nutrition bill into law. It was paid for by cutting more than $2.2 billion from food stamps.

Michelle Obama lobbied for the nutrition bill as a way to combat obesity and hunger. About half of the $4.5 billion cost was financed by a cut in food stamps several years in the future. In early December 2010, the Evil Lame Duck Congress passed the Child Nutrition Act of 2010 (the Healthy, Hunger-Free Kids Act). However, controversy surrounded the bill because of the cuts to the food-stamp fund to pay for the act.

Whether the bill passed didn't seem to matter much: Either way, more skinny kids are in America's future!

One suspected that by signing the bill, President Obama at least preserved marital harmony in the Obama household.

Nationwide, 14 percent of the population relied on food stamps as of September 2010 but in some states the percentage was much higher. In Washington, D.C., and in Mississippi and Tennessee—the states with the largest share of citizens receiving benefits—more than a fifth of the population was collecting food stamps.

With each report from the USDA during the two years of Obama's presidency, an increase appeared in the numbers of enrollees, setting a new record each time, beginning at 33.5 million people in 2009 and rising to 42.9 million people in October 2010. With the number of enrollees in the food-stamp program and unemployment hovering around 10 percent, the outlook for decreasing the food-stamp rolls is bleak.

In the eyes of Barack Obama and the Democrats (all but seventeen Republicans in the House opposed the cuts), this had all the makings of a perfect bill: It cut food stamps, raised prices for school lunches for middle-income families, and started an entire new program to compete for future funding. What wasn't to like?

8. Inspiring the Angry Masses

Quotations from the Barackalypse: seven therapeutic quotations from America's postracial Healer in Chief that referred to those who didn't share his point of view:

"They Bring a Knife . . . We Bring a Gun" (June 14, 2008)
"Get in Their Faces!" (August 4, 2008)
"I don't want to quell anger. I think people are right to be angry! I'm angry!" (March 2009)
"Punch Back Twice As Hard" (August 6, 2009: Quotation has also been attributed to senior White House advisor David Axelrod and deputy chief of staff Jim Messina)
"I think it's tempting not to negotiate with hostage-takers, unless the hostage gets harmed" (December 7, 2010)
"We're gonna punish our enemies and we're gonna reward our friends" (October 25, 2010)
"So I know whose ass to kick" (June 7, 2010)

Those who were disturbed by the president's increasingly overheated oratory when he referred to Americans who disagreed with his policies did have reason to take heart. At least there doesn't appear to be much room for President Obama to ratchet up his rhetoric, right? Despite the Obama rhetoric listed here, after the January 2011 Tucson shootings, Obama cautioned against "divisive rhetoric"—which basically meant disagreement with the White House's position.

9. Record Unemployment

Worried about record unemployment, which has stayed just above or below 10 percent nationally for Obama's entire term? Courage! The Obama administration had some encouraging words.

"I don't think the unemployment rate will be coming down significantly at any time in the near future," said President Obama's chairman of the Council of Economic Affairs (CEA) during an appearance on *Fox News Sunday* on September 12, 2010.

Barack Obama spoke of his presidency as being "unprecedented." He was correct: Obama is the worst jobs president since the Great Depression and possibly the worst jobs president in U.S. history. The U.S. unemployment rate did not fall below 10.8 percent for an unprecedented twelve months.

North Carolina, Oregon, Rhode Island, South Carolina, Florida, and Georgia all set new records for high unemployment. The previous record had been set in 1976—which, coincidentally, was the year Jimmy Carter was elected president. "Carteralypse" was a term that never caught on, despite some similarities in the economic policies of Carter and Obama.

It only took Barack Obama eighteen months. Another record—and another sign of the Barackalypse.

Of course, the reader may have been one of the lucky ones who landed one of Obama's phantom "three million jobs, saved or created." If that's the case, there's a couple of questions begging to be asked.

How's the pay? Are the benefits "saved" or "created"? How's

that work? How does one know when one's vacation has started? To those unemployed during the Barackalypse, every day is a holiday.

10. Number of Government Employees, Homeless Up

QUESTION: How can one tell whether a Democrat or Republican is inhabiting the Oval Office?

ANSWER: By the number of stories in the press about the "homeless." During Republican administrations, the homeless, like the poor, are always with us—or at least they are always in the minds of the Corporate Mainstream Media. During Democrat Barack Obama's administration—as in that of Democrat Bill Clinton before him—the plight of the homeless has disappeared from the pages of the newspapers and the anxieties of nightly newscasters. Perhaps the homeless problem has worked itself out?

Hardly. According to Fox News NY, "If you think you've been seeing more people sleep on city streets, statistics back up the perception. The homeless population living on New York City streets has gone up 50 percent in the past year, according to city statistics reported by the *HellsKitchenLife.com* blog."

A survey of homelessness covering twenty-seven cities, published by the U.S. Conference of Mayors, reported a "rise in family homelessness in many areas of the country, which reflected extreme failures of economic and social policy at all levels of government.

"Every city surveyed reported that requests for emergency

food assistance increased over the past year, and those requests increased by an average of 24 percent across the cities."

While there was a rise in homelessness, the public was hearing less about it from the media, so that was some small consolation. That situation should change in 2012 should a Republican win the White House. But while homelessness is up, so is the number of federal workers earning $150,000 or more a year. The number "soared more than tenfold in the past five years and doubled since President Obama took office," according to a *USA Today* analysis.

The year 2010 also saw the new dawn for labor. For the first time in American history, a majority of union members are government workers rather than private-sector employees, according to the Bureau of Labor Statistics: "According to Obama's proposed 2011 budget, federal civilian employment in the executive branch will be 15 percent higher in 2011 than it was in 2007."

The year 2010 was truly historic.

11. Christians Fear the Government

One of the signs of the Barackalypse. Christians in America fear their government more than in years past. According to an annual online poll conducted by *DefendChristians.org*, a ministry of the Christian Anti-Defamation Commission, "The surprising number one rated anti-Christian act of 2010 was the threat of the federal government interfering in the employment decisions of ministries."

The feared legislation was the proposed Employment

Non-Discrimination Act (ENDA), which forces ministries to hire people who don't uphold the faith and values of their organization.

In 2009 the federal hate crimes law was ranked number one.

TOP TEN ANTI-CHRISTIAN ACTS OF 2010 as chosen in the *DefendChristians* poll, according to their press release:

1. **Employment Non-Discrimination Act:** A proposed federal bill that would force ministries to hire people who oppose the beliefs or values of the organization.

2. **Vaughn Walker:** The California judge who overturned Proposition 8, a state constitutional marriage amendment that defined marriage as a union of one man and one woman. Earlier, another judge had overturned a previous election result by the voters of California on the same issue of marriage.

3. **Julea Ward and Jennifer Keeton:** Two women who were expelled from master's programs in counseling at two different universities because they wouldn't deny their faith and affirm the homosexual lifestyle.

4. **Elena Kagan:** President Obama's radical appointment to the Supreme Court bench. While serving under the Clinton administration, Kagan successfully conspired to twist unfavorable evidence against partial birth abortion to deceive the Supreme Court.

5. **Christian students arrested for passing out Christian literature in Michigan:** Christians were denied their civil rights and falsely arrested for disorderly con-

duct at an annual Arab festival in Michigan for peacefully sharing the gospel. They were falsely arrested in 2009, too.

6. **Chai Feldblum:** A law professor and open lesbian appointed to the Equal Employment Opportunity Commission. Feldblum stated that in any conflict that might arise between religious liberty and homosexual "rights," she would have a hard time coming up with any case in which religious liberty should win.

7. **Stephen Ocean and Tite Sufra:** Two young men murdered in Boynton Beach, Florida, while sharing the gospel.

8. **Larry Grard:** A Christian journalist fired from his job for sending an email from his personal account on his own time in support of traditional marriage.

9. **Southern Poverty Law Center:** A liberal ACLU-like organization that continued to label many mainstream Christian organizations that held traditional values as "hate groups" in lists that include violent racist groups. SPLC's list of "hate groups" casts a wide net. According to the *New American*, the SPLC list of thirty-six enemies "at the heart of the resurgent movement" opposing big government includes a mix of perfectly reasonable people along with some who have fallen for quirky but harmless conspiracy theories, as well as what the SPLC calls "enablers": Fox News contributor Judge Andrew Napolitano and Congressmen Ron Paul, Michele Bachmann, and Paul Broun. Among those who have made the list are the *New American*'s publisher John McManus, *New Ameri-*

can contributor Chuck Baldwin, Gun Owners of America chairman Larry Pratt, *World Net Daily* founder Joe Farah, radio talk-show host Alex Jones, and constitutionalist author Edwin Vieira, Jr. The list includes birthers, truthers, militia members, and other people the SPLC calls political heretics, but not one of which the SPLC accuses of advocating violence or law-breaking. Christians, as well as many others who don't sing the praises of the federal government, had much to fear from the Orwellian designs of the Southern Poverty Law Center.

10. **Eighty-eight prolifers were arrested for protesting President Obama's participation at a commencement ceremony at Notre Dame, a leading Catholic university:** Christians in America fearing the government didn't begin with Barack Obama, but their anxiety increased during the Barackalypse.

12. Non-Obamians Targeted as Cause for Increased Violence by the Insane

As 2011 began, the Obama administration had started a full-court press against opponents voicing their displeasure over the policies of the administration. The shrill rhetoric coming from politicians and the CMM alike after the Tucson shooting in January was surely a sign of the Barackalypse. It may have culminated in the bill proposed by Rep. Peter King (R-NY) to make it illegal for anyone to carry a firearm within one thousand feet of protected members of government. King never stated—nor was he asked by the media—what would happen if his bill became law and a congressman entered a restaurant where a citizen with a legal carry permit was eating. Would the patron have to run out of the restaurant to avoid being arrested?

The very fact that America is forced to ask such questions is not only a sign of the Barackalypse but a sign that we are being ruled by the New Mediocracy. A period of trial and tribulation needs a proper symbol, and the Barackalypse is no exception. But why limit the discussion to Obama only? The word "mediocracy" was made for his administration—as well as those of his three predecessors.

Mediocracy has been the political lot of the United States for at least the last twenty-three years. Leading the Mediocracy during that time have been George Herbert Walker Bush, William Jefferson Clinton, George Walker Bush, and Barack Hussein Obama—arguably the longest stretch of continual presidential mediocrity the United States has been asked to endure in its history.

A new national monument to commemorate this time period—a time when the United States has forsaken protected borders, currency, and citizens—is proposed. Let's call it Walk-Don't-Rushmore, and the visages of the four offending presidents who labored long and hard to drag the country down to its present state would grace this proud memorial. Of course, a corresponding national monument for the 101st through 111th Congresses would also be appropriate. Because of the massive amount of space needed to memorialize the miscreants responsible during that time, the use of more than one mountain would be needed: Mt. Stealalot and Porkout Point are two that come to mind.

Barack Hussein Obama only makes up one-fourth of the Mediocracy. It's hoped that the next president won't add a fifth to their number. At some point, the country could use a break.

There were many more signs than the dozen listed here. However, twelve is such an easy number to remember. There are sure to be many more signs to come before the end of 2012.

Welcome to the Barackalypse, baby!

All of America has a front-row seat.

20

Scenes from the
Upcoming Barackalypse!

Predictions are a tricky business.

—Anonymous

In 1972 a book was published that predicted what life would be like in 2010. The book was reprinted (with the title year changed to 2011) after attracting media attention and a cult following. *2010: Living in the Future*, by Geoffrey Hoyle, was a children's book, but thirty-eight years after it was released, it was adults who discussed how accurate Hoyle's many predictions turned out to be.

Hoyle predicted a three-day workweek, a world where jump-suits were the attire of choice and people shopped for groceries online using a combination TV-phone.

"I've been criticized because I said people [would] wear jumpsuits," explains Hoyle, the son of noted astronomer and science-fiction author Fred Hoyle. "We don't wear jumpsuits but to a certain extent the idea of the jumpsuit is the restriction of liberties."

Up to this point, the book the reader holds has been a collection of past events. But what about the future? What will happen over the coming months of the Barackalypse? While the author of this work is certainly no seer, there are events that are happening as this is being written that indicate which direction the wind will be blowing over the next few years.

The story about Hoyle's book should remind the reader that predictions are indeed tricky things. Be that as it may, based on what has already happened as of early June 2011, this is this writer's best guess at what is likely to happen over the next eighteen months, as it pertains both to Barack Hussein Obama and to related events.

Let's Get This Party Started: The Coming Barackalypse

Low poll numbers, as well as spiraling fuel and food prices, will haunt Obama's last two years in office to a greater degree than his first two. Unemployment will remain high, but even more important, job creation and the actual number of new jobs will remain low. No number of phantom "saved or created jobs" chicanery will fool the public. As with the audience that catches the magician pulling the card from his sleeve, the Obama magic of 2008 is gone, never to return.

No matter how hard the Corporate Mainstream Media tries to rekindle the fire from the good old days, the public won't buy it because Barack Obama will be *so* 2008. Voters will treat

Obama the same way they treat an old pair of parachute pants or a leisure suit they've discovered in the back of the closet: with a smile and a shake of the head before tossing them aside and selecting something better suited to their current needs. Possibly, this action might take place as they ask themselves "What was I thinking? *That* will never happen again!"

Obama was a product of a very particular time and that time has passed.

However, a portion of the CMM will continue pushing Barack Obama and the Obama Narrative™—at least for a while, until it's clear that the public doesn't trust the media any more than it does Obama.

Barring some civilization-changing, market-ready technological discovery in the next eighteen months, there are few large job-creation forces left in the economy. Decades of job-killing legislation by both parties and the steady grinding down by relentless regulation have finally put the heavy foot of government on the neck of small business. Politicians of both parties will continue to ask, "Why don't we make things here anymore?" and complain about "outsourcing" while passing more laws that make moving jobs overseas the only logical alternative to the noose they've put around the neck of any small company trying to make a buck.

The Obama EPA will continue to walk a delicate line: It will destroy jobs and create chaos out of order, while at the same time leaving large areas of the environment totally unprotected. This means that the EPA will continue to shut down places of middle-class employment: coal-fired power plants, coal mines, manufacturing plants, and various small businesses.

However, whenever BIG Business meets the environment, the EPA will huff and puff. Then do absolutely nothing. Exhibit A: the madcap fracking—much of it courtesy of Halliburton—in the Marcellus Shale natural gas field across the Eastern United States. Despite complaints from residents in Pennsylvania, New York, West Virginia, and Ohio, the EPA has been little more than a disinterested spectator.

As gasoline prices go up, expect the EPA to crack down harder on companies attempting to extract and produce energy from American sources. That's counterintuitive, but that's the EPA. Expect the EPA to continue its curious policies of protecting any environment devoid of human activity while giving the green light to destructive extractions that occur where people actually live.

The oil disaster at the BP Deepwater Horizon in the Gulf gave the president an excuse to shut down drilling in that area while simultaneously depopulating the Gulf via the frenzied spraying of toxic Corexit, a chemical dispersant that the EPA claimed it banned. That's an Obama environmental twofer!

The restrictions on domestic supplies, the series of faux "people's uprisings" in the Middle East, along with the Federal Reserve's relentless devaluation of the dollar, will push gasoline prices into the five- to seven-dollar range by the beginning of 2012. Big Oil should be the first to contribute to any possible Obama 2012 reelection bid. After all, his policies, both at home and abroad, have been instrumental in increasing their bottom line.

Expect Obama's artificial restricting of the oil supply to create shortages in different areas, which will be featured prominently in the CMM. This in turn will lead to stockpiling of both gasoline and other fuels.

Many of our political representatives, mostly Democrats but some Republicans, will react the way they usually do. They will bemoan our "dependence on foreign oil" while voting for laws that add to a regulatory regime that makes using domestic sources of energy legally and financially difficult. Countless trees will be sacrificed so the press can publish more nonsensical stories on "America's addiction to oil."

As oil and gasoline are saddled with increased costs, expect government to turn to other sources of energy—and expect Congress and the bureaucracy to move almost as quickly to jack up the costs of alternative fuels.

Obama's EPA has already pulled previously approved permits on working coal mines, throwing hundreds out of work. Obama famously vowed—though the media did their best to ignore it—to "bankrupt" any company that considered building a coal-fired electric plant in America. So, expect the price of electricity to continue rising.

One "solution" to be offered will be the installation of "smart electric meters" on homes and businesses. There will be no debate on the installation of smart meters. They will be required, as they already are in some parts of the country. In Cheyenne, Wyoming, where the devices are mandatory, a deputy sheriff accompanied the electric company to a man's home to install a smart meter after the man protested that the device would interfere with an existing medical condition.

The meters were made mandatory without any public meetings on the matter. The idea of the new devices will be sold to the public as a more intelligent way to manage the supply of electricity. If by "managing the supply" the government means "possessing the ability to cut off the supply with the push of a faraway button" it will be right. Regardless, smart meters and the power company's ability to cut off hundreds of customers via a central computer are making their debut in much of the nation during the Barackalypse.

While inflation ravages the savings of the middle class, the Federal Reserve will continue to fight "deflation." Evidence of falling prices (brought on by falling demand because no one will have the money to buy things) will be proof that it is necessary to print even more money. Continued use of such circular logic at the Fed is hardly to be considered a brave prediction, but one has to call 'em as one sees 'em.

While all of this is occurring, expect more permanent vacations, more White House parties (though more of the events will be "private, no-press-allowed" functions), and more golf outings from a man for whom the presidency increasingly seems more of a distraction than a job. Press accounts whispering of various Obama pharmacological dependencies will be more frequent.

As the part of the press that remains Obama-friendly struggles for positive stories in 2011–12, expect to see more "my little girls are growing up" coming-of-age stories about the daughters Obama. It's also difficult to see the "glamorous Michelle" angle ever going out of style. As pressures mount for Obama to step aside in 2012, press outlets still friendly to the president will trot out "Michelle is the Obama secret electoral weapon" pieces—again.

While problems mount during Obama's remaining time, expect more appointed Super-Special-Ultra-Blue-Ribbon Panels, like the much-heralded Debt Reduction Commission.

Announced with much fanfare, with no real power, and staffed with former failed politicians, just like the dog and pony show that was Simpson-Bowles, these new shams will accomplish every bit as much as their predecessors. Legal problems, both at the Department of Justice and at other administration agencies that have been kept off the public's radar by a compliant CMM, will get more press and, in some cases, a special prosecutor.

The years 2011 and 2012 will see the continued departure of key people from the Obama administration as their ship takes on more water. Expect the core inner circle to stay put or leave to position themselves advantageously for what they think will be another electoral bid (for example, Rahm Emanuel, Robert Gibbs).

However, because of the complete dissatisfaction with the president among key groups vital to his reelection, Obama will not be the Democratic nominee for 2012.

How this will unfold depends on the reaction of Barack Obama himself upon being told that he should step aside in 2012 "for the good of the party." Some of these events have already occurred and been reported.

First, it will be "suggested" that Obama step aside to make room for someone without his divisive history. This suggestion will be sugarcoated: Stories will appear in the press (some already have) suggesting that Obama has accomplished everything he set out to do or that the president's historic legacy is secure. There will be those who will suggest that America doesn't deserve such a man as Barack Obama. Gore Vidal has already declared in an interview that "Barack Obama is too smart for America." These types of statements will be made in an attempt to nudge Obama to come to the correct decision.

However, Obama's narcissism and his legendary self-regard will prevent him from taking the hints. Surrounded by his insular inner circle, he will be convinced that, even absent the magic from 2008, he controls enough patronage and power to make 2012 a repeat performance. There will be no end of advisors, as well as some in the press, who will constantly remind him how hard it is to defeat a sitting president.

In that case, the hints will become a little more explicit. Expect to see more news stories or commentary on those inconvenient or unpleasant aspects of Obama's past (personal BHO data, history) that never seemed to previously gain much traction in the Corporate Mainstream Media. Expect a few in the CMM to have epiphanies and suddenly strive for the rush that only investigative reporting can bring.

Questions from normally reliable allies could make the news, thrusting forward issues that Obama's team and the CMM successfully buried during 2008. This trend began at the end of 2010, when two reliable Obama "allies" brought up the issue of Obama's missing birth certificate. One reputed Obama ally, Hawaii governor Neil Abercrombie—who, coincidentally, happened to be the only person who ever gave media interviews claiming to have "been there" when Obama's parents, Stanley Ann Dunham and Obama Sr., were supposedly madly in love—brought up the issue of Obama's birth certificate as one of his first orders of business upon being elected, all in the guise of "helping the president out." From 2008 on, Abercrombie was the go-to guy—which is to say, the only guy—whom the media could run down who claimed to have memories of Obama as an infant in Hawaii. He was Representative Abercrombie (D-HI) at that time.

Just as "innocent" was Chris Matthews's on-air wondering on December 30, 2010, "Why doesn't Obama show his long-form birth certificate?" This is only one sample of how this scenario might play out—if the wrong path is chosen by Barack Obama after it's "suggested" that he step aside for the good of the party. Old Chinese saying: "Man with lots of skeletons in his closet doesn't want anyone to open door." Abercrombie and Matthews might not have opened the door, but they were rattling the knob, so to speak.

This clear shot across the Obama bow should do the trick. If not, the Chinese water torture of the steady drip, drip, drip of leaked Obama documents will continue and CMM "journalists" who were offended by the mere mention of "Obama's birth certificate" will clamor and badger the president and his spokesmen for information. The CMM will demand to see Obama records it totally ignored in 2008. Obama's secretiveness about his birth certificate will only be the beginning; there are many unrevealed Obama documents that the press might suddenly take an interest in. All in the service of the public's "right to know," of course.

This tension in the chess game between the forces of Barack Obama and the Democratic Party string-pullers was on display in April and May 2011. After Obama announced his intentions to seek reelection, the corporate media began focusing on Donald Trump. The sudden attention accorded Trump primarily dealt with his pronouncements about Obama's lack of public records, in particular, his elusive long-form birth certificate.

On April 27, after a constant two-week-long media beating by Trump, Obama released what he alleged was a copy of his Hawaiian birth certificate. Almost immediately, problems with the president's document were the subject of much discussion on the Internet.

On April 28, Trump fired back that he wanted to see Obama's college and university records. Obama upped the ante on May 1 by announcing that the U.S. had shot dead Osama bin Laden. This news promptly drove Donald Trump off the front pages for the next two weeks. That's where the game stood in mid-May as this was being written.

Obama will then receive the "Hillary Clinton treatment." The press will seriously consider, report, and debate the information that it ridiculed in 2008 whenever it surfaced elsewhere. The press first displayed this tactic with Clinton in 2008—when getting Obama elected was its mission—relentlessly pursuing information about her past that it had totally ignored while her husband was in the White House—information that might have actually mattered had it been reported in a timely manner.

Story lines of the type that dogged George W. Bush from 2002 to 2008 can then be expected to crop up: the sudden rediscovery of the homeless, the quagmire of Afghanistan, people giving up due to the terrible economy. Obama will find a press that's had its "Big Deal, 9.5 percent unemployment" attitude replaced by a sudden interest in times when unemployment rates were normally 5.4 percent—that is, the unemployment rate *before* Obama was elected.

Expect stories from "disillusioned" former Obama supporters, those young people who lived and breathed the slogans from the Obama Narrative™ of 2008—only to be slapped by the reality of Barack Obama's policies from 2008 to 2012. It has already begun.

After this round of persuasion, it will again be Obama's choice to pursue a "higher purpose" or continue his quest for a second term. If he chooses the former, the media will then break into hosannas for the Messiah once more. Barack Hussein Obama will be portrayed as a sort of Great Moral Force, a person relied upon to provide quotations and suggestions for the future "progress" of the United States and the world.

Barack Obama will become a well-compensated high official of the United Nations, perhaps secretary-general, where he can be depicted once again as a "unifying force." If Obama continues to pursue the Democratic nomination for a second term, it's likely that a progressive primary challenger could be found, draining his campaign of both money and manpower. Several names have already been floated in this regard—for example, former senator Russ Feingold of Wisconsin. Large donors who were counted on to provide electoral financial firepower will return Team Obama's calls, but will beg off, most probably with "Now's not a good time. It's the economy."

At some point, even a man with Barack Obama's huge ego might be persuaded. In that case, the Democratic nominee will be little-known nationally. A sacrificial lamb, groomed for the future, thrown to the Republican wolves in a political climate that will have changed almost 180 degrees from 2008. Regardless of the choices Obama ends up making, they won't have Barack Hussein Obama to kick around anymore.

After having lived through a four-year sentence of the Obama years, the electorate will be in a rather unforgiving mood. Remembering the misdeeds of two years of Democratic one-party rule under Obama, the country will be ready to switch to a Republican one-party situation after 2012.

Republican control of both houses of Congress and the presidency will make it possible for laws to be passed further limiting freedom and privacy in the name of "security" that the Democrats would never have been able to pass while in power. The Democrats passed laws limiting privacy and restricting freedom in the name of their pet causes (health care, financial regulation, "fixing" the economy the progressive way) while enjoying one-party rule. Expect the Republicans to continue along these lines in the name of their pet causes (security, helping business—Big Business, not small business—and national emergency preparation for possible future terror attacks, as well as the odd, unspecified "national emergency").

With or without Obama, left or right, Republican or Democratic, the beat will go on: The United States will be less free.

In the meantime, Americans should expect actions, which might include new laws or court rulings, that make voter fraud easier to accomplish by either Republicans or Democrats. While Republicans continually alleged that Obama allies ACORN and SEIU were involved in voter fraud, they also know how to play the game at the periphery. While it's been Democrats who have been attacked most frequently—and with good reason—over mobilizing the felon vote, one story that didn't get reported in the 2010 election was of a Mary Cheney–associated group that conducted robocalls in the days before the 2010 election that targeted felons, and those in jail, for the Republican GOTV effort.

More unelected federal judges will routinely circumvent the will of the voters in those states that resist the government take-over of everyday life, especially the loss of freedom and privacy and the attempts to prevent further erosion of public morality. Expect incest and pedophilia to become the next gay marriage–type issues, further eroding thousands of years of civilization in the name of "personal choice" and "privacy."

In a similar vein, more appointed local officials serving on unaccountable boards will pass more regulations having the force of law to restrict more everyday personal choices. Voters, as they are now, will be helpless to remedy this situation through the ballot box. Public nudity will be winked at; public smoking, not so much.

After the election, look for calls for a constitutional convention as a "quick fix" to correct the overreaching of Obama's term. Expect the solutions at such a convention, if it materializes, to be far worse than the cure. CMM pundits will attribute the resulting loss of constitutional safeguards to "unintended consequences."

Regardless of what events happen to ensure that Obama is not the 2012 Democratic nominee, be assured that a massive Obama rehabilitation campaign will be conducted in the Corporate Mainstream Media and the part of the Internet controlled by well-funded progressive interests. This will continue for years after Barack Obama has left office, and eventually, many conservative websites will join the effort. Expect more "Obama was too intelligent" and "Obama was too far ahead of his time" and "The country didn't deserve Obama" stories to appear after 2012. These will continue for years.

Continued economic turmoil, both while Obama finishes out his term and after the new president takes office, will cause the government to pass more job-killing regulations and laws in the name of "job creation" and "stimulus." Schemes that limit personal liberty and basic constitutional rights will be floated as solutions to the economic problems created by both the Republicans and the Democrats over the last twenty-five years. Trading liberty for security will be the favorite tactic of the coming "War on Want" just as surely as it has been in the "War on Terror."

Whoever becomes the president after 2012, the continued nonenforcement of existing laws will lead to more crime problems, making additional, more-restrictive laws necessary. Of course, the criminals will pay no attention to the new laws precisely because they are criminals. Local police forces will become even more militarized, and the militarization will extend to the forces of even the smallest of villages and towns. In desperation, citizens from local communities will attempt to band together to protect themselves from crime and will be prosecuted for violating laws that the criminals they seek to control routinely ignore.

Fear will play a big part in promoting these tradeoffs, and the CMM will play its usual part in ushering in a new age of restrictions in America—just as it did in the months after 9/11. A dress rehearsal was the aftermath of the Tucson shooting, when political hacks of both parties climbed over the bodies of the victims in the rush to pass even more restrictive measures to control Americans who were nowhere near Arizona.

The divisive rhetoric against divisive rhetoric will escalate. Expect more TV cable "experts" to fix their hair, go on the air, and provide justifications along the lines of "The Constitution is a great thing, but, you know . . ."

Whoever becomes president, expect more cameras and more surveillance in more public places as Americans go about their everyday lives. Expect the appearance of TSA-type scanners beyond airports. Obtaining permission to travel, purchase particular products, bank, move, and spend one's own money will consume more time than those living a couple of generations ago would have believed possible. Government will become the third "partner" in every marriage, needed to be consulted before important decisions are made, especially those concerning "the children." More personal information about more Americans will wind up on more government and corporate databases. More spokesmen will then assure the public that "safeguards are in place to ensure that the information collected is not misused." Of course, that information will be.

The CMM will continue to profile Big Banks, Big Business, and Big Money Men as the face of business in America. However, more Americans will no longer buy this particular propaganda and will equate Big Business with Big Government. After the massive corporate bailouts, more Americans will find it hard to believe that "what's good for Bill Gates is good for America."

Accounting trickery and cooking the books on General Motors and Chrysler won't fool anyone, and the Green Jobs scam—the idea that Big Government can create jobs at will by throwing Chinese money at them—will elicit the laughter it so richly deserves.

Both Democrats and Republicans will continue the charade, so as to be portrayed as "probusiness" while passing legislation that destroys small businesses. Progressives will rejoice to see more people agreeing with their view that Big Business Is Evil, because so many conservatives will cling to a variation of the falsehood that "business" means Big Business.

The country will trust the Corporate Mainstream Media even less—if that is possible. The crackdown on Internet freedom, both to read and to publish, will continue on a broad front. As in an ever-more-restricted everyday life, "security" will be the excuse used to control America's last free frontier. Registration to use, to read, and to publish will be required, and an attempt will be made for the government to register every computer before it's allowed to connect to the Internet.

A free Internet has almost destroyed the credibility of the CMM and the political hacks it has grown to love, protect, and cherish. Fraudulent narratives and memes are exploded within hours after they are floated by the traditional news organizations. Literally thousands of videos captured by ubiquitous cellphones and flip cams, uploaded to *YouTube*, and publicized by hundreds of bloggers sank many a candidate's version of the "truth" during the 2010 election campaign.

If the CMM is to retain its power to shape events and politics as usual are to continue, this situation cannot be allowed to stand. Therefore, a free Internet will be less free. Obama regulations have already begun the assault. It's been sold as being for the greater good of society, regardless of the negative impact on the individual members of that society.

Regardless of which party controls Washington, D.C., don't expect the southern border to be secured. Because of this, there will be more frequent checkpoints throughout the land—all in the name of security, some in the name of controlling illegals. Expect Americans to have to produce more documentation, while those here illegally will produce less and experience almost no consequences once apprehended.

Extragovernmental agencies, representing the United States, Mexico, and Canada, operating in the name of "cooperation," "goodwill," and "efficiency," will continue to proliferate. These got their start under George H. W. Bush, expanded under presidents Clinton and George W. Bush, and have flowered under Barack Obama. They will continue and multiply, despite government press releases to the contrary.

Border security will decline and the violence that is making parts of the American Southwest uninhabitable will grow worse. The United States government has already lost control of parts of Arizona and Texas. Since this is happening by design, this area will grow larger and will be ruled by the Mexican drug cartels. Local inhabitants will continue to be on their own and local law enforcement will be outgunned and, eventually, coopted and turned against the locals by the immense wealth of the cartels. The federal government will continue to vehemently deny that this is happening. The national media will continue to ignore the problem, though local U.S. news outlets will accurately document events until their journalists begin turning up missing, murdered, or bribed.

The CMM will continue its silence on these happenings, and Americans who depend on these organizations for their news will continue to remain in the dark.

The Corporate Mainstream Media will produce less news, but more words of ridicule will be coined to describe opponents who record the CMM's lack of curiosity and investigation. Americans will read more stories in the newspaper and hear more newscasts that "don't make any sense." It's useful to remind the reader that stories that "don't make any sense" do make perfect sense—if one keeps in mind that many in power are purposely trying to subvert the country's traditions and strengths. Barack Hussein Obama is but the most prominent.

More stories about "misunderstood" government employees who are experiencing stress when they carry out unpopular, oppressive measures will be featured in the CMM. People who resist these measures will be labeled "eccentric" or "difficult," and if possible, embarrassing details of their private lives will be leaked. The treatment of Joe the Plumber was only the dress rehearsal.

All the while, the partisan divide in the country will grow wider as the media play up differences between groups. People will be encouraged by the media to think in terms of "us" and "them" instead of being Americans with differing points of view. Upcoming dubious legislation will be offered by both parties, while commentators and pundits will urge their followers to support such legislation because "we can't let the other side win."

Keeping Americans divided will be a necessity; the country must not unite to fix the problems that arise from existing and proposed legislation from both parties. Although this practice began in earnest under George W. Bush, the Obama administration has turned it into an art form.

In light of the above, the government will crack down on the protests that will occur—increasingly by the middle-aged and senior citizens. The young will approve. After years of being brainwashed by a corrupt education establishment, being indoctrinated by universities with speech codes and desensitized by the popular culture, the young will become the generation of oppression.

Unlike in the 1960s, the young will become enforcers for "the Man" before becoming "the Man" himself. As Big Government sucks up and wastes more resources, the battle for survival will be decided not by ambition and hard work, but by which groups the government can count on for support. The elderly will be considered inconvenient, inconsiderate, irrelevant, and expendable.

Expect more candidates and spokesmen on the right to implore their followers to "pull a Mitch Daniels." In June 2010, Daniels, a former Bush director of OMB and Republican governor of Indiana, made a plea for a "truce on social issues." Daniels's rationale for checking morality at the door of the Republican National Convention is of course "tactics" and "concentrating on what's really important." Daniels was only publicly stating what his ex-boss, George W. Bush, did behind the scenes.

A few days before Christmas 2010, a so-called prolife leader wrote a piece at *Red State* urging conservatives to forget the attempt to place "personhood initiatives" (initiatives that amend various state constitutions to state that life begins at conception and thus, at that point, deserves the legal protection of the state) on state ballots. As social conservatives make up a tiny part of Democrats, expect more of these calls for politically expedient morality from the Republican side.

Obama's and the Democrats' unlooked-for nemesis, the Tea Party, will still be attacked in the press. Attempts will be made behind the scenes to coopt various Tea Party groups, either to water down their message or to discredit the entire grassroots movement. Expect money to pour into Tea Party groups—with strings attached, of course (compromising the original message of small government), all in the name of "winning" and "tactics." This has already happened to several organizations that started out as representative Tea Party groups.

One Tea Party organization was taken over by a group of outsiders and hosted what it billed as the "National Tea Party Convention" in Nashville, Tennessee. That fifty other Tea Party leaders in the Volunteer State protested the convention, with some picketing outside the convention hall, didn't receive nearly as much press. The spokesman from this group is now referred to in the press as a "Tea Party founder" and his words, no matter how controversial or ill-timed, are assumed to represent the entire Tea Party movement. Expect this situation to be repeated.

Beware of groups claiming to speak for the entire movement or the "nationalization" of the Tea Party, which is a decentralized, highly localized movement. Expect more "national voices of the Tea Party" to appear in the CMM before the 2012 election.

The Tea Party was the group to which many frustrated Americans—especially conservatives—turned as a way of expressing their unhappiness with the utter recklessness of the policies of the two major parties. As the Tea Party gets infiltrated and corrupted, expect more Americans to express not just interest, but enthusiasm, for another major party. When that third party appears, expect the corrupting influences of Washington and the behind-the-scenes money changers to make it indistinguishable from the Democrats and Republicans within ten years.

The government will still be picking winners and losers. The phrase "hate speech" will still be a popular way to stifle discussion, especially if the speaker is a Christian or someone who resists special benefits for a particular group the government has designated as a "winner."

The politicization of terror attacks—real or imagined, attempted or realized—will increase. Lawmakers will be pressured by events to pass difficult legislation tightening the screws on surveillance and overseeing everyday life (going to the mall, owning a gun, traveling, using the Internet, protesting the government). None of these measures will make Americans safer. They will, however, make Americans easier to control.

Expect one party to set up rules making it easier for the other party to ram through unpopular legislation, as the Democrats in the Senate are doing by seeking to dismantle Senate rules for the filibuster.

One final note about the 2012 election: If Barack Obama dumps Joe Biden as his running mate for 2012, then a completely different forecast is made. If Obama chooses another running mate instead of Biden, not only will Obama be the Democratic Party nominee, but he will win the 2012 election. Biden's "medical problems" will be cited—most likely, his previously reported brain aneurism.

Any number of uninspiring Democratic pols might replace Biden in such a scenario; speculation is likely to touch on a number of hardened Democratic warhorses. These include, but aren't limited to, John Kerry, Hillary Clinton, and Joe Lieberman. On a hunch, John Kerry is a slight favorite in this corner over Hillary Clinton. This hunch is based solely on the number of freelance "diplomatic missions" Kerry has undertaken for the Obama administration since the summer of 2010.

Regardless, the Barackalypse will rumble along until 2012—when it will accelerate, either under the direction of Barack Hussein Obama, a new Republican president, or someone else.

21

The Gift of Barack Hussein Obama

When the author was much younger, Christmas was celebrated a bit differently from how it is in many homes today. There were no bars open on Christmas; no Christmas TV cable "marathons" featuring twenty-four hours of continuous reruns of sitcoms that were of dubious value when they first appeared; no fear that wishing others a "Merry Christmas" might offend the sensibilities of a shadowy, unseen "minority." Christmas was a time to eat, get in the car, travel to see the grandparents—and open the presents!

All of the "most wanted" presents—the new bicycle, the cool fighting robots in the bright plastic boxing ring, the James Bond 007 attaché case—were immediately seen for what they were: truly valuable additions to a kid's personal stash. Then came the

"Gifts of Utility": the coats, the pants, the shirts, socks. They were mentally noted and quickly forgotten. How is one to get excited over a new pair of socks when there were Hungry Hungry Hippos to maneuver?

In fact, there was something secretly like resentment at having received those gifts: The time spent to try on blue jeans, shirts, and socks to make sure they fit was time not spent outside test-firing the Jr. NASA X500 Rocket—complete with authentic Launch Pad.

The socks were appreciated weeks later, when standing in the below-freezing morning weather, waiting for the school bus to arrive. However, no instances of children rushing home in the afternoon to thank a parent for that wise gift of a pair of socks have been recalled.

Sometimes, the true value of a gift isn't realized by the recipient until long afterward. And so it is with our forty-fourth president, Barack Hussein Obama. Obama really has been a gift to the United States. Whether the United States sees the true value in such a gift will be determined over the next decade or so. Barack Obama should be a name to be celebrated and remembered—but not in the manner Team Obama and its many Corporate Mainstream Media pimps would desire.

In December 2010, this idea was touched upon by Peter Heck, a public-high-school government teacher and radio talk-show host in central Indiana. Heck, who wrote from a conservative perspective in "The Presidency That Saved America" at *American Thinker*, had some cogent thoughts along this line:

In fifty years I have little doubt that we will regard the administration of Barack Obama as the presidency that saved America. No, not in the sense that Chris Matthews, Keith Olbermann, and all the other media John the Baptists foretold as they proclaimed the coming of our political messiah just over two years ago. Rather, the history of our time will show that it was the radical nature of Obama's dogged devotion to a liberal progressive philosophy far out of the American mainstream that jolted awake a generation of apathetic and passive citizens just in time to save the republic.

Heck seemed to be saying that Obama's gift to apathetic Americans of a conservative bent will be the gift of Awakening. Conservatives will no longer ignore smiling Democrats who come in the guise of Republicans, no longer ignore the threat to the American way of life from socialism and the far left. Heck is right, but it's hoped that Barack Obama's endowment will prove to be more comprehensive and multifaceted.

Of course, the presidency of Barack Obama will be used by conservatives as an allegory of the dangers of Democratic Party governance, just as the presidency of Bill Clinton was employed—and quickly forgotten by the nation—as an allegory of the dangers of Democratic governance. "Bill Clinton" became conservative shorthand for "garish self-indulgence" and "using the power of the U.S. government for personal gain."

The "Legend of Bill Clinton, Womanizing Wastrel," however, was a tale that was passed along orally among conservatives, much like the oral history of primitive tribes. Many Americans never heard that tale, because history is not a strong point for the corporate media, especially the history of one of its chosen favorites. To the CMM, and to many Americans, Bill Clinton was known only as "The Great Triangulator."

Clinton's shortcomings were not discovered by many Americans until his wife ran against Barack Obama eight years after Clinton left office. It was only during the Democratic Party primary season that the public was enlightened by the same stories about Hillary Clinton that had appeared in conservative publications a decade earlier. Only when it benefited the latest corporate media darling, Barack Obama, did the conservative oral history become fare for the *New York Times*.

There is a lesson to be learned here for the next Democratic Party darling: What the CMM giveth, the CMM can taketh away.

Heck's final take on Obama's Gift is, again, from a conservative viewpoint:

> And with a 2012 election cycle that already sees Democrats poised to face even more devastating Congressional losses (they are defending far more Senate seats than Republicans, and could lose upward of thirty House seats due to redistricting), Obama's persistent, unapologetic left-wing crusade is shaping up to be the political equivalent to Pickett's Charge.
>
> In the end, the era of Obama will do more damage to the progressive left than any Republican presidency could have ever done. For that, posterity will owe him a debt of gratitude.

All of that is true—as far as it goes. Barack Obama, however, could prove to be a great gift to American progressives—if they realize it. The progressive left embraced Barack Obama as truly one of their own: He would end vile foreign wars, take on the evil Big Bankers, roll back the excesses of the hated Bush years. The Age of Obama would grant progressives political victories hitherto available to them only through the courts.

However, Obama used the progressives to get elected and then kicked them to the curb. He renewed the Patriot Act, maintained the Guantanamo Bay detention facility, and escalated the war in Afghanistan. Obama proved anything but a warrior against Big Business and Big Banking. How could someone who was the largest recipient of money from Big Banking, Fannie Mae, and Freddie Mac prove otherwise?

When conservatives questioned the Obama Narrative™, progressives were Obama's fiercest defenders—even though they knew nothing more of Obama's past than his detractors. Progressives not only didn't know, they didn't want anyone else to know either—or even to ask questions about it. The Gift of Obama to progressives is that they should never again trust a Chicago machine politician whose background is largely unknown, based solely on their vague assumption, amplified by the CMM, that "he is one of us." George W. Bush gave a similar gift to conservatives.

Obama's biggest gift to all Americans of any or no political persuasion is skepticism. This is a gift that the public should not need, especially after the presidencies of the last twenty-odd years. Americans should be skeptical of anyone sold by the CMM on the basis of "trust us." After Barack Obama, more Americans have become aware of a corporate media that operates not as a watchdog but as a lapdog. The difference between what Barack Obama promised and his actions was so huge, especially during the implementation of ObamaCare, that a skeptical public's trust in the Corporate Mainstream Media has been shattered for the immediate future.

This shattering of trust should cut both ways: Progressives should no more trust the shills at MSNBC and the alphabet networks to objectively keep them informed than conservatives should trust Fox News. For months, MSNBC was one continuous infomercial for a man who would betray and eventually attack the "professional left." Fox News ignored two issues that would have awakened many viewers immediately: Obama's call for a national civilian military force and the lengthy gaps in his history about which nothing—except what was offered by Obama himself—was known.

Barack Hussein Obama, like the ancient Greeks outside the walls of Troy, will prove to be a bearer of gifts. If Americans examine his gifts closely and learn a few lessons from his meteoric rise to fame via the corporate media, much good can come from the bad years of the administration of Barack Obama. Will America come to appreciate these?

Or will they change the channel to the latest music awards show or text someone they really don't care about before they begin another video game?

Appendix

Thwarting the CMM: Where to Go for More Reliable Information on Obama

This book has attempted to acquaint the reader with Obama lore that somehow escaped inclusion in the Obama Narrative™. But this effort covers only a finite period. What's the curious reader to do for future events—after the time covered herein?

If the reader can't depend upon the Corporate Mainstream Media news to deliver all of the information about Barack Hussein Obama, where can one turn in the future for information on Barack Obama and news about important events?

In a word: the Internet. (Okay, that's actually two words.)

According to a January 2011 Pew Research Center survey, more Americans depend upon the Internet for their news than ever before. Only television supplies more Americans with their news—and the Internet is gaining. Some 66 percent say they get most of their news from television; 41 percent from the Internet; 31 percent from newspapers; and 16 percent from radio. In 2010, for the first time, among people under the age of thirty, the Internet passed television as their main source of news.

One reason for this shift: With some notable exceptions in the conservative press, it was the Internet that investigated and published information unfavorable to Barack Obama during the 2008 election—including the now-familiar Obama method of dealing with "inconvenient" information that comes to light.

The history of Barack Obama is a study in the incredible power of coincidence. Whatever the document, whatever the question, the Obama campaign/administration has ignored it—until the issue became troublesome. Then they would release only enough information to satisfy the very few in the CMM who'd had the brass to inquire further. Supporters and apologists would then rush in to condemn anyone who wanted follow-up information. One of the favorite ways to squelch debate was to yell "Conspiracy theorist!"

Readers are once more reminded that the term "conspiracy theorist" was applied to those publications (notably *American Spectator*) that, during the Clinton administration, uncovered embarrassing information about Bill and Hillary Clinton's past. Interestingly, it was Hillary Clinton who coined the famous phrase "vast right-wing conspiracy." The CMM have become ardent believers and promoters of the concept ever since.

Barack Obama and his apologists apparently remember that, as for the Clintons in the 1990s, persistent questions about the sanitized version of Barack Obama have mainly come from those branded as "conspiracy theorists." Once more, it's not as if the CMM has been guilty of mere "bias"; active "content management" prevented many Americans from reading important information about Obama until after the election—months after the election, in many cases. Two years after the fact, news about Obama's campaign financing shenanigans still haven't been featured in most of the corporate media.

The Corporate Mainstream Media did a scandalous job of vetting our forty-fourth president during the 2008 campaign, both in the primaries and in the general election. Almost all of the corporate media (ABC, CBS, CNN, MSNBC, NBC, the *New York Times* and most of the rest of big-city, urban newspapers, *Time*, *Newsweek*, and associated websites) have shirked their constitutionally protected duties.

The smart money says that the corporate media will continue to be slackers. Why change now? Therefore, Americans will trust the CMM even less than they do now—if that is possible. The 2008 election profoundly changed the way Americans viewed the CMM. For the worse.

In the 2009 Pew Research survey on trust in the media, the poll found that only 29 percent said that the media generally "get the facts straight." Some 63 percent of respondents said news articles were often inaccurate; 74 percent said news organizations favored one side or another in reporting on political and social issues; 74 percent said the media were often influenced by powerful interests. These were the worst marks Pew has ever recorded. A 2010 Gallup Poll found a similar dive in public trust in major media.

So, what's a body to do? Several things. First, turn off the TV. Television, while the most popular, is the most restrictive of all news media. If your goal is the uncensored, unfiltered free flow of information, television is undoubtedly the worst source. Because ABC, NBC, CBS, and Fox, as well as the cable news networks, reach such a wide audience, their news is refined, filtered, homogenized, and then streamlined and endlessly repeated for mass consumption. How many of the news networks covered the John Edwards scandal? Zero—and it's not hard to figure out why. The number of reporters that CNN, MSNBC, Fox News, ABC, CBS, and NBC assigned to the Edwards story totaled zero. Combined. This contrasted to the *National Enquirer*, which usually had seven—and had at one time a high of twelve—reporters working the story.

Fortunately, in today's Internet Age, there are many options available for the concerned citizen who wants to find sources of unreported information concerning the president. Information that never makes the daily newspapers or the nightly newscasts can easily be accessed on the Internet. But there's a catch: It takes work on the part of the reader to sift through the many different accounts and decide what information is valid and what should be ignored. To regular news consumers of the Corporate Mainstream Media, doing some work and being much better informed may require more time and effort than they're prepared to commit.

Of course, the motto of most news junkies might be "Better more information to sift than no information at all."

DBKP—Death By 1000 Papercuts maintains a list of more than one hundred Internet news sources/websites at *DBKP's* "Thwarting the Corporate Mainstream Media" list. Readers will find listed news from every conceivable viewpoint: progressive, conservative, libertarian, alternative, conspiracy, and more. The site is updated regularly to reflect new fairly reliable sources of news as well as to drop those websites that discontinue their service.

NOTE: The list can be accessed at the following URL: http://deathby1000papercuts.com/thwarting-the-corporate-mainstream-media-list-of-websites/.

If the reader forgets the URL, a quick way to find the information is to Google "Thwarting the Corporate Mainstream Media."

Bibliography / Sources

Chapter 1: Who Is Barack Hussein Obama?

Mondo Frazier, Obama College, Medical, Birth Records: Who Is Barack Obama?; *DBKP—Death By 1000 Papercuts,* October 12, 2008. http://deathby1000papercuts.com/2008/10/obama-college-medical-birth-records-who-is-barack-obama/.

Wayne Madsen, Obama's White House Press Corps warned about asking certain questions, *Online Journal,* January 10, 2010. http://www.onlinejournal.com/artman/publish/article_5430.shtml.

Mondo Frazier, Barack Obama: Our First President of Self-Esteem, *DBKP—Death By 1000 Papercuts,* April 6, 2010. http://deathby1000paper cuts.com/2010/04/barack-obama-our-first-self-esteem-president/.

Mondo Frazier, Who Is Barack Obama: BHO v8.0, *DBKP—Death By 1000 Papercuts,* April 8, 2010. http://deathby1000papercuts.com/2010/04/who-is-barack-obama-bho-v8-0/.

Mondo Frazier, Elaine Marlow, Who Is Barack Obama: Library of DBKP Articles and Videos, *DBKP—Death By 1000 Papercuts,* December 4, 2008. http://deathby1000papercuts.com/who-is-barack-obama-library-of-dbkp-articles-and-videos/.

Mondo Frazier, Obama Selective Service Registration: Another Obama Record, Another Question, *DBKP—Death By 1000 Papercuts,* November 17, 2008. http://deathby1000papercuts.com/2008/11/obama-selective-service-registration-another-obama-record-another-question/.

Chris Hedges, Buying Brand Obama, *Truthdig,* May 3, 2009. http://www.truthdig.com/report/item/20090503_buying_brand_obama/, taken from Hedges' book, *Empire of Illusion: The End of Literacy and the Triumph of Spectacle* (New York: Nation Books, 2009).

Jon Swaine, Barack Obama: The 50 facts you might not know, *Telegraph,* November 7, 2008. http://www.telegraph.co.uk/news/worldnews/northamerica/usa/barackobama/3401168/Barack-Obama-The-50-facts-you-might-not-know.html.

Barry O'Sullivan, Fun and weird Barack Obama facts you maybe didn't know, *Mirror,* January 20, 2011. http://www.mirror.co.uk/news/top-stories/2009/01/20/fun-and-weird-barack-obama-facts-you-maybe-didn-t-know-115875-21056021/.

Barack Obama, *The Audacity of Hope,* Crown, 6th edition (October 17, 2006).

Chapter 2: Twenty Things Most Americans Don't Know about Barack Hussein Obama

Kyle, Illinois winning lottery number on election day—666, *Our Rising Sound,* November 6, 2008. http://www.ourrisingsound.com/2008/11/06/illinois-winning-lottery-number-on-election-day-666/.

Denny, Is Barack Hussein Obama the First "Beast" Spoken of in the Book of Revelation? Let's Look at Some Available Information, *777Denny,* December 31, 2010. http://777denny.wordpress.com/2010/12/31/is-barack-hussein-obama-the-first-beast-spoken-of-in-the-book-of-revelation-lets-look-at-some-available-information/.

Mondo Frazier, Obama, Hagel, Cantwell: Fighting Global Poverty— One Speech at a Time, *DBKP—Death By 1000 Papercuts,* June 13,

2008. http://deathby1000papercuts.com/2008/06/obama-hagel-cantwell
-fighting-global-poverty-one-speech-at-a-time/.

Elaine Marlow, McCain Works on Financial Crisis While Obama
Touts $845 Billion Global Poverty Bill Funded by US Taxpayers,
DBKP—Death By 1000 Papercuts, September 25, 2008. http://death
by1000papercuts.com/2008/09/mccain-works-on-financial-crisis-while
-obama-touts-845-billion-global-poverty-bill-funded-by-us-taxpayers/.

Mondo Frazier, Obama's Global Poverty Act: Spread U.S. Wealth Around
the World, *DBKP—Death By 1000 Papercuts,* October 28, 2008.
http://deathby1000papercuts.com/2008/10/obamas-global-poverty-act
-spread-us-wealth-around-the-world/.

Ann Coulter, Investigate This!, *Human Events,* January 5, 2011. http://www
.humanevents.com/article.php?id=41005.

Edward Cline, Obama's Global Poverty Act, *Investors Business Daily,* April
3, 2008. http://www.capitalismmagazine.com/index.php?news=5152.

Barry O'Sullivan, Fun and weird Barack Obama facts you maybe didn't
know, *Mirror,* January 20, 2009. http://www.mirror.co.uk/news/top
-stories/2009/01/20/fun-and-weird-barack-obama-facts-you-maybe-didn't
-know-115875-21056021/.

Jocelyn Noveck, Obama's related to Palin, AP, October 13, 2010. http://
news.yahoo.com/s/ap/20101013/ap_on_re_us/us_obama_and_palin.

Andrew Malcolm, Barack Obama related to Sarah Palin, Rush Limbaugh
and George W. Bush, ancestory website claims, *Los Angeles Times,* October 13, 2010. http://latimesblogs.latimes.com/washington/2010/10/
barack-obama-related-to-sarah-palin-rush-limbaugh-bush.html.

Top 10 interesting Obama facts, *Obama Zone.* http://obama-zone.com/
interesting-facts/.

Barack Obama: The 50 facts you might not know, *Telegraph,* November
7, 2008. http://www.telegraph.co.uk/news/worldnews/northamerica/
usa/barackobama/3401168/Barack-Obama-The-50-facts-you-might-not
-know.html.

N. S. Gill, Myth—Religion—Hanuman, *About.com,* 2002. http://ancient
history.about.com/library/bl/bl_myth_gods_hindu_hanuman.htm.

Robert Parham, A Word of Thanks, A Note That Leadership Is Fragile—
Like Holding an Egg, *Ethics Daily,* November 10, 2010. http://www

.ethicsdaily.com/a-word-of-thanks-a-note-that-leadership-is-fragile-like -holding-an-egg-cms-17054.

Amy Sullivan, No Churchgoing Christmas for the First Family, *Time,* December 23, 2009. http://www.time.com/time/politics/article/ 0,8599,1949879,00.html.

Pam Geller, Obama's "Non-Religious" White House Christmas and No Christmas Gifts for His Kids, *Atlas Shrugs,* December 8, 2009. http:// atlasshrugs2000.typepad.com/atlas_shrugs/2009/12/obama-planned -to-take-christmas-out-of-christmas-a-nonreligious-christmas.html.

A conversation with Jon Meacham and Evan Thomas, *Charlie Rose* show, November 5, 2008. http://www.charlierose.com/view/interview/9341.

Obama's India visit: 4 weird facts, *The Week,* November 5, 2010. http:// theweek.com/article/index/209060/obamas-india-visit-4-weird-facts.

Steve Pendlebury, What the Obama School Teleprompter Photos Really Show, *USA Today,* January 10, 2010. http://www.aolnews.com/2010/ 01/25/what-the-obama-school-teleprompter-photos-really-show/.

Bill Carter, Comedians find Obama jokes a tough sell, *New York Times,* July 15, 2008. http://www.nytimes.com/2008/07/15/world/americas/ 15iht-humor.1.14503508.html.

Allahpundit, Marlon Wayans: It's hard to joke about Obama because he's "trying to do good," *Hot Air,* May 6, 2010. http://hotair.com/archives/ 2010/05/06/marlon-wayans-its-hard-to-joke-about-obama-because-hes -trying-to-do-good/.

Mondo Frazier, Late Night Joke Dump, *DBKP—Death By 1000 Papercuts,* August–December 2010. http://deathby1000papercuts.com/2010/12/ late-night-joke-dump-december-31-2010/.

Jokes, *Newsmax,* August–December 2010. http://www.newsmax.com/ Jokes/226.

What brand of cigarettes did Barack Obama smoke? *Answers.com.* /Q/ What_brand_of_cigarettes_did_Barack_Obama_smoke#ixzzlAEA4 dljx.

Adrienne LaFrance, Obama's Winter White House an Illegal Rental, *Honolulu Civil Beat,* January 5, 2011. http://www.civilbeat.com/articles/ 2011/01/05/7920-obamas-winter-white-house-an-illegal-rental/?sl=1.

Another Michelle Obama gaffe, *New-Con News,* March 26, 2010. http://www.neoconnews.com/2008/03/26/another-michelle-obama-gaffe/.

Michelle Obama Quotes, *Brainy Quotes.* http://www.brainyquote.com/quotes/authors/m/michelle_obama.html.

Ed Morrissey, Obamateurism of the Day, *Hot Air,* January 5, 2011. http://hotair.com/archives/2011/01/05/obamateurism-of-the-day-422/.

Super Weird: Obama leaves Clinton to conduct White House press conference, *Daily Caller,* December 10, 2010. http://dailycaller.com/2010/12/10/obama-leaves-clinton-at-helm-in-white-house-press-room/#ixzzlAEN9VQOb.

Peter Finn, Key coordinator of detainee policy quits, *Washington Post,* November 25, 2010. http://www.washingtonpost.com/wp-dyn/content/article/2009/11/24/AR2009112402503.html.

Who has left the White House so far? BBC, October 8, 2010. http://www.bbc.co.uk/news/world-us-canada-11430109.

Jason Horowitz, Gibbs says he'll serve Obama better from outside, *Washington Post,* January 5, 2011. http://www.washingtonpost.com/wp-dyn/content/article/2011/01/05/AR2011010506274.html.

Mondo Frazier, Obama's Constant Time Cover Status: TIME Hearts Obama, *DBKP—Death By 1000 Papercuts,* October 16, 2008. http://deathby1000papercuts.com/2008/10/obamas-constant-time-cover-status-time-hearts-obama/.

Domenico Montanaro, Obama appeared on half of Time covers, MSNBC, December 17, 2008. http://firstread.msnbc.msn.com/_news/2008/12/17/4432215-obama-appeared-on-half-of-time-covers.

Mondo Frazier, Contributions: Obama, Dodd and the Freddie Fannie Five, *DBKP—Death By 1000 Papercuts,* September 26, 2008. http://deathby1000papercuts.com/2008/09/contributions-obama-dodd-part-of-the-freddie-fannie-five.

Chapter 3: The Media and the Messiah

Mondo Frazier, Obama: If TV Interviews Were Jobs, U.S. Would Have Full Employment, *DBKP FLASH Headline News,* November 25, 2009.

http://deathby1000papercuts.com/headlines/2009/11/obama-if-tv
-interviews-were-jobs-u-s-would-have-full-employment/.

Barack Obama Credits, *TV.com*. http://www.tv.com/barack-obama/person/
334864/appearances.html.

Mark Knoller, Obama's First Year: By the Numbers, CBS News, January 20, 2010. http://www.cbsnews.com/8301-503544_162-6119525
-503544.html.

Chapter 4: The Missing Obama Records

Mondo Frazier, Obama College, Medical, Birth Records: Who Is Barack
Obama? *DBKP—Death By 1000 Papercuts,* October 12, 2008. http://
deathby1000papercuts.com/2008/10/obama-college-medical-birth
-records-who-is-barack-obama/.

Mondo Frazier, Obama Medical Records: Still Missing in Action, *DBKP
@ Blogger,* October 16, 2008. http://deathby1000papercuts.blogspot
.com/2008/10/obama-medical-records-missing-in-action.html.

Mondo Frazier, Obama Medical Records: MSM's Don't Ask, Obama's
Don't Tell Policy, *DBKP—Death By 1000 Papercuts,* October 16, 2008.
http://deathby1000papercuts.com/2008/10/obama-medical-records-msms
-dont-ask-obamas-dont-tell-policy/.

Mondo Frazier, Obama Records: Obama Campaign Still Refuses to Release Medical, Other Records, *DBKP—Death By 1000 Papercuts,*
October 23, 2008. http://deathby1000papercuts.com/2008/10/obama
-records-obama-campaign-still-refuses-to-release-medical-other-records/.

Mondo Frazier, Obama Records: Obama Medical, College, University,
Other Records Still Hidden, *DBKP—Death By 1000 Papercuts,* October
25, 2008. http://deathby1000papercuts.com/2008/10/obama-records
-obama-medical-college-university-other-records-still-hidden/.

Obama's Missing Illinois State Senate Documents, *Obama's Records,* October 27, 2009. http://obamarecords.com/?p=22.

Of Barack Obama, Judges, Private Papers, Marxofascist Moves, & the
Various Meanings of "Bastard," *Gulag Bound*, October 25, 2010. http://
gulagbound.com/7403/of-barack-obama-judges-private-papers-marx
ofascist-moves-the-various-meanings-of-bastard.

Eye-opening list of Obama's missing-hidden documents: "The American People Demand to Know: WHO SENT YOU???" *Newsgroups. DerKeiler.com,* December 7, 2008. http://newsgroups.derkeiler.com/Archive/Misc/misc.consumers/2008-12/msg00041.html.

Education, *Obama Files,* 2008. http://www.theobamafile.com/obamaeducation.htm.

Executive Order 13489, *FAS.org,* January 21, 2009. http://www.fas.org/sgp/obama/presidential.html.

Obama Details Promises for Transparency, *Pro Publica,* November 7, 2008. http://www.propublica.org/article/obama-details-promises-for-transparency-1107.

Chapter 5: Has Anyone Seen My Birth Certificate?

Elaine Marlow, Obama's Million Dollar Birth Certificate Mystery, *DBKP –Death By 1000 Papercuts,* July 29, 2009. http://deathby1000papercuts.com/2009/07/obamas-million-dollar-birth-certificate-mystery/.

Mondo Frazier, Elaine Marlow, Obama College, Medical, Birth Records: Who Is Barack Obama? *DBKP—Death By 1000 Papercuts,* October 12, 2008. http://deathby1000papercuts.com/2008/10/obama-college-medical-birth-records-who-is-barack-obama/.

Mondo Frazier, Obama Birth Certificate Federal Lawsuit: The Curious Behavior of the Obama Campaign, *DBKP—Death By 1000 Papercuts,* October 9, 2008. http://deathby1000papercuts.com/2008/10/obama-birth-certificate-federal-lawsuit the-curious-behavior-of-the-obama-campaign/.

Elaine Marlow, Hawaii Governor Neil Abercrombie Adds Fuel to Obama Birth Certificate Fire, *DBKP—Death By 1000 Papercuts,* December 30, 2010. http://deathby1000papercuts.com/2010/12/hawaii-governor-neil-abercrombie-adds-fuel-to-obama-birth-certificate-fire/.

Mondo Frazier, Obama Birth Certificate: Neil Abercrombie Plays Footsie Obama's Birth Document, *DBKP—Death By 1000 Papercuts,* January 30, 2011. http://deathby1000papercuts.com/2011/01/obama-birth-certificate-neil-abercrombie-plays-footsie-obamas-birth-document/.

Obama birth certificate lawsuits, *Conservapedia*. http://www.conservapedia
.com/Obama_birth_certificate_lawsuits.

Jerome Corsi, Obama 'mama': 15 days from birth to Seattle class, *World
Net Daily,* August 4, 2009. http://www.wnd.com/?pageId=106018#ixzz
lCgD8WnUn.

Mark Niesse, HI bill would give anyone Obama birth info for free,
AP, January 28, 2011. http://hosted.ap.org/dynamic/stories/U/US_
OBAMA_BIRTH_CERTIFICATE?SITE=FLTAM&SECTION=US.

Elaine Marlow, Abercrombie and the Obama Birth Certificate: Abercrombie Pal Says He Misspoke in Radio Interview, *DBKP—Death By
1000 Papercuts,* January 26, 2011. http://deathby1000papercuts.com/
2011/01/abercrombie-and-the-obama-birth-certificate-abercrombie
-pal-says-he-misspoke-in-radio-interview/.

Jana Winter, Celebrity Journalist: I Never Spoke to Hawaii Gov About
Obama Birth Certificate, Fox News, January 26, 2011. http://www.fox
news.com/politics/2011/01/26/celebrity-journalist-says-he-never-talked
-hawaii-governor-obama-birth/#ixzzlCgFzdDpO.

Mondo Frazier, Obama Birth Certificate: A Birther is a Racist is a Truther
is a Nazi, *DBKP—Death By 1000 Papercuts,* December 30, 2010. http://
deathby1000papercuts.com/2010/12/obama-birth-certificate-a-birther
-is-a-racist-is-a-truther-is-a-nazi/.

Allahpundit, Chris Matthews and liberal panelists: Where's the birth
certificate? *Hot Air,* December 27, 2010. http://hotair.com/archives/
2010/12/27/chris-matthews-and-liberal-panelists-wheres-the-birth
-certificate/.

Amanda Ripley, The Story of Barack Obama's Mother, *Time,* April 9, 2008.
http://www.time.com/time/nation/article/0,8599,1729524-3,00.html.

Aliyah Shalid, Neil Abercrombie, Hawaii governor drops mission to dispel birthers, prove Obama was born in state, *New York Daily News,*
January 22, 2011. http://www.nydailynews.com/news/politics/2011/
01/22/2011-01-22_neil_abercrombie_hawaii_governor_drops_mission
_to_ dispel_birthers_prove_obama_wa.html.

David Corn, The Birther Plan to Block Obama's Reelection, *Mother Jones,*
January 31, 2011. http://motherjones.com/politics/2011/01/arizona
-birther-bill-deny-obama-reelection.

Is Obama constitutionally eligible to serve? *World Net Daily,* updated February 1, 2011. http://www.wnd.com/index.php?fa=PAGE.view&pageId =98546.

Joe Kovacs, Obama on MySpace: I'm now 4 years younger! *World Net Daily,* August 4, 2010. http://www.wnd.com/?pageId=187933#ixzzlCg ScZFEE.

Joe Kovacs, Hawaii elections clerk: Obama not born here, *World Net Daily,* June 10, 2010. http://www.wnd.com/index.php?fa=PAGE.view &pageId=165041.

Chapter 6: A Birther Is a Racist Is a Truther Is a Nazi

Mondo Frazier, Obama Birth Certificate: A Birther Is a Racist Is a Truther Is a Nazi, December 30, 2010. http://deathby1000papercuts .com/2010/12/obama-birth-certificate-a-birther-is-a-racist-is-a-truther -is-a-nazi/.

Chapter 7: Columbia, the Obama Narrative™, and Other Conspiracy Theories

Declan McCullagh, Did Barack Obama Actually Attend Columbia? CBS News, November 6, 2009. http://www.cbsnews.com/8301-504383_162 -5556507-504383.html.

Macon Phillips, Change has come to WhiteHouse.gov, *The White House Blog,* January 20, 2009. http://www.whitehouse.gov/blog/change_has _come_to_whitehouse-gov/.

Mondo Frazier, Unreleased Obama Records: Did Obama Attend Columbia? *DBKP—Death By 1000 Papercuts,* November 1, 2008. http:// deathby1000papercuts.com/2008/11/unreleased-obama-records-did -obama-attend-columbia/.

Barack Obama Education, *The Obama File.* http://www.theobamafile .com/ObamaEducation.htm.

Mencius Moldburg, Did Barack Obama Go to Columbia? *Unqualified Reservations,* October 31, 2008. http://unqualified-reservations.blog spot.com/2008/10/did-barack-obama-go-to-columbia.html.

Ross Goldberg, Obama's Years at Columbia Are a Mystery, *New York Sun*, September 2, 2008. http://www.nysun.com/new-york/obamas-years-at -columbia-are-a-mystery/85015/.

Larry Gordon, Occidental recalls "Barry" Obama, *Los Angeles Times*, January 29, 2007. http://articles.latimes.com/2007/jan/29/local/me-oxy29.

Naomi, Barack Obama's GPA and College Records, *EDU in Review*, October 7, 2008. http://www.eduinreview.com/blog/2008/10/barack-obamas -gpa-and-college-records/.

Obama's Lost Years, *Wall Street Journal*, September 11, 2008. http://on line.wsj.com/article/SB122108881386721289.html.

Jim Cook, Did Wayne Allyn Root really claim Barack Obama didn't go to Columbia? *Irregular Times,* May 26, 2010. http://irregulartimes.com/ index.php/archives/2010/05/26/wayne-allyn-root-obama-not-at-columbia/.

Matt Welch, Wayne Allyn Root's Million-Dollar Challenge, *Reason*, September 5, 2008. http://reason.com/archives/2008/09/05/wayne-allyn -roots-million-doll/1.

Mondo Frazier, Wayne Allyn Root, Libertarian Party Presidential Candidate: DBKP Interview, *DBKP—Death By 1000 Papercuts*, March 14, 2008. http://deathby1000papercuts.com/2008/03/wayne-allyn-root -libertarian-party-presidential-candidate-dbkp-interview/.

Recollections of Obama's Ex-Roommate, *New York Times*, January 20, 2009. http://cityroom.blogs.nytimes.com/2009/01/20/recollections-of -obamas-ex-roommate/.

Obama at Columbia University, *FactCheck*, updated February 23, 2010. http://www.factcheck.org/2010/02/obama-at-columbia-university/.

A Columbia Classmate Remembers Obama, *FactCheck*, February 23, 2010. http://www.factcheck.org/2010/02/factcheck-mailbag-week-of-feb-16 -feb-22/.

Victor Davis Hanson, The End of Journalism, *National Review Online*, October 31, 2008. http://www.nationalreview.com/articles/226135/end -journalism/victor-davis-hanson.

Zombie, Barack Obama's Close Encounter with the Weather Underground, *ZombieTime*, October 27, 2008. http://www.zombietime.com/obama _and_the_weather_underground/.

Jim Davidson, I met Obama at Columbia and told Wayne Root about it, *Independent Political Report*, May 17, 2010. http://www.independent politicalreport.com/2010/05/jim-davidson-i-met-obama-at-columbia -and-told-wayne-root-about-it/.

Tom Maguire, Why Obama's Columbia Years Went AWOL, *Just One Minute*, October 14, 2008. http://justoneminute.typepad.com/main/2008/ 10/why-obamas-colu.html.

Ace, How Did Obama Not Know about Ayers and Dohrn, Given That Weathermen Terrorists Killed Brinks' Armored Car Guard and Two Cops in a Heist in NYC While He Was Attending Columbia? *Ace of Spades HQ,* October 7, 2008. http://minx.cc/?post=275067.

Radley Balko, Wayne Allyn Root: Bonkers, *Agitator,* May 16, 2010. http:// www.theagitator.com/2010/05/16/wayne-allyn-root-bonkers/#comment -396482

Linda Bentley, The People v. Columbia and Obama trial convenes in Harlem church, *Sonoran News*, May 19, 2010. http://www.sonoran news.com/archives/2010/100519/ftpgObamaTrial. html.

Barack Obama Never Attended Columbia University, *Firetown,* September 30, 2010. http://www.firetown.com/blog/2010/09/30/barack-obama -never-attended-columbia-university/.

Lysandra Ohrstrom, The Local: Obama on Morningside Heights, Morningside Heights on Obama, *New York Observer*, September 12, 2008. http://www.observer.com/2008/real-estate/local-obama-morningside -heights-morningside-heights-obama.

Old friends recall Obama's college years, AP, May 16, 2008. http://dyn .politico.com/printstory.cfm?uuid=F1C46FDE-3048-5C12-00ED1702 A906DC5F.

Serge F. Kovaleski, Old Friends Say Drugs Played Bit Part in Obama's Young Life, *New York Times*, February 9, 2008. http://www.nytimes .com/2008/02/09/us/politics/09obama.html?_r=1.

Chapter 8: Obama and the CIA: Agent Double O Bam!

Wayne Madsen, Who We Are, *Wayne Madsen Report*. http://www.wayne madsenreport.com/categories/20070329

Tom Blumer, More Obama Resume Inflation: His Days at Business International, *News Busters*, September 15, 2008. http://newsbusters .org/blogs/tom-blumer/2008/09/15/more-obama-resume-inflation-his-days -business-international#ixzzlAmBWhiTE.

Steve Gilbert, Co-Workers: Obama Inflated His Resume, *Sweetness & Light*, September 14, 2008. http://sweetness-light.com/archive/ did-obama-turn-down-a-wall-street-career.

Barack Obama, Senior Lecturer in Law, Curriculum Vitae, University of Chicago. http://web.archive.org/web/20010509024017/http://www.law .uchicago.edu/faculty/obama/cv.html.

Sasha Issenberg, Obama shows hints of his year in global finance, *Boston Globe*, August 6, 2008. http://www.boston.com/news/nation/articles/ 2008/08/06/obama_shows_hints_of_his_year_in_global_finance/? page=1.

Dan Armstrong, Barack Obama embellishes his resume, *Analyze This*, July 9, 2005. http://www.analyzethis.net/2005/07/09/barack-obama -embellishes-his-resume/.

James Simon Kunen (June 1970), The Strawberry Statement: Notes of a College Revolutionary, Avon, pp. 130–31.

CIA Established Many Links to Journalists in US and Abroad, *New York Times*, December 12, 1977.

Joseph Cannon, The name's Obama—BARACK Obama, *Info Wars*, August 30, 2009. http://www.infowars.com/the-names-obama-barack -obama/.

Video, Barack Obama Worked for the CIA—John Pilger, *YouTube*, October 31, 2009. http://www.youtube.com/watch?v=ezcr18NTOtA.

Janny Scott, Obama's Account of New York Years Often Differs from What Others Say, *New York Times*, October 30, 2007. http://www.ny times.com/2007/10/30/us/politics/30obama.html?ex=1351396800&e n=631bf83f428647f9&ei=5089&partner=rssyahoo&emc=rss.

Lobster, Issue 14, 1987.

Andrew McCarthy, Why Won't Obama Talk about Columbia? *National Review*, October 7, 2008. http://www.nationalreview.com/articles/225910/why-wont-obama-talk-about-columbia/andrew-c-mccarthy.

Dr. Stuart Jeanne Bramhall, Who Pulls Obama's Strings? *Op-Ed News*, August 10, 2010. http://www.opednews.com/articles/Who-Pulls-Obama-s-Strings-by-Dr-Stuart-Jeanne-B-100809-898.html.

David McGowan, *Center for an Informed America*, April 2000–present.

Adil Najam, Barack Obama's Pakistan Connections, *Pakistan. Pakistani. Pakistaniat*, September 1, 2008. http://pakistaniat.com/2008/09/01/barack-obama-pakistan/.

Obama's Mother Stayed in Pakistan for 5 Years, *Daily Waqt*, September 3, 2008.

Tim Jones, Barack Obama: Mother not just a girl from Kansas, Stanley Ann Dunham shaped a future senator, *Chicago Tribune*, March 27, 2007.

Webster Tarpley, Confirmed on MSNBC: Obama Is Puppet of Zbigniew Brzezinski, Trilateral Revanchist, *Tarpley.net*, March 21, 2008. http://tarpley.net/2008/03/21/confirmed-on-msnbc-obama-is-puppet-of-zbigniew-brzezinski-trilateral-revanchist/.

Cliff Kincaid, New START and Obama's Mysterious Trip to Russia, *Accuracy in Media*, July 13, 2010. http://www.aim.org/aim-column/new-start-and-obama%E2%80%99s-mysterious-trip-to-russia/.

Cloak's Aug 2005 Story Exposing Obama's Kenyan Birthplace Forces Sanitizing Passport, *Free Republic*, September 15, 2008. http://www.freerepublic.com/focus/f-news/2340129/posts.

http://www.cloakanddagger.de/home%20page%20items/CLOAK%20STATE%20SECRETS%20TWO.htm.

James Petras, The Ford Foundation and the CIA, *Center for Research and Globalization*, December 5, 2001. http://globalresearch.ca/articles/PET209A.html.

Charles Digges, Lugar delegation detained for three hours in Perm after inspecting nuke weapons facility, *Bellona*, August 29, 2005. http://www.bellona.no/bellona.org/English_import_area/international/russia/nuke_industry/co-operation/39511.

Joseph Cannon, Obama, the passport scandal, and a murder, *Cannonfire*, April 22, 2008. http://cannonfire.blogspot.com/2008/10/money.html.

The Obama Timeline, *The Obama Timeline and thoughts on restoring American Liberties.* http://www.colony14.net/id41.html.

Joseph Cannon, Spies, Lies, Barry and his Mom, *Cannonfire,* November 3, 2008. http://cannonfire.blogspot.com/2008/11/spies-lies-barry-and-his-mom.html.

http://www.thenews.com.pk/daily_detail.asp?id=108690, visited August 17, 2010.

Chapter 9: Obama the Socialist

Mondo Frazier, Barack Obama, Socialist: Obama a Member of Socialist New Party, *DBKP—Death By 1000 Papercuts,* October 8, 2008. http://deathby1000papercuts.com/2008/10/barack-obama-socialist-obama-a-member-of-socialist-new-party/.

Jarid Brown, Web Archives Confirm Barack Obama Was Member of Socialist "New Party" in 1996, *Politically Drunk on Power,* October 8, 2008. http://politicallydrunk.blogspot.com/2008/10/web-archives-confirm-barack-obama-was.html.

New Party, October 1996 Update: Running to Win: The Key Races, *Internet Archives,* October 1996. http://web.archive.org/web/20010306031216/www.newparty.org/up9610.html.

Editorial: The Next Campaign, *Progressive Populist,* November 1996. http://www.populist.com/11.96.Edit.html.

Elaine Marlow, Obama Video Shows Pattern of Socialist Lingo, Socialist Ties, *DBKP—Death By 1000 Papercuts,* October 9, 2008. http://deathby1000papercuts.com/2008/10/obama-video-shows-pattern-of-socialist-lingo-socialist-ties/.

Bruce Bentley, New Party Update, *Chicago DSA,* July–August 1996. http://politicallydrunk.blogspot.com/2008/10/web-archives-confirm-barack-obama-was.html.

Thomas Lifson, Archives prove Obama was a New Party member (updated), *American Thinker,* October 8, 2008. http://www.americanthinker.com/blog/2008/10/archives_prove_obama_was_a_new.html.

Alan Blinder, Obama Is No Socialist, *Wall Street Journal,* March 20, 2009. http://online.wsj.com/article/SB123751241072091037.html.

Video, ABC News, Obama Talks with "Joe the Plumber," October 15, 2008. http://abcnews.go.com/Video/playerIndex?id=6031110.

Patricia Murphy, Top U.S. Socialist Says Barack Obama Is Not One of Them, *Politics Daily*, July 21, 2010. http://www.politicsdaily.com/2009/09/09/top-u-s-socialist-says-barack-obama-is-not-one-of-them/.

Donald J. Boudreaux, Is Barack Obama really a socialist? Not exactly, but his "socialist-lite" policies should still be cause for concern, *Christian Science Monitor*, October 30, 2008. http://www.csmonitor.com/Commentary/Opinion/2008/1030/p09s01-coop.html.

Transcript of Larry King's interview with John McCain, CNN, October 29, 2008. http://articles.cnn.com/2008-10-29/politics/larry.king.mccain.transcript_1_john-mccain-public-financing-larry-king?_s=PM:POLITICS.

Sunder Katwala, Obama not Socialist say Socialists, *Next Left*, October 20, 2008. http://www.nextleft.org/2008/10/obama-not-socialist-say-socialists.html.

Rick Moran, Obama is not a socialist, *Right Wing Nuthouse*, October 9, 2008. http://rightwingnuthouse.com/archives/2008/10/09/obama-is-not-a-socialist/.

David Lightman and William Douglass, You may not like Obama's tax plan, but it's not socialism, *McClatchy Newspapers*, October 21, 2008. http://www.mcclatchydc.com/2008/10/21/54546/you-may-not-like-obamas-tax-plan.html#ixzzl9NpBCh6r.

Jeff Dunetz, Barack Obama ran on a MARXIST PARTY line in 1996, *Yid With Lid*, May 29, 2008. http://yidwithlid.blogspot.com/2008/05/barack-obama-ran-on-marxist-party-line.html.

Warner Todd Huston, Obama Sought Endorsement of Marxist Third Party in 1996, *Red State*, May 29, 2008. http://archive.redstate.com/blogs/warner_todd_huston/2008/may/29/obama_sought_endorsement_of_marxist_third_party_i n, sf1996.

New Party (NP), *Discover the Networks*. http://www.discoverthenetworks.org/groupProfile.asp?grpid=7434.

Rick Moran, Obama's Alliance with Marxists, *American Thinker*, June 3, 2008. http://www.americanthinker.com/blog/2008/06/obamas_alliance_with_marxists.html.

Rick Moran, Obama's radical political alliances, *Right Wing Nuthouse*, May 30, 2008. http://rightwingnuthouse.com/archives/2008/05/30/obamas -radical-political-alliances/.

Peter J. Orvetti, Is "Socialist" a Dirty Word? *Moderate Voice*, August 16, 2010. http://themoderatevoice.com/82918/is-socialist-a-dirty-word/.

Erick Erickson, Barack Obama sought the New Party's endorsement knowing it was a radical left organization, *Red State*, May 2008. http:// archive.redstate.com/stories/elections/2008/barack_obama_sought_ the_new_partys_endorsement_knowing_it_was_a_radical_left_organi zation.

John Blake, Ask the card-carrying socialists: Is Obama one of them? CNN, April 14, 2010. http://articles.cnn.com/2010-04-14/politics/Obama .socialist_1_socialist-agenda-democratic-socialists-health-care-bill?_s =PM:POLITICS .

Stanley Kurtz, Inside Obama's ACORN, *National Review*, May 29, 2008. http://www.nationalreview.com/articles/224610/inside-obamas-acorn/ stanley-kurtz.

Edward Cline, Obama's Global Poverty Act, *Investors Business Daily*, April 3, 2008. http://www.capitalismmagazine.com/index.php?news=5152.

Mondo Frazier, Obama, Hagel, Cantwell: Fighting Global Poverty—One Speech at a Time, *DBKP—Death By 1000 Papercuts*, June 13, 2008. http://deathby1000papercuts.com/2008/06/obama-hagel-cantwell -fighting-global-poverty-one-speech-at-a-time.

Elaine Marlow, McCain Works on Financial Crisis While Obama Touts $845 Billion Global Poverty Bill Funded by US Taxpayers, *DBKP— Death By 1000 Papercuts*, September 25, 2008. http://deathby1000 papercuts.com/2008/09/mccain-works-on-financial-crisis-while-obama -touts-845-billion-global-poverty-bill-funded-by-us-taxpayers/.

Mondo Frazier, Obama's Global Poverty Act: Spread U.S. Wealth Around the World, *DBKP—Death By 1000 Papercuts*, October 28, 2008. http://deathby1000papercuts.com/2008/10/obamas-global-poverty-act -spread-us-wealth-around-the-world/.

Chapter 10: The Obama Narrative™

Obama to disciples: You will experience an epiphany, *Is Barack Obama the Messiah?* January 9, 2008. http://obamamessiah.blogspot.com/2008/01/obama-to-disciples-you-will-experience.html.

George Will, As the Oceans Rise, *Newsweek*, June 7, 2009. http://www.newsweek.com/2008/06/07/as-the-oceans-rise.html.

AP, Text of Obama's speech Tuesday, *Breitbart TV*, June 3, 2008. http://www.breitbart.com/article.php?id=d912vd200&show_article=1.

Chapter 11: Campaign 2008: The Big
Lie and the Obama Narrative™

Joseph Goebbels, *Die Zeit ohne Beispiel*, January 12, 1941, Munich: Zentralverlag der NSDAP, 1941, pp. 364–69.

Media Credibility Plummets, Just 30% Believe "Most Trusted" CNN, *Media Research Council*, August 2008. http://www.mrc.org/cyberalerts/2008/cyb20080813.asp#1.

Rasmussen, 55% Say Media Bias Bigger Problem than Campaign Cash, *Media Research Council*, August 2008. http://www.mrc.org/cyberalerts/2008/cyb20080813.asp#5.

Ken Doyle, TV is a psycho-social weapon, *OneworldScam*, August 9, 2010. http://oneworldscam.com/?p=7130.

Jerry Mander, Four Arguments for the Elimination of Television, March 1, 1978, by *Harper Perennial*. http://www.goodreads.com/book/show/228250.Four_Arguments_for_the_Elimination_of_Television.

Joe McGinniss, The Selling of the President, *Parade*, September 21, 2008 http://www.parade.com/articles/editions/2008/edition_04-27-2008/3 Selling_Of_President.

Joe McGinniss, *The Selling of the President 1968*, New York: Trident Press (Simon & Schuster), 1969.

Mondo Frazier, MSM Content Management More Visible, Less Effective, *DBKP—Death By 1000 Papercuts*, October 23, 2010. http://deathby1000papercuts.com/2010/09/msm-content-management-more-visible-less-effective/.

Mondo Frazier, MSM Censorship: Is the NY Times Censoring Comments? *DBKP—Death By 1000 Papercuts*, September 21, 2010. http://deathby1000papercuts.com/2010/09/msm-censorship-is-the-ny-times-censoring-comments/.

Mondo Frazier, Sarah Palin: Why No Amount of Newsweek Reporting Will Hurt Palin, *DBKP—Death By 1000 Papercuts*, September 2, 2010. http://deathby1000papercuts.com/2010/09/sarah-palin-why-no-amount-of-newsweek-reporting-will-hurt-palin/.

Mondo Frazier, Mainstream Media Decline: Corrupt Rules Lead to a Defective News Product-UPDATED, *DBKP—Death By 1000 Papercuts*, August 13, 2010. http://deathby1000papercuts.com/2010/08/mainstream-media-decline-corrupt-rules-lead-to-a-defective-news-product/.

Mondo Frazier, MSM Silent on Norton Holmes' Shakedown Call, AP Says Bloggers Not Trusted, *DBKP FLASH Headline News*, September 17, 2010. http://deathby1000papercuts.com/headlines/2010/09/msm-silent-on-norton-holmes-shakedown-call-ap-says-bloggers-not-trusted/.

Wilson Research Strategies survey: Controversial Zogby Poll Duplicated and Confirmed Presidential Campaign Media Coverage "Creates Two Americas," *Wilson Research Strategies*, December 3, 2008. http://www.w-r-s.com/blog/2008/12/03/wilson-research-strategies-survey-controversial-zogby-poll-duplicated-and-confirmed-presidential-campaign-media-coverage-%E2%80%9Ccreates-two-americas%E2%80%9D/.

John Ziegler, Zogby Poll Results, Media Malpractice: *How Obama Got Elected*, November 2008. http://www.howobamagotelected.com/.

Poll: News media biased for Obama, *Washington Times*, July 22, 2008. http://www.washingtontimes.com/news/2008/jul/22/poll-news-media-biased-for-Obama/.

Van Helsing, Another Day in the Year Journalism Died, *Moonbattery*, October 2, 2008. http://www.moonbattery.com/archives/2008/10/another_day_in.html.

Myra Adams, 2008—The year journalism really died, *Daily Caller*, July 23, 2008. http://www.blogger.com/post-create.g?blogID=3036599788274013578.

Philip Kotler, Gary Armstrong, Veronica Wong, John Saunders (2008), *Marketing defined. Principles of marketing* (5th ed.), p. 7. http://books

.google.com/books?id=6T2R0_ESU5AC&lpg=PP1&pg=PA7#v=onepage &q=&f=true.

Richard Baehr, Obama's campaign built on lies, *American Thinker*, October 21, 2008. http://www.americanthinker.com/2008/10/obamas_cam paign_built_on_lies_1.html.

Jay Newton-Small, Reaction to the Obama Speech, *Time*, March 18, 2008. http://www.time.com/time/politics/article/0,8599,1723442-2,00 .html.

Transcript: Barack Obama's Speech on Race, NPR, March 18, 2008. http://www.npr.org/templates/story/story.php?storyId=88478467.

Jeff Poor, Gore Vidal: Obama "Too Intelligent" for America, Vidal Adds He Wanted to "Murder" Bush, *NewsBusters*, October 23, 2009. http:// newsbusters.org/blogs/jeff-poor/2009/10/23/gore-vidal-obama-too-intell igent-america-vidal-adds-he-wanted-murder-bush#ixzz1A3K Qv8Le.

David M. Halbfinger and Nicholas Confessore, Cuomo's Former Boss, Bill Clinton, Is an Admirer, *New York Times*, October 27, 2010, http:// www.nytimes.com/2010/10/28/nyregion/28clinton.html.

Kyle Drennen, Newsweek's Evan Thomas: Obama Is "Sort of God," *NewsBusters*, June 5, 2009. http://newsbusters.org/blogs/kyle-drennen/ 2009/06/05/newsweek-s-evan-thomas-obama-sort-god#ixzz1A3SSA21s.

Sam Smith, How the media is rigging the 2008 election, *Undernews*, June 28, 2007. http://www.prorev.com/2007/06/how-media-is-rigging-2008 -election.htm.

Jeffrey Lord, Media Malpractice: Tom Brokaw's World Implodes, *American Spectator*, September 19, 2009. http://spectator.org/archives/2009/ 09/15/media-malpractice-tom-brokaws.

Mondo Frazier, Media: It Took 50 Years to Destroy Trust in Establishment Media, *DBKP—Death By 1000 Papercuts*, September 15, 2009. http:// deathby1000papercuts.com/2009/09/media-it-took-50-years-to-destroy -trust-in-establishment-media/.

Mondo Frazier, Elaine Marlow, et al., John Edwards Love Child Scandal, Library of DBKP Articles, *DBKP—Death By 1000 Papercuts*, December 17, 2007–present. http://deathby1000papercuts.com/john-edwards -love-child-scandal-library/.

Chapter 12: Campaign 2008: Rogue Democrat

Obama Campaign's National Network Separate from the Democratic Party, *DBKP—Death By 1000 Papercuts*, September 24, 2008. http://death by1000papercuts.com/2008/09/obama-campaigns-national-network -separate-from-the-democratic-party/.

Moderate Democrats Turn Away From Barack Obama . . . Ohio Gov Ted Strickland Says No to VP Position, *Scared Monkeys*, June 11, 2008. http://scaredmonkeys.com/2008/06/11/moderate-democrats-turn-away -from-barack-obama-ohio-gov-ted-strickland-says-no-to-vp-position/.

AP-Yahoo Poll, *Yahoo*, September 2008. http://ap.google.com/article/ ALeqM5gP-1Puq75vWi4w3xx8ARg7_JBjqAD93CC8A80.

Why Obama doesn't want Clinton Democrats, *Insight Analytical*, September 24, 2008. http://insightanalytical.wordpress.com/2008/09/24/ why-obama-doesnt-want-clinton-democrats/.

No Biden Rumor: No Obama-Biden Campaign Materials in Obama Offices, *DBKP—Death By 1000 Papercuts*, September 11, 2008. http:// deathby1000papercuts.com/2008/09/no-biden-no-obama-biden-cam paign-materials-in-obama-offices/.

Democrats Take Control of Obama's "Web.org," MSNBC, February 7, 2009. http://www.msnbc.msn.com/id/29069515/ns/politics-white_house/.

Chapter 13: Campaign 2008: The Human Gaffe Machine

Obama: Return of the Great Orator, *New American Media.org*, March 4, 2008. http://news.newamericamedia.org/news/view_article.html?article _id=1fa1d4ab5f737b8cb2a5e316848d02c2.

Barack Obama: The Great Orator, *American Chronicle*, March 30, 2008. http://www.americanchronicle.com/articles/view/56984.

Barack Obama: Orator in the mould of history's best, *TimesOnline*, November 9, 2008. http://www.timesonline.co.uk/tol/news/world/us_and _americas/us_elections/article5114841.ece.

Obama's Oratory Grabbing Spotlight, CBS News, February 14, 2008. http://www.cbsnews.com/stories/2008/02/14/earlyshow/main3829938 .shtml.

Great American Orators of My Lifetime: Kennedy, King, Obama, *Salon*, November 7, 2008. http://open.salon.com/blog/dogwoman/2008/11/05/great_american_orators_of_my_lifetime_kennedy_king_obama.

Mondo Frazier, Barack Obama Quotes: Twelve Famous Obama Gaffes, *DBKP—Death By 1000 Papercuts*, April 1, 2010. http://deathby1000papercuts.com/2010/04/barack-obama-quotes-ten-famous-obama-gaffes/.

Chapter 14: Our Very First President of Self-Esteem

Mondo Frazier, Barack Obama: Our First President of Self-Esteem, *DBKP—Death By 1000 Papercuts*, April 6, 2008. http://deathby1000papercuts.com/2010/04/barack-obama-our-first-self-esteem-president/.

Chapter 15: The Obama Enemies List

Mondo Frazier, Obama: Punish Our Enemies: The Ravings of Our Littlest President, *DBKP—Death By 1000 Papercuts*, October 26, 2010. http://deathby1000papercuts.com/2010/10/obama-punish-our-enemies-the-ravings-of-our-littlest-president/.

Mondo Frazier, Obama As Nixon: Enemies List First Appeared in Campaign, *DBKP—Death By 1000 Papercuts*, October 20, 2009. http://deathby1000papercuts.com/2009/10/obama-as-nixon-enemies-list-first-appeared-in-campaign/.

Mondo Frazier, Smear, Inc.: Obama Enemy List Published on Fightthe Smears.com, *DBKP—Death By 1000 Papercuts*, July 9, 2008. http://deathby1000papercuts.com/2008/07/smear-inc-obama-enemy-list-published-on-fightthesmearscom/.

David Limbaugh, Barack's Enemies List, *Town Hall*, October 20, 2009. http://townhall.com/columnists/DavidLimbaugh/2009/10/20/baracks_enemies_list.

Chris Stirewalt, Obama's Long and Evolving Enemies List, Fox News, October 12, 2010. http://politics.blogs.foxnews.com/2010/10/12/obamas-long-and-evolving-enemies-list.

Howard Portnoy, Obama's "Enemies" List Includes You, *Hot Air*, October 27, 2010. http://hotair.com/greenroom/archives/2010/10/27/obamas-enemies-list-includes-you/.

Mark Hyman, Obama's Enemies List, *American Spectator*, February 18, 2009. http://spectator.org/archives/2009/02/18/obamas-enemies-list.

Chapter 16: The Complete Guide to Obama Creepiness

Jim Wolfe, Obama does turn as comedian in chief, Reuters, May 10, 2009. http://www.reuters.com/article/idUSTRE54904320090510.

Mondo Frazier, Obama Photo Ops: We Are All Props Now, *DBKP FLASH Headline News*, March 28, 2010. http://deathby1000paper cuts.com/headlines/2010/03/obama-photo-ops-we-are-all-props-now/.

Rick Moran, Top ten things that creep me out about Obama, *Right Wing Nuthouse*, July 27, 2008. http://rightwingnuthouse.com/archives/2008/07/27/top-ten-things-that-creep-me-out-about-obama/.

Bonnie Erbe, Barack Obama's Mounting Ethical Tone Deafness, Now with Jim Johnson's Mortgage Scandal, *U.S. News*, June 11, 2008. http://www.usnews.com/opinion/blogs/erbe/2008/06/11/barack-obamas-mount ing-ethical-tone-deafness-now-with-jim-johnsons-mortgage-scandal.

Michael Dobbs, Obama's Fannie Mae "Connection," *Washington Post Fact-Checker*, September 19, 2008. http://voices.washingtonpost.com/fact-checker/2008/09/obamas_fannie_mae_connection.html.

Mondo Frazier, Obama: Former Fannie Mae CEO Franklin Raines Advising Obama on Housing Policy, *DBKP—Death By 1000 Papercuts*, September 16, 2008. http://deathby1000papercuts.com/2008/09/obama-former-fannie-mae-ceo-franklin-raines-advising-obama-on-housing-policy/.

Eamon Javers, Inside Obama's bank CEOs meeting, *Politico*, April 3, 2009. http://www.politico.com/news/stories/0409/20871.html.

Mondo Frazier, Ft. Hood Shootings: President Appears to Begin Ft. Hood Remarks with "Shout Out," *DBKP—Death By 1000 Papercuts*, November 5, 2009. http://deathby1000papercuts.com/2009/11/ft-hood-shootings-president-appears-to-begin-ft-hood-remarks-with-shout-out/.

Mondo Frazier, Obama Ft. Hood Remarks: People Are Upset, *DBKP FLASH Headline News*, November 7, 2009. http://deathby1000paper

cuts.com/headlines/2009/11/obama-ft-hood-remarks-people-are-up
set/.

Robert A. George, Obama's Frightening Insensitivity Following Shooting,
NBCChicago, updated October 6, 2010. http://www.nbcchicago.com/
news/politics/A-Disconnected-President.html#ixzz19HhHGmzf.

Ed Morrissey, Obamateurism of the Day, *Hot Air*, November 9, 2010.
http://hotair.com/archives/2010/11/09/obamateurism-of-the-day
-395/.

Susan Anne Hiller, Obama Remembers Mumbai Massacre, Forgets Ft.
Hood First Anniversary, *Big Peace*, November 8, 2010. http://bigpeace
.com/sahiller/2010/11/08/obama-remembers-mumbai-massacre-forgets
-ft-hood-first-anniversary/.

T. Paine, Obama: Tone Deaf and Heading on $2 Billion Trip to India
and Southeast Asia, *Saving Common Sense*, November 3, 2010. http://
savingcommonsense.blogspot.com/2010/11/obama-tone-deaf-and-head
ing-on-2.html.

Elaine Marlow, Obama India Trip: 34 US Warships to Guard Obama,
DBKP—Death By 1000 Papercuts, November 4, 2010. http://deathby
1000papercuts.com/2010/11/obama-india-trip-34-us-warships-to-guard
-obama/.

Kathleen Parker, Michelle Obama: Tone deaf on the Costa del Sol?
Washington Post, August 11, 2010. http://www.washingtonpost.com/wp
-dyn/content/article/2010/08/10/AR2010081004224.html.

Lynn Sweet, Michelle Obama, Sasha on Lavish Vacation While President Turns 49, *Politics Daily*, August 7, 2010. http://www.politicsdaily
.com/2010/08/04/michelle-obama-sasha-on-lavish-vacation-while-presi
dent-turns-4/.

John Kinsellagh, A politically tone-deaf Obama gratuitously slaps
wounded military veterans in the face, *Examiner*, March 18, 2009.
http://www.examiner.com/republican-in-boston/a-politically-tone-deaf
-obama-gratuitously-slaps-wounded-military-veterans-the-face.

Yahoo News, March 17, 2009. http://news.yahoo.com/s/usnw/20090316/
pl_usnw/the_american_legio . . .

Joseph Farah, Obama's "civilian national security force," *World Net Daily*,
July 15, 2008. http://www.wnd.com/index.php?pageId=69601.

Bob Unruh, Obama's "Big Brother" vanishes from speech, *World Net Daily*, July 16, 2008. http://www.wnd.com/index.php?fa=PAGE.view&pageId=69784.

Ed Morrissey, Are the media airbrushing Obama's speeches? *Hot Air*, July 8, 2008. http://hotair.com/archives/2008/07/17/are-the-media-air brushing-obamas-speeches/.

Bob Unruh, House adopts plan for "volunteer" corps, *World Net Daily*, March 19, 2009. http://www.wnd.com/index.php?fa=PAGE.view&pageId=92288" http://www.wnd.com/index.php?fa=PAGE.view&pageId=92288.

RAPH, Obama New Civilian Volunteer Force Bill, H.R. 1388: Parallels to 1930's Germany and Hitler? *DBKP— Death By 1000 Papercuts*, March 27, 2009. http://deathby1000papercuts.com/2009/03/obama -new-civilian-volunter-force-bill-hr-1388-parallels-to-1930s-germany -and-hitler/.

Library of Congress, Thomas, Bill Summary & Status 111th Congress (2009–2010) H.R.1388. http://thomas.loc.gov/cgi-bin/bdquery/z?d111: HR01388:@@@L&summ2=m&.

Mondo Frazier, Obama: 16 Signs of the Obamalypse, *DBKP—Death By 1000 Papercuts*, November 2, 2010. http://deathby1000papercuts.com/ 2010/11/obama-16-signs-of-the-obamalypse/.

"Office of the President Elect" seal violates 18 USC Sec. 713?? *Obama Shrugged*, November 8, 2008. http://obamashrugged.com/?p=225.

Despite Bells and Whistles, "Office of President-Elect" Holds No Author-ity, FoxNews, November 25, 2008. http://www.foxnews.com/politics/ 2008/11/25/despite-bells-whistles-office-president-elect-holds-authority #ixzzl19IdAKbR6.

Michelle Malkin, What the hell is the "Office of the President-Elect?" And why is it still attacking McCain?, *Michelle Malkin.com*, November 7, 2008. http://michellemalkin.com/2008/11/07/what-the-hell-is-the -office-of-the-president-elect/.

Joe Gandelman, Emerging Question: Is Barack Obama politically tone deaf? *Moderate Voice*, June 17, 2010. http://themoderatevoice.com/ 76812/emerging-question-is-barack-obama-politically-tone-deaf/.

Aaron Klein, American flag disappears from Obama campaign jet, *World Net Daily*, July 21, 2008. http://www.wnd.com/index.php?fa=PAGE .printable&pageId=70236.

Nancy Morgan, Obama: Not a Leader, Not Elected, *DBKP—Death By 1000 Papercuts*, July 28, 2008. http://deathby1000papercuts.com/2008/07/obama-not-a-leader-not-elected/.

Marc Ambinder, Obama Team Begins Work on Presidential Transition, *Atlantic*, July 24, 2008. http://www.theatlantic.com/politics/archive/2008/07/obama-team-begins-work-on-presidential-transition/53902/.

Dan Amato, Change.gov Removes Immigration Agenda—I Have a Screenshot [Pic], *Digger's Realm*, November 8, 2008. http://www.diggersrealm.com/mt/archives/003006.html.

Mondo Frazier, Changes You Can Believe In: Change.Gov Changes America Serves Post, *DBKP—Death By 1000 Papercuts*, November 8, 2008. http://deathby1000papercuts.com/2008/11/changes-you-can-believe-in-changegov-changes-america-serves-post/.

Mondo Frazier, Barack Obama: Compulsory Service REQUIRED of Middle, High School, College Students, *DBKP—Death By 1000 Papercuts*, November 7, 2008. http://deathby1000papercuts.com/2008/11/barack-obama-community-service-required-of-middle-high-school-college-students/.

America Serves, *Change.gov*, November 2008. http://change.gov/americaserves/.

ArrMatey, Five things that are creepy about the change.gov website, *Stop the ACLU*, November 7, 2008. http://www.stoptheaclu.com/2008/11/07/five-things-that-are-creepy-about-the-changegov-website/.

Mondo Frazier, Barack Obama: Supporters Propose National Obama Holiday, *DBKP—Death By 1000 Papercuts*, November 9, 2008. http://deathby1000papercuts.blogspot.com/2008/11/barack-obama-supporters-propose.html.

Steven Watson, "Pocket Obama" Compared to Mao's Little Red Book by Irate Amazon Customers, *Info Wars*, January 26, 2009. http://www.prisonplanet.com/pocket-obama-compared-to-maos-little-red-book-by-irate-amazon-customers.html.

White House Christmas Decor Featuring Mao Zedong Comes Under Fire, Fox News, December 24, 2009. http://www.foxnews.com/politics/2009/12/23/white-house-christmas-decor-featuring-mao-zedong-comes #ixzz1AKzWqV2N.

Matthew Balan, Newsweek's Thomas: "Slightly Creepy Cult of Personality" Around Obama, *NewsBusters*, November 6, 2008. http://newsbusters .org/blogs/matthew-balan/2008/11/06/newsweek-s-thomas-slightly-creepy -cult-personality-around-obama#ixzzlANpE5xRO.

Chapter 17: D.C. Scuttlebutt: Dirty Filthy Obama Gossip

Mondo Frazier, DC Scuttlebutt: Obama a "Chainsmoking, Nervous Wreck," *DBKP—Death By 1000 Papercuts*, September 6, 2010. http://death by1000papercuts.com/2010/09/dc-scuttlebutt-obama-a-chainsmoking -nervous-wreck/.

Ulsterman, White House Insider on Obama: President Losing It, *News Flavor*, September 7, 2010. http://newsflavor.com/opinions/white-house -insider-on-obama-president-losing-it/#ixzz10A072pqv.

Mondo Frazier, DC Scuttlebutt: Obama a Chainsmoking Nervous Wreck Confirmed? *DBKP—Death By 1000 Papercuts*, September 21, 2010. http://deathby1000papercuts.com/2010/09/dc-scuttlebutt-obama-a -chainsmoking-nervous-wreck-confirmed/.

Mondo Frazier, Hillary-Obama 2010 Rematch: Not going to happen, but not for the reasons given, *DBKP—Death By 1000 Papercuts*, September 23, 2010. http://deathby1000papercuts.com/2010/09/hillary -obama-2010-rematch-not-going-to-happen/.

Wayne Madsen, White House: Obama Conducting Reign of Terror, *Opinion Maker*, November 6, 2010. http://www.opinion-maker.org/2010/ 11/white-house-obama-conducting-reign-of-terror/.

Elaine Marlow, Obama Effigy Burned by Students in India, Small Protest in Mumbai, *DBKP—Death By 1000 Papercuts*, November 7, 2010. http://deathby1000papercuts.com/2010/11/obama-effigy-burned-by -students-in-india-small-protest-in-mumbai/.

Mike Allen and Jim VandeHei, Obama isolated ahead of 2012, *Politico*, November 8, 2010. http://dyn.politico.com/printstory.cfm?uuid=29E5067 E-EFA1-0AD0-9AC494FA064A0B1C.

Mondo Frazier, Obama's Increasingly-Bizarre Behavior: D.C. Scuttlebutt, *DBKP—Death By 1000 Papercuts*, November 9, 2010. http://death

by1000papercuts.com/2010/11/obamas-increasingly-bizarre-behavior
-d-c-scuttlebutt/.

Reuters, Obamas on vacation in Hawaii, *Yahoo News*, January 5, 2011.
http://news.yahoo.com/nphotos/slideshow/photo//110104/ids_photos_
ts/r2107112856.jpg/.

Mail Foreign Service, Is "Barack n Bones" Obama thin as a rail because
he's skipping too many meals to run the country? *Daily Mail* (U.K.),
January 5, 2011. http://www.dailymail.co.uk/news/worldnews/article
-1224723/Is-skinny-Barack-Obama-losing-MORE-weight-U-S-website
-slams-president-rail.html#ixzz1A8ARbOfE.

Chapter 18: One All-Purpose Positive
Chapter about Barack Obama

Obama Refers to Himself 132 Times in One Speech, *Real Clear Politics*,
January 26, 2010. http://www.realclearpolitics.com/video/2010/01/26/
obama_refers_to_himself_132_times_in_one_speech.html.

Proof Barack Obama Is the AntiChrist, read on, *Topix*, July 22, 2007.
http://www.topix.com/forum/topstories/TUAMH99M1STQE3C5Q.

Barack Obama will be the Anti Christ, *Above Top Secret*, January 27,
2008. http://www.abovetopsecret.com/forum/thread329728/pg1.

The 27 Characteristics of the AntiChrist: Know how to recognize the
beast and not be swayed into believing that someone is the AntiChrist
who doesn't match the Biblical characteristics, *Eads Home Ministries*,
updated July 17, 2006. http://www.eadshome.com/antichrist.htm.

Who Is the AntiChrist?—32 Characteristics of the Real AntiChrist,
The AntiChrist Is Not, March 28, 2010. http://theantichristis
not.com/archives/who-is-the-antichrist-32-characteristics-of-the-real
-antichrist.

Andrew Malcolm, Brazen Obama sells White House Super Bowl cheers
for political support, *Los Angeles Times*, January 29, 2009. http://
latimesblogs.latimes.com/washington/2009/01/obama-super-bow.html.

President Obama Revokes Bush Presidential Records Executive Order
(updated January 26), *National Coalition for History*, January 21,

2009. http://historycoalition.org/2009/01/21/president-obama-revokes
-bush-presidential-records-executive-order/.

Michael Grunwald, One Year Ago: The Republicans in Distress, *Time*,
May 7, 2009. http://www.time.com/time/politics/article/0,8599,1896
588,00.html.

John Hindraker, Something Good about Barack Obama, *PowerLine*,
June 20, 2010. http://www.powerlineblog.com/archives/2010/06/026572
.php.

Kristen Gosling, Florida man launches "Bama" cigarettes with nod to
smoker in chief, *KSDK*, October 25, 2010. http://www.ksdk.com/
news/watercooler/story.aspx?storyid=223456&catid=71.

Barack Obama is the Anti-Christ and I have proof! *Godlike Produc-
tions*, January 4, 2008. http://www.godlikeproductions.com/forum1/
message483746/pg1.

132: The Number of Times Barack Obama Refers to Himself in One
Speech, *Breitbart TV*, January 26, 2010. http://www.breitbart.tv/132
-the-number-of-times-obama-refers-to-himself-in-one-speech/.

Obama Linked to Master Number 11, *Reobama.com*. http://www.reobama
.com/ObaMath.

Swooning Supporters Fainting for Obama, *World Net Daily*, February 16,
2008. http://www.wnd.com/?pageId=56559.

Why Barack Obama's Fans Are Fainting, *US News*, February 29, 2008.
http://health.usnews.com/health-news/blogs/on-women/2008/2/29/why
-barack-obamas-fans-are-fainting.

Bama Cigarettes Named after President, *Newport Cigarettes*, October
31, 2010.

Where does the Republican Party go from here? NPR, November 11,
2010. http://www.npr.org/templates/story/story.php?storyId=96863596.

The Republicans in Distress, *Time*, May 9, 2009. http://www.time.com/
time/politics/article/0,8599,1896588,00.html.

Republican enthusiasm reaches record high, *Political Wire*, July 2, 2010.
http://politicalwire.com/archives/2010/07/02/republican_enthusiasm_
hits_record_high.html.

100 Fun Facts about Obama for 100 days as Prez, *NewsOne*, April 29,
2009.

10 Events surrounding September 11, *Listverse*, August 27, 2010. http://listverse.com/2010/08/27/10-events-surrounding-september-11/.

The C-SPAN lie? See eight clips of Obama promising televised health care negotiations, *Breitbart TV*, January 6, 2010. http://www.breitbart.tv/the-c-span-lie-did-obama-really-promise-televised-healthcare-negotiations/.

Chapter 19: Welcome to the Barackalypse, Baby! Snapshots from Obama's America

Terrence P. Jeffrey, Obama Added More to National Debt in First 19 Months Than All Presidents from Washington through Reagan Combined, Says Gov't Data, *CNSNews*, September 8, 2010. http://www.cnsnews.com/node/72404.

Mondo Frazier, Obama: 16 Signs of the Obamalypse, *DBKP—Death By 1000 Papercuts*, November 2, 2010. http://deathby1000papercuts.com/2010/11/obama-16-signs-of-the-obamalypse/.

CPUSA Political Action Committee, 12 days to go: The election depends on you! *Communist Party USA*, October 21, 2010. http://www.cpusa.org/12-days-to-go-the-election-depends-on-you/.

Doug Ross, It's Come to This: Communist Party USA Openly Collaborates with Democrats, *Hot Air*, October 30, 2010. http://hotair.com/greenroom/archives/2010/10/30/its-come-to-this-communist-party-usa-openly-collaborates-with-democrats/.

Bob Unruh, Rangel plan gives prez "civilian security force," *World Net Daily*, October 28, 2010. http://www.wnd.com/index.php?fa=PAGE.view&pageId=220869.

Bob Unruh, Obama's "Big Brother" vanishes from speech: "Civilian security force" missing from "call to service" transcript, *World Net Daily*, July 16, 2008. http://www.wnd.com/index.php?fa=PAGE.view&pageId=69784.

Cordell Eddings and Daniel Kruger, Treasury Draws Negative Yield for First Time during TIPS Sale, *Bloomberg*, October 25, 2010. http://www.bloomberg.com/news/2010-10-25/treasury-draws-negative-yield-for-first-time-during-10-billion-tips-sale.html.

Laurie Segall, Ex-Shell president sees $5 gas in 2012, CNN, December 27, 2010. http://money.cnn.com/2010/12/27/markets/oil_commodities /index.htm?hpt=T2?dirty.

Jacob Goldstein, A Grim Record: One in Seven Americans Is on Food Stamps, NPR, December 8, 2010. http://www.npr.org/blogs/ money/2010/12/08/131905683/a-grim-record-one-in-seven-americans -is-on-food-stamps.

Susan Anne Hiller, With Record Number of Food Stamp Recipients, Congress Continues to Loot Fund, *Big Government*, December 30, 2010. http://biggovernment.com/sahiller/2010/12/13/with-a-record-number -of-food-stamp-recipients-congress-still-loots-fund/.

Robert Pear, Congress Approves Child Nutrition Bill, *New York Times*, December 2, 2008. http://www.nytimes.com/2010/12/03/us/politics/ 03child.html.

Linda Feldman, Angry Obama defends tax deal, with harsh words for both left and right, *Christian Science Monitor*, December 7, 2010. http://www.csmonitor.com/USA/Politics/2010/1207/Angry-Obama-de fends-tax-deal-with-harsh-words-for-both-left-and-right.

Allahpundit, Obama's turnout pitch to Latinos: Get out there and punish your "enemies," *Hot Air*, October 25, 2010. http://hotair.com/ archives/2010/10/25/obamas-turnout-pitch-to-latinos-get-out-there-and -punish-your-enemies/.

Jeff Zeleny, As the Public Simmers, Obama Lets Off Steam, *New York Times*, March 20, 2009. http://www.nytimes.com/2009/03/21/us/poli tics/21memo.html?,_r=3.

Frank of Queens and John of Staten Island, A History of Obama's Violent Rhetoric, *Right Perspective*, June 12, 2010. http://www.theright perspective.org/2010/06/12/a-history-of-obamas-violent-rhetoric/.

Record unemployment rates in eight states, AP, June 6, 2009. http://www .msnbc.msn.com/id/31445338/ns/business-stocks_and_economy/.

Jim Hoft, Top Obama Official: Record Unemployment Not Coming Down Anytime Soon, *Gateway Pundit*, September 12, 2010. http://gateway pundit.rightnetwork.com/2010/09/top-obama-official-record-unemploy ment-not-coming-down-anytime-soon/.

Jim Hoft, It's Official: Barack Obama Is Worst Jobs President since Great Depression, *Gateway Pundit*, August 3, 2010. http://gateway pundit.rightnetwork.com/2010/08/its-official-barack-obama-is-worst-jobs-president-since-great-depression/.

King Banaian, Negative job growth for 2009–2010, says OMB, *Hot Air*, August 30, 2010. http://hotair.com/archives/2009/08/30/negative-job-growth-for-2009-2010-says-omb/.

Michelle Chen, Homelessness Creeps Up on Working Americans, *Ms Blog*, January 4, 2010. http://msmagazine.com/blog/blog/2011/01/04/homelessness-creeps-up-on-working-americans/.

U.S. Conference of Mayors, *2010 Hunger and Homelessness Survey*, December 21, 2010. http://www.usmayors.org/pressreleases/uploads/2010_Hunger-Homelessness_Report-final%20Dec%2021%202010pdf.

Kelly Bennett, Homelessness Up 7.8 Percent, *Voice of San Diego*, June 18, 2010. http://www.voiceofsandiego.org/survival/article_891caa60-7b2f-11df-b9ec-001cc4c002e0.html.

Toni Randolph, Study: Homelessness up sharply in Minn., *Minnesota Public Radio News*, March 31, 2010. http://minnesota.publicradio.org/display/web/2010/03/31/homelessness-rise/.

Luke Funk, Homelessness Up 50% in New York City, *Fox NY*, August 30, 2010. http://www.myfoxny.com/dpp/news/local_news/nyc/homelessness-up-in-new-york-city-20100830-lgf.

Dennis Cauchon, More federal workers' pay tops $150,000, *USA Today*, November 10, 2010. http://www.usatoday.com/news/nation/2010-11-10-1Afedpay10_ST_N.htm.

Steve Greenhouse, Most U.S. Union Members Are Working for the Government, New Data Shows, *New York Times*, January 22, 2010. http://www.nytimes.com/2010/01/23/business/23labor.html.

Tad DeHaven, Growth in Government Employment, Cato Institute, June 29, 2010. http://www.cato-at-liberty.org/growth-in-government-employment/.

Tad DeHaven, The Government IS creating jobs, Cato Institute, February 5, 2010. http://www.downsizinggovernment.org/the-government-is-creating-jobs.

Chapter 20: Scenes from the Upcoming Barackalypse!

Finlo Rohrer, Futurology: The tricky art of knowing what will happen next, *BBC News Magazine*, December 22, 2010. http://www.bbc.co.uk/news/magazine-12058575.

Smart Meters in Every British Household? *Utility Charges.* http://www.utilitycharges.co.uk/smart-meters-every-british-household.html.

Josh Mitchell, Residents Blast Smart Meters, *Wyoming Tribune Eagle*, January 5, 2011. http://www.wyomingnews.com/articles/2011/01/05/news/19local_01-05-11.txt.

Jason Easley, Rachel Maddow: Obama Has Accomplished 85% of First Term Agenda in 2 Years, *Politics USA*, December 22, 2010. http://www.politicususa.com/en/maddow-obama-agenda.

Joseph Lawler, Mitch Daniels's Truce, *American Spectator*, June 8, 2010. http://spectator.org/blog/2010/06/08/mitch-danielss-truce.

S. Ertelt, Put Personhood Amendments Aside to Defeat Obama, Stop Abortion, *Red State*, December 21, 2010. http://www.redstate.com/sertelt/2010/12/21/put-personhood-amendments-aside-to-defeat-obama-stop-abortion/.

Paddy, Audio—Tea Party Founder Judson Phillips Says Only Property Owners Should Vote, *Political Carnival*, November 30, 2010. http://thepoliticalcarnival.net/2010/11/30/video-tea-party-founder-judson-phillips-says-only-property-owners-should-vote/.

Kenneth P. Vogel, Latest tea party target: Its own convention, *Yahoo News*, January 21, 2010. http://news.yahoo.com/s/politico/20100121/pl_politico/31816.

World's Worst Predictions—Famously Wrong Predictions, *That's Weird.* http://www.thatsweird.net/facts13.shtml.

Incorrect predictions, *WikiQuote.* http://en.wikiquote.org/wiki/Incorrect_predictions.

Claudia, What's Good for the Goose . . . ; *I Own the World*, January 16, 2011. http://iowntheworld.com/blog/?p=55071.

Chapter 21: The Gift of Barack Hussein Obama

Peter Heck, The Presidency That Saved America, *American Thinker*, December 4, 2010. http://www.americanthinker.com/2010/12/the_presi dency_that_saved_amer.html.

Mondo Frazier, Mainstream Media: Other Names for the MSM, *DBKP— Death By 1000 Papercuts*, October 23, 2009. http://deathby1000pa percuts.com/2009/10/mainstream-media-other-names-for-the-msm/.

Appendix—Thwarting the CMM: Where to Go for More Reliable Information on Obama

Mondo Frazier, Thwarting the Corporate Mainstream Media: List of Websites, *DBKP—Death By 1000 Papercuts*, December 2010–present. http://deathby1000papercuts.com/thwarting-the-corporate-mainstream -media-list-of-websites/.

Mondo Frazier, Obama Selective Service Registration: Another Obama Record, Another Question, *DBKP—Death By 1000 Papercuts*, November 17, 2008. http://deathby1000papercuts.com/2008/11/obama -selective-service-registration-another-obama-record-another-question/.

Internet Gains on Television as Public's Main News Source, Pew Research Center for People and the Press, January 4, 2011. http://people -press.org/report/689/.

Moe Lane, Gallup: Big Media's underwater trust numbers, *Red State*, September 29, 2010. http://www.redstate.com/moe_lane/2010/09/29/ gallup-big-medias-underwater-trust-numbers/.

Richard Perez-Pena, Trust in News Media Falls to New Low in Pew Survey, *New York Times*, September 13, 2009. http://www.nytimes .com/2009/09/14/business/media/14survey.html.

Mondo Frazier, Top 100 Conservative Websites, *DBKP Reports.* http:// deathby1000papercuts.com/dbkpreport.

Mondo Frazier, Liberal-Progressive 100 Websites, *DBKP Reports.* http:// deathby1000papercuts.com/dbkpreport.

Mondo Frazier, Alternate News 60, *DBKP Reports.* http://deathby1000 papercuts.com/dbkpreport.

Acknowledgments

Thank you to:

God—for finally knocking some sense into me;
Carrie, Darcy, and January—lost but not forgotten;
Gene Brissie—who plucked me from obscurity;
Andrea at Threshold Editions—an ace;
Barack Obama—for NOT being a Muslim (no other U.S. president has killed as many Muslims);
The long-suffering American people—on Day 927 of the Barackalypse.

Index

INDEX

INDEX

INDEX

INDEX